utely delightful, surprisingly useful and pleasingly absurd'

Rachel Parris

ity'

The Times

vie and Tessa are two of the least qualified people to advise
one. Thankfully they are two of the funniest people I know'

Nish Kumar

unny funny women, I love them'

Suzi Ruffell

'Brilliant and honest. Expect to laugh and totally relate'

Stylist

'Hilarious and brilliant writing. I wish Stevie and Tessa were available
to hire to sort all my life problems, but instead you can just read
this tremendously funny book'

Cariad Lloyd

'Life lessons from a cracking comedy duo . . . laugh-out-loud
funny'

The Mail on Sunday

'That perfect straddle between helpful advice and a good laugh'

Refinery29

'This book is a rarity: absolutely hilarious and yet, incredibly
helpful. I always wanted a Stevie and a Tessa in my handbag to
consult when things get tough, and now I have'

Pippa Evans

Praise for Tessa and   'Absol

'This book is VERY funny and wise and war
my plants are thriving, my groupchats are ma   'Jau
know how to use my oven. If you are a huma
about anything, or if you want to read an absol   'St
about the UK's tax system, this is the book for   an

'*Nobody Panic* [the podcast] has comforted me and   '
and this brilliant book does exactly the same'

E

'Hilarious and brilliant'

'Stevie and Tessa deliver solid, empathetic and hilarious li
a must-read for anyone struggling to be a convincing gr
Which, let's face it, is all of us'

Richard H

'Funny AF'

Time C

'I'd expected this book to be bloody funny (which it is) but I hadn'
accounted for it being genuinely informative. Thanks to Stevie and
Tessa I now know everything from how to be productive, how to
keep a plant alive, how Stevie's dad packs a suitcase and most importantly, why you should always eat the dead frog first'

Ellie Taylor

'Witty, smart and oh-so-relatable. Trust me, you'll love it'

Evening Standard

NOBODY PANIC

Tessa Coates and
Stevie Martin

First published in Great Britain in 2021 by Hodder Studio
An Imprint of Hodder & Stoughton
An Hachette UK company

1

Illustrations: © Emma Cowlam
Select illustrations (p3 and p385): © Margie Martin
Emojis: © Shutterstock

A CIP catalogue record for this title is available from the British Library

Hardback ISBN 9781529364408
eBook ISBN 9781529364415

Typeset in Sabon MT by Palimpsest Book Production Limited, Falkirk, Stirlingshire

Printed and bound in Great Britain by Clays Ltd, Elcograf S.p.A.

Hodder & Stoughton policy is to use papers that are natural,
renewable and recyclable products and made from wood grown in sustainable
forests. The logging and manufacturing processes are expected to conform
to the environmental regulations of the country of origin.

Hodder & Stoughton Ltd
Carmelite House
50 Victoria Embankment
London EC4Y 0DZ

www.hodder-studio.com

For everyone who has no idea what they're doing

Contents

How to Use This Book   1

How to Overcome Imposter Syndrome   4

How to Look After a Houseplant   8

How to Be On Time   14

How to Cure a Hangover   21

How to Say Sorry   24

How to Deal with Jealousy   30

How to Understand the Oven   34

How to Be Incredible at Dating   41

How to Ask for a Pay Rise   47

How to Make a Rental House a Home   54

How to Listen   70

How to Drink More Water   77

How to Handle Job Rejection   78

How to Understand Wine   86

How to Be More Assertive   92

How to Spot Relationship Red Flags   98

How to Make Friends   107

How to Bleed a Radiator   116

How to Get into Ethical Fashion   121

How to Be More Organised   128

How to Cope with Grief   133

How to Be Impressive in the Kitchen   141

How to Write a CV   149

How to Get Over a Broken Heart   153

How to Leave a WhatsApp Group   158

How to Read Tarot   168

How to Change a Light Bulb   176

How to Be More Body Positive   179

How to Nail a Job Interview   188

How to Sleep   194

How to Break Up with a Friend   199

How to Have a Smear Test, Colposcopy
or Biopsy   207

How to DIY   216

How to Care Less About Life's Milestones   223

How to Respond to Catcalling   229

How to Poo   234

How to Network   243

How to Understand Tax   249

How to Behave When Your Friend's New
     Partner Is Trash   255

How to Move Back In with Your Parents   260

How to Put Up a Shelf   265

How to Survive Your Stopgap Job   270

How to Be Single   277

How to Budget   284

How to Deal with Online Bullying   288

How to Quit Your Job   293

How to Restart a Dead Friendship   298

How to Be More Productive   303

How to Break Up with Someone   310

How to Pack   322

How to Go to Therapy   330

How to Have a Live-in Lover   337

How to Go Travelling Alone   346

How to Survive the Post-education Wasteland   352

How to Be Creative   358

How to Go to a Wedding   364

How to Be Brilliant at Public Speaking   372

How to Work Out What You Want to Do with
    Your Life   381

Read in Case of Emergency: You're Crying
    on the Bus   386

Read in Case of Emergency: You're In Need of a
    Confidence Boost   393

Read in Case of Emergency: You Want to
    Text Your Ex   397

Actually Useful Resources   401

Acknowledgements   403

How to Use This Book

Hello!

Thank you for buying our book! Or receiving it as a gift. Or reading it standing up in a bookshop, deciding whether you should buy it (we think yes).

STEVIE: I'm Stevie.
TESSA: I'm Tessa.

And this is our book. It's born out of a podcast called *Nobody Panic*. Every episode is a 'How to . . .', and we cover everything from houseplants to taxes to broken hearts to how to leave a WhatsApp group.

It was originally called *The Debrief Podcast*, and then *The Debrief* website closed down. We found out our podcast was going to be stopped in 2017 while sitting in a Pret a Manger. Tessa had just run the London Marathon without doing any training so she couldn't walk, and Stevie had to carry her out. We had a little cry, decided to strike out on our own – and look at us now!

If you've never heard of us or the podcast, that absolutely doesn't matter; this book is a totally stand-alone experience. We went through our twenties feeling like we'd missed out on the orientation day. It seemed like everyone else had read a manual on how to do everything, so we've written the manual we wish we'd had.

This book is the sum of everything we've learnt, with the addition of some experts and some painstaking research. It's a 'How to . . .' guide to life. Dip in, dip out, jump around. Skip over some chapters and come back to them one day if they become relevant. By all means read it straight through from start to finish like a novel, but you will be disappointed by the lack of narrative arc. Sometimes you will think, 'Sorry, who doesn't know how to do that?' in which case fantastic, good for you, move on to a different bit. If it's in here, it's because we had to learn how to do it. At the back there are helpful resources, and some emergency chapters to read if you're currently crying on the bus, in need of an immediate confidence boost or about to text your ex.

If you're looking to learn from two people who have made some quite frankly outrageous mistakes, this book will help. This book is intended to hold your hand and remind you that you're not alone.

It's important to say that our experience is of two white cis straight women. One working class, one a bit not working class. One city slicker, one so rural she's practically feral. One much too confident, one really working on it.

Always good to know who you're reading, but we hope that whoever you are and wherever you're from, there's something in here that'll make you smile or make you do something that you've always worried about doing.

We'll be bobbing in and out –

STEVIE: Like this!

– in a way that's both illuminating and hopefully not too distracting.

We've got you, champ. So nobody panic.
Love, Stevie and Tessa x

How to Overcome Imposter Syndrome

Imposter syndrome strikes us all down at one time or another. We progress higher and further than we think we deserve, convince ourselves we got there by mistake and then we tie ourselves in knots waiting to be found out.

> TESSA: I once won a writing competition and told everyone I had won 'due to a clerical error'.
>
> STEVIE: I once told someone I wasn't a real journalist while I was interviewing them for a magazine I worked for as a journalist.

It's estimated that around 70% of the population feel like they don't deserve to be where they are,[1] so let's see – are you an imposter?

Question 1: How did you get this job?

A) I saw it advertised and I applied. There was an interview but I think I made myself appear way more qualified than I am.

B) I intercepted the advertisement before it could go in the paper and

---

1 Sakulku, J. 'The Impostor Phenomenon', *The Journal of Behavioral Science*, Vol.6, no.1, 1, pp.75–97.

changed the phone number so no one else could apply. Then I placed a number of prank calls so my ex-wife would lose hope of ever finding someone suitable, bought myself a latex mask and bodysuit and infiltrated my own family home posing as a nanny.

Question 2: When you feel like people are going to 'find you out', what do you mean?

A) They'll realise I'm not very talented, and they'll admit they should never have hired me.

B) Following an incident at a cursed fairground attraction where I wished to be big, I appear to be 30 but am in fact a child in an adult's body.

Question 3: What is your biggest worry at work?

A) I'll overhear someone judging my work or laughing at me.

B) An enemy defector will walk into my office and reveal that I am a Russian sleeper agent operating undercover. I will be forced to kill several of my colleagues and flee.

STEVIE: What film is this?

TESSA: *Salt*. Angelina Jolie plays the sleeper agent and at one point she takes her knickers off to put over a CCTV camera, when she could have used literally anything else, and then you can't focus for the rest of the film because she's running all over the city and you know she hasn't got any pants on.

Question 4: Did you have any inside knowledge or feel that you were given a leg-up?

A) A friend recommended me, which helped me get the job. I feel so weird about it.

B) My estranged twin I didn't know I had prepped me on a working knowledge of our mother's home.

Question 5: You are offered a very exciting career progression. How do you feel?

A) So overwhelmed because of course this is a great opportunity, but I'm convinced I'm going to mess it up!

B) Nervous because no woman has ever infiltrated the Chinese imperial army pretending to be a man before. Plus, the talking dragon that sounds like Eddie Murphy keeps getting me into trouble.

Question 6: Why do you feel like an imposter?

A) I guess I'm just self-sabotaging, but it's so hard to feel like I truly deserve to be here!

B) I am in witness protection pretending to be a nun.

If you answered B to any of the above questions then yes, you're a legitimate imposter. If you got mostly As, you join nearly three-quarters of the adult population who secretly worry they're not worthy of the job, position or life that they're leading. Success makes people uncomfortable, and there's no easy fix.

The big secret to adult life is that no one has any idea what they're doing. Everyone is winging it, and some people are just styling it out better than others.

Every time you pause before applying for that job, remember a study conducted by Hewlett-Packard that we read about in the *Harvard Business Review* –

TESSA: We're always reading the *Harvard Business Review*.
STEVIE: I can't stop.

– revealed women only applied to a position if they fulfilled 100% of the requirements, while men applied for the same position when they fulfilled just 60% of them.[2] Sure, there will be lucky breaks and leg-ups, but that's life. Everyone else is getting leg-ups and lucky breaks too! Back yourself! You've got the job, someone believes you can do it, so unless you're three children standing on top of each other wearing a trench coat, there's no reason to feel you don't belong in this room full of adults.

---

2 Internal report at Hewlett-Packard, cited in the *Harvard Business Review*: https://hbr.org/2014/08/why-women-dont-apply-for-jobs-unless-theyre-100-qualified

How to Look After a Houseplant

Obituaries for plants we have known and loved. And murdered.

STEVIE'S VICTIMS

Planty

(2016–2018)

A Boston fern with a lust for life, Planty enjoyed being watered, sitting in soil and reading, even spending a full year on a bookshelf with such tomes as *He's Just Not That Into You* and *How to Stop Smoking*. A creature of habit, Planty encountered problems when he was forced to move house, to a room with floor-to-ceiling windows. Rather than 'finally getting some sunlight', he tragically burnt to death.

How to prevent murder: Low humidity and direct sunlight will kill Boston ferns so keep them away from sunny windows. Unless you live in a greenhouse, or in the middle of a bog, chances are your flat/house/flat house (bungalow) isn't very humid, so spray them once or twice a week and check the soil daily – if it feels dry, your fern needs a drink.

The Thirsty Boys
(February 2018–September 2018)

Hydrangeas are renowned for their thirstiness and these rooty boys – one in pink, and one in violet, like two pastel-shirted finance bros about to close a sale – were no exception. Huge, bushy and full of sparring badinage, their liquid lunches were a thing of legend on the balcony. Going so much as a long weekend without their daily pints just wasn't tenable, so they were given to a neighbour to look after for a week. Unfortunately, said neighbour also went away, a heat wave struck and they both burnt to death.

How to prevent murder: Liberally water hydrangeas three times a week, sometimes more in heat waves. Whenever their leaves droop, it's time for a gulp. Don't allow them to sit in water, though, or they'll get root rot. They need to be in a plant pot with a hole, and sitting in a tray with drainage stones so your Thirsty Boy doesn't have a soggy bottom 24/7.

Susan the Succulent
(December 2018)

Kept well away from direct sunlight, Susan was a quiet sort of plant, happy to sit by the TV enjoying sports-related documentaries, period dramas and true crime. She never spoke during the show or ruined the ending. Nowhere near direct sunlight, Susan seemed hardy, happy and healthy, until it became clear that you're not supposed to water succulents every day, her leaves started bursting open and she drowned.

How to prevent murder: The cruel thing about succulents is that when they look thirsty and shrivelled, they're actually getting too much water. Don't water them every week; more like every three. Each succulent is different, so make sure you know exactly what type you just bought ('It looks a bit like a starfish' doesn't count) and how much water it needs.

Susannah the Succulent
(January 2019–March 2020)

Proclaimed as 'unkillable', Susannah thrived in Susan's old spot by the TV, getting just the right amount of water and sunlight. But this wasn't enough. Unlike those before her, she craved adventure. The bright lights of the living room drew her in, until one day she upped sticks to join an arrangement of ornaments on the floor. This proved her undoing: Susannah was immediately, and regrettably, eaten by a tortoise.

How to prevent murder: Obviously don't put any plant at tortoise-level if you have a pet tortoise. Or even if you don't. Tortoises are everywhere. There could be one lurking behind you right now, ready to eat an entire plant in under five minutes before getting Ubered straight to the vet, who will say: 'Thankfully it isn't poisonous, but she's quite hardy – didn't she eat a kitchen sponge last summer?'

TESSA'S VICTIMS
The Sunflower Twins
(June 2020–June 2020)

These two vibrant, zesty twins were bought on a drunken lunchtime whim from a florist whose outdoor display had intense *Amélie* vibes, and who *promised* that two potted sunflowers were extremely easy to look after. They withered within 24 hours of getting home and then, in a sort of Cain and Abel fight for survival, one pushed the other to his death out of a five-storey window, and the remaining twin promptly died of a broken heart.

How to prevent murder: Don't knock one sunflower out of a five-storey window and then blame it on the other one; sunflowers take these things personally. Also, they are really high maintenance, only flowering once (WHAT IS THE POINT?) and needing six hours of direct sunlight a day. Water them once a week, but if they start to wilt you've watered them too much. With all due respect, sunflowers need to get a grip. But also, with all due respect, the moment you buy them from the florist is the moment they are looking their best. It's all downhill from there.

Fern the Fern
(September 2018–October 2018)

Fern arrived at a party as a house-warming gift from a well-meaning but extremely overconfident friend, and from the moment she entered the room, she shone. She was soft, quick-witted, a real party hit.

11

But the moment the party guests left, she withered. Starved of attention and, crucially, water, she curled up into herself, a shadowy husk of her former self, before ultimately crumbling away to dust.

How to prevent murder: Water your fern. There are many types of fern, and we'll never know Fern's origin story and exactly what care and attention she needed, but in general you need to keep them humid, well watered and away from direct sunlight.

The Leek

(June 2020–June 2020)

During a particularly over-zealous commitment to recreational indoor farming, The Leek was rescued out of the food bin, after he'd given most of himself to a disappointing yet nutritional soup, and put in

a small glass of water. From there he began to flourish. In astonishingly little time, he was regrowing himself. Bright-green shoots of life rose upwards, relentlessly beating back the waves of time. The Leek was not only surviving, but thriving. Surely he would soon be a brand-new leek? His water was carefully changed every day, his progress monitored, his height lovingly measured in pencil against the door frame. One particularly sunny day, in order to soak up some life-giving rays, he was ceremoniously placed on the windowsill, where he was immediately eaten by a bird.

How to prevent murder: Don't let your leek get eaten by a bird.

The Cactus: A Story of Survival
(November 2017–fingers crossed never)

 During the same move that killed beloved Planty, a cactus was thrown to the floor of the moving van. Over the course of two years, he slowly browned and withered in the window, never named and, towards the end, never watered, because Stevie couldn't bear to look at him. It was decided that he had died the day before Christmas 2019, but, when picked up for his last journey towards the recycling bin – what's this? A flower! On his face! Or the back of his head! It's unclear which way round a cactus goes! Anyway, he had bloomed a flower in a final attempt at communication and so, watered back to life, now stands at four times his original size, a deep-green colour and named Callum. What a lovely tale of redemption to end on.

How to Be On Time

You're a late person! Come on in! Maybe a loved one keeps leaving this page open for you in various rooms around the house. Maybe 'be less late' has been written on your New Year's resolutions list for the last decade. You're a late person and you're ready to get in our cult and journey on the path to punctuality.

The main advice when you're a late person is just 'be on time', which is profoundly unhelpful. The first exciting discovery you get to make on this journey is that there are different types of late people all running to work under the Late People umbrella. Late – obviously – but for different reasons.

In her book *Never Be Late Again*, Diana DeLonzor identifies five different types of late personalities – the Deadliner, the Producer, the Absent-minded Professor, the Rationaliser and the Rebel – and how they can fix themselves. We've condensed everything we've learnt from her game-changing book here (and gave each personality a name to make them more personable). Most people are a melting pot of several of these, with one dominant – see if you can find yourself, and what you can do to de-stress your journeys.

DEBBIE DEADLINE (THIS IS TESSA)

Debbie Deadline enjoys the rush of the last minute. She doesn't start her essays until midnight the night before, and thrives on a crisis. She claims she 'works best under pressure'. The thrill of getting on the train just as the doors shut far outweighs the nine times out of ten when the doors closed mid-run and she cried on the train platform. Debbie is the personification of the feeling of Indiana Jones rescuing his hat.

What can Debbie do? Learn not to live down to the wire

Here's a wonderful secret about life: you can fill the car up with petrol before the red light goes on. And if you think, as Debbie Deadline does, 'Where's the fun in that?' you can find fun elsewhere! Create your own external fun that doesn't run the risk of running out of petrol at midnight in the middle of the M4. (Which has happened to Tessa *on more than one occasion*.) Practise being early to things, paying bills in advance, doing things well before the deadline and realise how extremely calm and more pleasant life can be when your adrenaline isn't constantly through the roof. If you miss the adrenaline kicks, take up base jumping or something.

PAULA THE PRODUCER

Paula only feels calm when she's got a massive to-do list and is ticking things off. She tends to engage in 'magical thinking', consistently underestimating the time a task will take. Paula truly believes she can walk the dog, build a bookcase, bake a cake, have a shower, roast a yam and paint her nails in an hour. Paula hates wasted time, and loves when her schedule is packed with absolutely no margin for error. Waiting time is wasted time, so she's always squeezing in one more thing, even when there's no more space left to squeeze.

What can Paula do? Time yourself

Part of the problem for the temporally challenged is that we actually perceive time differently. Pick another chapter of this book at random, start a stopwatch and stop reading when you think you've hit 90 seconds. Chances are you'll overshoot or undershoot by some distance.

> TESSA: I just did it, got distracted, panicked and stopped the clock at 44 seconds.
> STEVIE: I just did it, completely forgot what I was doing and kept reading.

We wildly underestimate how long things take. How long do you think it would take you to leisurely walk a mile? Tessa once believed she could do it in five minutes. In 1954 Roger Bannister broke the four-minute mile, one of the defining sporting achievements of the twentieth century, so no, she couldn't walk the same distance in five minutes.

Guess how long it takes you to do all these activities, write it down, then time yourself.

	my guess	actual time
Having a shower		
Getting dressed		
Eating breakfast		
Walking a mile		
The journey from home to work, door to door		

This way, as you lie in bed, you can't trick yourself that you're not late yet because you can shower and get dressed in 2 minutes and 37 seconds. You can't.

THE ABSENT-MINDED PROFESSOR (THIS IS STEVIE)

The Professor is extremely bright –

STEVIE: Why, thank you.

– but easily distracted.

STEVIE: What?

They commit to appointments and then immediately forget them. They start researching one topic on the internet and end up moderating a forum about Guam. They can't find their shoes and they lose a lot of keys.

What can the Professor do? Get a diary

This can be digital, physical or a calendar, but it has to be one thing and you have to stick to it. Don't have three on the go, because you won't be able to keep track of anything. Got a meeting coming up? Put it in the diary, rather than just beaming and nodding. Dentist? In the diary. Capoeira Club? In the diary. The diary goes with you everywhere. It's a shame that 'testicles, spectacles, wallet and watch' doesn't have a catchy modern equivalent. Maybe 'vagina, retainer, iPhone and keys'. Every time you leave the house you say out loud, 'Diary, phone, keys, money,' and touch all these things to check you've actually got them – don't just proudly say it and close the door.

RAYMOND THE RATIONALISER

Raymond skimmed over this chapter because lateness isn't a problem for him. Sure, he's late all the time, but it's never his fault. It was the traffic, the kids, a colleague held him up talking, the lift was broken. Raymond thinks everyone is too uptight about punctuality. He's been known to say, 'What even is time?' and, on more than one occasion, 'A wizard arrives exactly when he means to.'

What can Raymond do? Learn to be 20 minutes early for everything

A friend who went to drama school reported that one day a willowy teacher with an enormous scarf sashayed into the room and said: 'The only lesson I have to teach you is . . . always be 20 minutes early!' Then sashayed out, never to be seen again.

If the meeting starts at 10 a.m. and you walk in the door at 10 a.m., sure, you made it on time, but you spend the first 20 minutes gently sweating and trying to silently get the right things out of your bag. If the play starts at 7.30 p.m. and you get to your seat as the lights are going down, sure, you made it, but everyone in your group is cross with you and you have to stay in your coat for the whole first half because you can't risk drawing more attention to yourself. When you show up to shared activities late, you impact how the other person feels – they were nervous you were going to miss the start of the play, worried you were lost, had to stall for time in the meeting. Your life will improve dramatically if you learn to get addicted to the feeling of being 20 minutes early. Thanks, mystery drama teacher!

TROY THE REBEL

Troy is late on purpose as a power play because of a need for control. Troy might be controlling in other areas too, or perhaps being late makes them feel like they have taken back some control in an otherwise control-less life.

> STEVIE: I used to turn up at 9.31 a.m. on purpose for work because I hated the fact that I had to be there at 9.30 a.m. and felt I needed to claw back one iota of independence. Am I a Troy?
> TESSA: As long as you are not purposely late to meet friends, you're not a Troy.
> STEVIE: What a RELIEF.

What can Troy do? Have a really good think

Lots to unpack here, Troy. Diana DeLonzor writes: *'Tardiness by rebellion comes in three basic flavours: competing for power, resisting authority, or attempting to feel special or unique.'* Artists, musicians and actors often fall into the last group; it's a way of appearing more exciting and creative by saying, 'The rules don't apply to me.'

19

We've all read interviews where the interviewer was kept waiting for seven hours while the celebrity went to the zoo or something.

And we've all been guilty of being in the middle group, resisting authority in a horrible job. It's natural to attempt to wrestle back some power by showing up late, but ultimately it will get you fired. Instead, try rebelling by arriving early, starting your shift and then going to the toilet for 45 minutes and thinking about how that horrible boss is paying you to do a poo.

The competing-for-power group brings to mind dick-swinging corporate meetings, in which everyone wants to be the silverback. Purposefully keeping everyone waiting so you can feel like the king might give you a feeling of short-term power, but in the end all it suggests is that you lack power in the rest of your life. And that you have a small penis. The bigger the penis, the earlier you arrive. We don't make the rules.

> STEVIE: It feels prudent to point out that this rule is not in Diana DeLonzor's book.
> TESSA: She actually suggests the smaller the penis, the *earlier* you arrive.
> STEVIE: It feels prudent to point out that this is a joke.

To summarise: nobody is just 'late'; there's always more going on. Time yourself if you keep being surprised by your own lateness; try being actively early to give yourself time to prepare; remember that waiting time is not wasted time and if you have a large penis, you'll arrive a lot sooner. Simple.

How to Cure a Hangover

Some hangover tips – not from Tessa (who was known for many years as Tap Water Tessa), but from Stevie, whose nickname was Stevie Is Drunk Again in a Non-addiction Way, Sure, But Where Did She Get That Bollard From?

> TESSA: Sure thing, kid, take it away. I'll just tidy things up in here and maybe pop this bollard outside.

You will have read a variety of articles on hangover cures already, probably including the following:

1. Drink a glass of water between each alcoholic beverage.
2. Line your stomach with a carbohydrate and protein-rich meal beforehand.
3. Why does so much hangover advice involve going back in time and doing things before you've got yourself into this state? Who is reading a 'How to Cure a Hangover' chapter before a night out?
4. Drink water before you go to bed.
5. Again, too late. I got in, ate a can of kidney beans because I thought they were something else, ordered a Deliveroo for next

Thursday and fell asleep wearing one shoe.

6. Have a hearty protein-and-fat-and-carbohydrate-rich breakfast.

7. Don't have any breakfast because you'll throw up. Even if you just ate a single satsuma segment. You may think that throwing up one satsuma segment on the way to work will go unnoticed by those around you, and you'd be right. But YOU know. You will wrap the satsuma segment in an old receipt and put it deep in your pocket and commute alongside hordes of normal people who don't have thrown-up citrus tucked in their pockets and you will feel Shame. This Shame never leaves you and may even put you off satsumas for the remainder of your adult life until someone accidentally puts them in a fruit salad and you think, 'I missed out on this sweet snack for six whole years – what was I doing?' Just an example off the top of my head.

8. Hair of the dog.

9. Avoid hair of the dog because it promotes an unhealthy relation-ship with alcohol.

10. Eat a raw egg with some Tabasco.

11. Obviously don't eat raw eggs – who are you, Gaston? What if you get one with a weird red bit in the yolk?

TESSA: Do you want me to tell you what the red bit is?
STEVIE: Absolutely not.

12. Exercise.

13. Don't exercise because, again, you'll throw up. And if you don't throw up, you will sweat pure Sauvignon (even if you didn't drink Sauvignon) and will put off all the nice people at the yoga class

because they'll think you're an alcoholic. If exercising by yourself, the smell of Sauvignon will put YOU off because you'll think you're an alcoholic.

The reason these cute lists of hangover cures don't work is because there isn't a cute cure for hangovers. Alcohol is a poison. When you drink it, you wee loads because your brain registers poison entering the body (wine, gin, rum if you're a pirate, brandy if you're a CEO getting away from it all at your hunting lodge in Vermont), and so signals for your kidneys to release loads of wee to flush everything out. Which makes you incredibly dehydrated the next day. So dehydrated that your brain shrinks and pulls away from your skull, causing hangover headaches.

Once more for people at the back – that hangover headache is your brain becoming so starved of water it's shrinking away from your skull. No wonder you're lying in bed making a noise like a blocked drain.

All you can do is drink water, sleep and eat as well as you can. And avoid coffee because it dehydrates you further, which, yes, is a shame, but remember that brain thing?

Oh, and feel free to buy expensive sports drinks to 'replenish your electrolytes', but there's apparently just as many electrolytes in, say, a glass of milk, so eat and drink whatever you fancy. Whisper 'it's for the electrolytes' if that helps, and get back in bed.

How to Say Sorry

It's a cliche that sorry is the hardest word, but unfortunately cliches are popular because they're mostly true. Apologising can feel awful, but it's also one of the most useful life skills you can learn. That and being able to bleed a radiator (which is on page 116).

The only thing worse than saying sorry when you've done something wrong is refusing to say sorry and regretting it later down the line. Every time you dodge an apology, you make it harder for yourself.

If you've broken something, or done something by accident, own up to it straight away. Apologising is a thousand times easier than trying to get away with it. Even in the rare circumstances when you do get away with it, the guilt will eat you up and you'll be forced to publish a self-help book years later where you finally admit it was you who let the guinea pigs out of their cage in the neighbour's garden in 1997. And while they were eventually caught, you're truly very sorry.

When the hurt wasn't physical, instead it was someone's feelings, it can be even harder to apologise. People rarely do things out of malice; they just don't think through how their actions will affect others. But just because you didn't *mean* for people to get hurt, it doesn't mean that people didn't get hurt. You need to be very brave

24

and own up to what you did. Doesn't matter that you didn't mean it, you still did it.

Being unable to apologise is a weakness rather than a strength, and something that needs to be practised and worked on as we go through life – so why not start now?

Here's an example of an ideal apology for general use:

DO SAY:

I'M SORRY . . .

Every apology, regardless of what it's for, should start with these two words. If your apology doesn't include 'I'm sorry' then it's not an apology so much as some words you've just said out of your mouth.

DO NOT SAY:

. . . BUT

ABORT. ABORT. The words 'I'm sorry' should never be followed with 'but'. If you're tempted to do this then you're not ready to say sorry and you've still got some intense psychological untangling to do. An apology must be pure and without mud-flinging or passing the blame. There will be time later to discuss what your intentions were, but not right up top. You've got to start with a bit of humility.

DO SAY:

I'M SORRY. I REALISE THAT [INSERT ACTIONS AND/OR BEHAVIOUR] HAVE BEEN HURTFUL.

It's important to show that you have been moved to apologise because you've realised your actions were upsetting.

DO NOT SAY:

I'M SORRY YOU'RE UPSET or **I'M SORRY IF MY ACTIONS COULD BE PERCEIVED AS HURTFUL.**

What are you, a psychopath? These lay the blame on the response, rather than the actions. You're saying it's their fault they got upset about it. Even if you secretly think this is true (and, listen, it might be), keep it out of the apology and write it in your diary. Or your little notebook of secrets. Or on a little bit of papyrus and then float it down the river. Just keep it out of the apology, because it'll just pour gasoline over the situation.

ALSO AVOID:

I CAN'T BELIEVE I DID THAT. I'M SO UPSET! I LITERALLY CAN'T STOP CRYING!

Again, might well be true, but going on about how upset *you* are just conveniently shifts the focus over until you're the victim. You're not the victim. And you're not upset that you did it, you're upset that you're in trouble. Keep your feelings out of this.

DO SAY:

I FELT LIKE [POSSIBLE REASON BEHIND THE ACTIONS] BUT I NOW SEE THAT THIS WASN'T THE RIGHT WAY TO GO ABOUT IT.

Often skipped, this section contains a much-needed depth that soothes the person you are apologising to, and lets them know you aren't just reading an apology template out loud from a book. Be as thorough and as clear as you possibly can be. Really investigate why you did the thing you did.

'I'm sorry I pushed your mattress onto a lake on this camping trip while you were sleeping, I realise that must have been very upsetting. My recently discovered twin and I are scared you will replace our mother in our father's affections and are behaving badly out of fear.'

If you tried to do something positive and got it wrong, explain that. Show that you've thought about how, regardless of any positive intentions, the result was negative. They will appreciate hearing what you were trying to achieve. It will help them understand why you did what you did.

DO SAY:

I THOUGHT ABOUT HOW I COULD MAKE THINGS RIGHT, AND CAME UP WITH [INSERT SUGGESTIONS] . . .

Sometimes there isn't any way to make amends because what we've done is dogshit. But if there is anything you can think of that could help the situation or the person you are apologising to, let them know. It shows you're fully engaged rather than going through the motions of a robo-apology, hoping they'll let you off the hook and tell you what to do.

DO SAY:

I'M STRUGGLING TO COME UP WITH SUGGESTIONS FOR HOW TO MAKE THINGS RIGHT, BUT I'D LOVE TO TALK TO YOU AND SEE IF WE CAN FIND A WAY THROUGH IT TOGETHER.

If you really can't think of any way to make it right, then offering to work through it together is much better than just laying the apology at their feet and running off feeling proud of yourself. If it's work-related, organise a time when you can sit down together. If it's a friend, take them for a drink to work through it. Show you're willing to put the time and effort in.

DO SAY:

I WILL MAKE SURE IT DOESN'T HAPPEN AGAIN.
This is relevant for some apologies –

> STEVIE: For example, when I didn't close the back door of my flat properly, causing it to blow off during a storm.

– and less relevant for others.

> STEVIE: For example, when my ex-boyfriend(s) cheated on me multiple times.

If it feels helpful and relevant, then promise you'll prevent a repeat performance.

DO SAY:

THANK YOU FOR LISTENING TO ME.
Again, often skipped, but it's nice to thank someone for listening to your apology, especially if things have been very tense or you feel there is a lot of animosity flowing out of their eyes towards your eyes. While this isn't the point, showing humility and the strength of character to own up to a mistake can often soften someone's feelings towards you. There's nothing like a genuine, humble apology to douse the fury-fire raging within.

And there you have it. Copy it out, memorise it, make sure you fill in the correct words rather than telling people to 'insert suggestions', and congratulate yourself on having mastered the art of the apology. Now it's time to really piss someone off so you can test it out.

How to Deal with Jealousy

Now technically what we're describing here is envy, but the two are so confusing and interchangeable, and we prefer the word jealousy. Also we didn't know there was a difference and one of us has a degree in English literature.

Technically, you are jealous of your friend if they start hanging out with a new friend and you feel threatened. You are envious of your friend if they get a new job and you really wanted that job. But the more common term for both is jealousy.

To add in more linguistic complications, there are also two types of jealousy: benign and malicious.[3] In Russian, there is white envy and black envy. In Dutch, *benijden* and *afgunst*. Benign jealousy is to covet something that is within your grasp. Someone has a new iPhone, you're jealous, so you save up and get the iPhone. Your friend got great marks in an exam, you're jealous, so you revise really hard next time.

Malicious jealousy is something much darker and comes from a deep, gnarled place within you that believes this person does

---

3 van de Ven, Niels et al., 'Leveling up and down: the experiences of benign and malicious envy', *Emotion (Washington, D.C.)*, Vol.9, 3 (2009), pp.419–29.

not deserve their success. They're rich, or they fell upwards, or they come from the right family, or they were in the right place at the right time. They always have a new iPhone because their dad gives them the best stuff. They only did well in the exam because they're the teacher's favourite. Malicious jealousy finds you sneering in the corner, filled with bitterness and resentment.

Whether your feelings are benign or malicious, there's no point denying them. You need to admit they're there, decide which one they are and work out what you're going to do next.

If you're dealing with malicious jealousy, there's a whole lot of unpacking to do. If your friends are being gifted houses, or popping out babies left, right and centre, or getting married, or being given career opportunities, or doing things that you desperately crave but that are physically, financially or in some other way beyond your means, that is really, really tough. Be honest, be open, talk about it, admit it out loud.

Friendships have crumbled over much less than the cognitive dissonance of being genuinely happy for your friends and desperately jealous of them at the same time.

STEVIE: I was so jealous of one of my close friends that one day I snapped and said: 'I'm being such a dick, but it's only because I'm really jealous of you. It's absolutely on me. I'm going to work on it and I couldn't be more sorry.' She was excellent about it and, if anything, it brought us much closer. I didn't mean to be so impressively communicative, I'd drunk several gins and had run out of excuses so just went for it.

Admitting to feeling jealous is such an astonishingly competent and mature move it will leave people breathless. Very few of us are brave enough to articulate it, and no wonder. Unlike Russia, or the Netherlands, who have two clear words for benign and malicious, we're still interchanging envy and jealousy. Of course we lack the skills to talk about this properly.

Not only is it so important to talk about it, but if you can channel it, jealousy can be excellent for you. It makes you admit to yourself what you secretly want. As a great woman (Stevie) once said: 'I never lie awake at night thinking about the guy who won the Grand Prix.' This is because Stevie doesn't want to win the Grand Prix (best wishes to everyone who does and literally Godspeed to you). Stevie lies awake at night thinking about the people doing all the things she wants to do and hasn't.

If you're dealing with benign jealousy, and the thing is within your grasp, the only way to deal with it is to Do The Thing.

If you're jealous of people who are travel bloggers, off you go.

If you're jealous they've written a book, go right ahead and write a book.

If you're jealous of your friend's career, set out a plan and take meaningful steps along that career path.

If you are coveting your neighbour's ass, because your neighbour is an Instagram star with a mind-blowing ass, put in the money, time and effort into building yourself an equally covetable ass.

If you're jealous that they're married, be honest with yourself, admit that you'd like to find a partner and get back in the dating ring.

You are not too old and it is not too late! Go! Channel that jealousy! Do The Thing!

How to Understand the Oven

The oven is deceitful. Please see our bestselling hobsman-only cookbook, *Fuck the Oven*.

> TESSA: It's no excuse for still not being able to use the oven, but I grew up in the deep countryside in a house that has occasionally been compared, favourably and otherwise, to the Weasleys' house, The Burrow, where we had an AGA. An AGA is hot all the time, runs off gas, has two lids on the top (one very hot, one slightly less hot) and two doors (one very hot, one slightly less hot). It heats the whole kitchen. You can use it to dry laundry and something was always either dying or being born on or near it. The cat lived in front of it 'til he was nearly 30 and so old and motionless that people thought he was a piece of taxidermy. Baby ducks lived in a box on the back of it. Chicken eggs went there to hatch out. If you left the bottom door open, you could put orphan baby lambs in there, wrapped in a towel, to heat up. Anyway, I describe this to you because you can't set the temperature on an AGA, you don't have to preheat it, there are no settings; you just cook things in the top door and you keep things warm in the bottom door. Occasionally

all the heat goes out if you leave the lids up too long, and sometimes it goes out by accident. Then you have to call the very expensive and ethereal 'AGA Man', who rides from town to town like a mysterious pedlar and is the only person with the powers to light the AGA.

STEVIE: I have never even seen an AGA other than in Tessa's house.

It has been the battle of our adult lives to attempt to understand the oven. Things go in, and it is anybody's guess what comes out. This is partly because half the symbols have rubbed off our oven dial and we refuse to learn what the remaining ones mean. So:

Welcome to our quiz, called 'Is this a symbol for the oven or an ancient rune?'

Oven symbol or Norse rune? It's . . . an oven symbol!

We call this symbol 'Man who doesn't want to talk about his day'. Stevie, what do you think it means?

STEVIE: That the oven will purely be heating the food from below? Like hell?

Correct! It means 'Lower heat elements only'. In other words, only the bottom is going to heat up, and the air isn't going to circulate.

This is for when you want to cook something slowly, like a casserole or a stew. If things have gone awry and you've cooked the top but not the bottom of something, you can put it back in on this setting.

> TESSA: I don't have one of these symbols and I've just investigated and, yes, there's no heating element at the bottom of my oven. So no stew for me.

Oven symbol or Norse rune? It's . . . a Norse rune!

This is Dagaz, the ancient symbol meaning the day, or the dawn. It is a rune of hyper-consciousness and the process of concept becoming realised. It is not an oven symbol.

Oven symbol or Norse rune? It's . . . an oven symbol!

Bit of a trick question, because this is also the hieroglyph for water and the zodiac symbol for Aquarius. It's also recognised as 'the two pieces of corrugated iron'. Stevie, any thoughts?

> STEVIE: Mine has two STRAIGHT lines at the top. Going off the fact that a line at the bottom meant heating from the bottom, I'm going to say heating from the . . . top?

This one is the GRILL. The heat is coming from the top only and this is ideal for grilling sausages, bacon – any kind of meat. Do NOT put a cake under the grill; it will be charred black on the outside and raw on the inside. Huge reveal: some people change the settings while they're cooking. So you might cook your lasagne or your pizza on a different setting, and then put it under the grill for a few minutes at the end to get just the top extra crispy and cheesy. Extraordinary.

Oven symbol or Norse rune? It's . . . an oven symbol!

STEVIE: Wait. OK, this is what I have but two of these! I thought this was the grill!

TESSA: And this is why we hate the oven.

This symbol means 'upper heat elements only', but after extensive research if you've got two straight lines, it usually means 'very hot from the top'. Zig-zag is always grill, but grill might not always be zig-zag, which feels unfair because 'grilling' when you put something on the barbecue is from below! And cooking from above in the oven is technically called 'broiling'.

Oven symbol or Norse rune? It's . . . an oven symbol!

We call this, 'Man with a fringe who doesn't want to talk about his day'.

STEVIE: Our first combo! Heating from the base of hell but also the zig-zag grill is involved?

Correct! This is the ideal pizza setting if you have this one.

Oven symbol or Norse rune? It's . . . a rune! This is Inguz, the ancient rune meaning seed, or new life.

It is not an oven symbol.

STEVIE: I was going to say 'clothes rail you hang wet laundry on'.

Oven symbol or Norse Rune? It's . . . an oven symbol!

STEVIE: A snowman has pissed himself?

Very close. This means 'defrost', so there's no heat but the fan is on, and apparently moving air will defrost something much more quickly than just leaving it on the kitchen counter.

Oven symbol or Norse rune? It's . . . BOTH! This is Gebo, the ancient symbol of gifts, fair exchange, sacrifice and sacred marriage, and also the symbol for the oven fan.

How to Understand the Oven

TESSA: I include this one because my oven has this exact cross, but you might also have:

The international plug

The Spirograph

Three pieces of Chocolate Orange on the floor

Four pieces of Chocolate Orange on a plate

TESSA: My oven has both the cross and the cross in the circle, and you'll never guess – the cross in the circle means 'fan' but the cross with no circle means 'defrost'! No wonder I thought my oven was broken! I've only got four settings and one of them just blows air around. I've got fan, defrost, grill and grill with fan, and the grill is broken, so I've just got fan, nothing, nothing, fan again!

The fan is the thing that makes the noise, and the fan in the circle symbol is the jack-of-all-trades option to go for if you're not confident. There's a circular heating element at the back of the oven and then the fan circulates the heat. A classic all-rounder, good for every meal. If in doubt, use Gebo, the ancient symbol for the sacred gift. And fuck the oven.

How to Be Incredible at Dating

We are not incredible at dating. We're telling you that right off the bat. Stevie has been on one date. It lasted 42 minutes and ended with her, in a desperate bid to leave, saying she needed to 'move some boxes'. Tessa once left her number for the waiter in a restaurant because he looked like Dave Franco and then they met that night at midnight and walked up Primrose Hill and then he made a reference to his A levels and it turned out he'd just left school.

This chapter is not about how to make anyone fall in love with you, but how you can get the most out of the dating experience. How to make it the most fun and the least stressful, given that people talk about dating apps and use words like 'soul-crushing'. If you want to know how to ensure that every date ends with them catatonic with lust, we don't know how to help you. And not for lack of trying. We've scoured the internet and all the advice is just 'be confident', 'wear red, the colour of passion' and 'remember to brush your teeth'. One article suggested putting a grape in your pocket to give you a feeling of power because you now have a secret. The secret being 'I've got a grape in my pocket'.

There's no way to trick people into falling for you. You've just got to keep showing up and spinning the wheel to see if you land

41

on someone whose body and mind you dig, and who digs yours back.

Because of Stevie's technique of never speaking to or looking directly at anybody she fancies lest they guess that she fancies them, and the time Tessa's WhatsApp picture was a chicken and when a boy from Tinder asked her why, she said she was a chicken who had learnt to use the phone and was typing with her beak, we have taken the executive decision to hand this over to friends who know what they're talking about.

In order to protect their identities, we have ascribed them names from the IKEA product range.

SMORBOLL SONGESAND

Smorboll dates like it's a job. 'When being single gets me down, dating makes me feel like I'm proactively moving forward. Taking matters into my own hands. Dating is just a numbers game, so it's easy to feel like you should be dating all the time, but it's really exhausting if you do it more than once or twice a week. You need evenings with people you actually like, and evenings for yourself. Booking up every single night with dates will mean you'll look at your diary on a Monday and want to throw it – and yourself – out of the window.'

Smorboll's top tip is to pick the place. That way, you're in control and you can choose somewhere that's easy to get home from. Plus, there's nothing more boring than the constant back and forth about a venue, finding out you can't book, getting there and discovering it's too busy so you have to wander round for ages until settling on a Pizza Express because it's the only place with seats. Nothing wrong with Pizza Express, it's just that now you're locked in for at least two hours and you've committed to a Sloppy Giuseppe.

BEHANDLA SHIRMISHAMM

Behandla always has a back-up plan. 'You've got to have an established means of escape. Always arrange to be somewhere after the date. If the date goes well, you can bring them along! If the date does not go well, you don't have to worry about making excuses because you've already told them, "I've got something at 9 so shall we meet at 7.30 for a drink?" Flawless.

'Always hope for the best and plan for the worst. You will turn up after having great and lengthy message-badinage with someone, only to find they are absolutely nothing like you thought.' This is a real dating issue, and not even a modern one. Probably in Tudor times people were meeting people for the first time and thinking, 'God, he was so funny in his letters, and yet he's so boring in real life.'

Sometimes you arrive and you immediately think, 'NO!' but then you just stay for one drink and say you have to get to your 'thing'. You're relaxed, you're calm, because you've already established the time limit on this experience.

STEVIE: This is where I went wrong with boxesgate. Always, always have an established means of escape. I just spent the whole date in my head trying to come up with the boxes thing, finally said it, and then he said, 'What's in the boxes?' and of course I hadn't thought that far. It did not go down well.

TESSA: I lied and said I needed to get to the train station, but then he walked me all the way there and then said, 'Which one is your train?' So I had no option but to buy a ticket and get on a train!

Always have somewhere to go afterwards, or a friend to come home to or phone, so you can give them a blow-by-blow account of the whole experience. The weird-date energy needs to go somewhere, and you need to get it out of your system. Don't just go home and go to bed and stare at the ceiling.

TARNABY KLABB

But what about the date itself? How do you dazzle people with your sparkling wit, your charm, your knowledge of fine wine, when you go bright red every time anyone looks at you?

Tarnaby says, 'Rather than trying to impress them, I treat the date like my one aim is to find out as much about them as possible. I'm doing a documentary on them, and I want to get to the good stuff.'

> TESSA: I once went on a date (didn't plan ahead, didn't pick the place, did end up in a Prezzo) and we were both so nervous that to fill the silence I just started talking nineteen to the dozen and before our calzones had even arrived I was performing a sort of historical re-enactment of how the Gunpowder Plot was an inside job.

Chill out, and just keep asking questions. Pick any piece of information they've just told you and ask another question about that.

Don't leap about, cannon-firing unrelated questions without listening to the answers. It's a conversation, not an interrogation. And don't judge your questions either. Boring-seeming questions like, 'What do you do?' are the gateway to more interesting topics like, 'What extinct animal would you most like to see reintroduced into the wild?'

'The interview thing works because it moves the perspective from, "Oh God, what do they think about me? Am I fit enough?" to "What do I think about THEM," and so I don't have to worry about me so much,' says Tarnaby. Absolutely Grade A advice there. Well done, Tarnaby.

You have no control over how attractive another person finds you – just google any gorgeous famous person and you'll find people being negative – but you do have control over how self-conscious you feel, and how much you can relax and have a nice time.

BILLY BOOKCASE

Billy says, 'If you think the date went well, ignore anyone who has any rules about how long you should leave it before messaging. If they fancied you, they're not going to stop fancying you because you messaged "too early".'

If you're here to play power games, by all means play hard to get. But otherwise, we're all adults here, and one adult would like to tell the other that they would like to see them again. Forget the weird rules or trying to second-guess them. If you fancy them, you fancy them. If it's a pass from them, best to get that information out now and then we can all move on.

You'll know if you had a frisson. And you'll also know, deep down, if the frisson only truly went one way. May we also suggest reading *He's Just Not That Into You* by Greg Behrendt and Liz Tuccillo? It's a terrible film, sure, but the book stands up remarkably well considering it was published in 2004. The advice is essentially: if someone is interested in you, this will be obvious and you will not need to guess. As the title suggests, it's heteronormative with the pronouns, but honestly, if you're in dire need and able to ignore the he/she-ing, the advice works for anyone dating anyone. If the 2004 vibes are too strong to work through, bypass the book and take this away: there are so many people in the world and loads of them will be into you. Don't waste time with the ones who are not.

Do everything you can to drag that perspective from 'What will they think?' over to 'How do I feel?' and don't settle for anyone who doesn't think you're the bee's knees.

Now if you'll excuse us, those boxes aren't going to move themselves.

How to Ask for a Pay Rise

*And now, a small dramatic realisation of Stevie's attempts to ask
for a pay rise, written by T. Coates Esq., playwright and raconteur.
Tessa will play The Boss. Stevie will play herself.*

*Raise curtain to reveal a grand office set-up: a desk of rich
mahogany, a plush leather chair, a number of awards in a glass-
fronted cabinet to illustrate that this is the office of someone
important. Perhaps a fully operational fountain.*

And . . . scene.

BOSS: *(A young Danny DeVito. He has a cigar)* Whaddayawant,
   kid?

STEVIE: What? Who am I in this? Why is Danny DeVito here?

BOSS: *(Emerging from behind the fourth wall)* It's actually me,
   Tessa, playing a young Danny DeVito, playing a boss. *(She coughs
   on her cigar)* Feel free to throw a penny in the fountain.

STEVIE: I'm OK, thank you.

BOSS: Say your lines.

STEVIE: Can I have a pay rise, please?

BOSS: No.

Exeunt. End of scene.

TESSA: OK, great, great, let's gather round and talk about how that went. Stevie, your performance was very lacklustre. Anything to add?

STEVIE: Well, I didn't get the pay rise.

TESSA: Hmmmmmm. No. I think it's because Danny DeVito was caught unawares. Also it's because you came to his house in the middle of the night – very unprofessional, quite weird.

STEVIE: I thought this was an office!

TESSA: Let's try it again, and this time have your character email him in advance and say why you want to arrange a meeting. And . . . scene

STEVIE: *(Typing)*

TESSA: Well, say it out loud so the audience knows what you're typing!

STEVIE: *(Typing but also speaking)* Dear Boss . . .

TESSA: No.

STEVIE: Hi, Mr DeVito, this is awkward but—

TESSA: No.

STEVIE: Please could we arrange a meeting to discuss an increase in my pay? Sorry for the bother—

TESSA: Cut that.

STEVIE: I'm *not* sorry for the bother—

TESSA: Just don't say it.

STEVIE: Should I definitely mention the pay in the email?

TESSA: As we learnt in the first scene, you can't catch them unawares! It makes it look like you're trying to ambush them. Go on, keep going.

STEVIE: Please could we arrange a meeting to discuss an increase in my pay? Would this Friday at 11 a.m. work for you? Let me know, Stevie.

Exeunt. End of scene.

TESSA: Lovely work! Why did you choose Friday at 11 a.m.?

STEVIE: Well, one study I found showed that people may have a higher moral awareness in the mornings.[4] Friday has been floated by some psychologists as a good day to ask because people are looking forward to the weekend and are therefore more amenable.[5] Monday is obviously the worst possible option, and Friday is the opposite of Monday. 11 a.m is not too early – gives everyone a chance to get a cup of coffee, settle in for the day.

TESSA: Genius. OK, here we go for the next scene: it's Friday at 11 a.m., the Boss knows you're coming, you look smart, you've got your best shoes on, this is your big moment. We're about to go in.

STEVIE: I'm nervous.

TESSA: Because of your terrible acting in front of Danny DeVito?

STEVIE: No! What if I ask for a pay rise and get fired?

TESSA: Let me be very clear: in the UK it is illegal for an employer to fire you for asking for a pay rise.

STEVIE: Really?

---

4 Kouchaki, M. and Smith, I.H., 2014, 'The Morning Morality Effect: The Influence of Time of Day on Unethical Behavior', *Psychological Science*, Vol.25, No.1, pp.95–102.

5 Suzanne Roff-Wexler as quoted in: Walton, A., 2015, 'When Is the Best Time of Day to Ask for a Raise? Psychologists Weigh In', Forbes.com.

TESSA: Hand on heart. The employer tribunal is on your side. Now get in there! Aaaaaand . . . scene.

STEVIE: Hello, Mr DeVito.

BOSS: Hello, Stevie, those are very interesting shoes. Take a seat. I hear you want to ask for a pay rise?

STEVIE: Yes.

Silence.

BOSS: No.

Exeunt. End of scene.

STEVIE: Well, that went badly.

TESSA: Did you think you could just ask and he would say yes? Let's pick that up and this time tell him why you deserve the pay rise. And scene.

STEVIE: Yes. I work very hard for this company and I really need the money. I've got holes in my weird shoes and rent is so much and my family— *(Starts crying)*

TESSA: Cut, cut, cut! Stop crying!

STEVIE: But my son!

TESSA: You haven't got a son! Definitely no tears in there, and no saying why you need the money. Everyone needs money. You're here to explain why your excellent work should be reflected by a pay increase. You recently did that good thing for the company and you're about to take on new responsibilities – both excellent reasons to ask for more money.

STEVIE: But he knows that and he still said no!

TESSA: He's got a lot on his plate! Bosses can't keep track of every employee's narrative arc – you need to remind him. And scene!

STEVIE: Thank you for taking the time to see me today, I've really enjoyed working for . . . Danny DeVito Enterprises these past two years. As account director, I've taken on more work since Susan Sarandon left, and last month won us that new client, Cigars 4 U. Considering there's been talk of me absorbing some of Tom Cruise's responsibilities in order to help increase our quarterly sales – sorry, what does this company do?

TESSA: Not important! Carry on.

STEVIE: Considering the new responsibilities I'm about to take on and that, in the open market, equivalent positions are worth £36,000 – which is 15% higher than my current wage – I'd like to discuss closing that gap.

TESSA: Oh my God, I've got GOOSEBUMPS. That was so slick and professional. How did you know that number?

STEVIE: I researched the average national pay for my job, and I asked around to make sure I knew what everyone else was getting.

TESSA: Information is power! You go get 'em, kid! OK, what's next? AND SCENE.

STEVIE: I was thinking perhaps somewhere in the region of—

TESSA: No.

STEVIE: I was wondering if—

TESSA: No.

STEVIE: I was hoping—

TESSA: Are you hoping? Or do you know this increase is what

you deserve? How can Danny DeVito be confident if you're not confident? Tell him what you think.

STEVIE: I think an increase of 7.8% would more appropriately reflect my work here.

TESSA: I'm loving these decimal points! Shows you're specific and you've really thought about it instead of just guessing at 10%. That's the kind of person we want on the team. OK, over to you, Danny DeVito.

BOSS: Thank you, Stevie, I really appreciate everything you do here and I'll see what we can do. I don't know if we can go to 7.8% but I'm sure we can manage something like 6%.

STEVIE: *(Looks to the audience)* That's OK because I asked for more than I wanted, ready for them to come down!

BOSS: I can hear you.

STEVIE: OK, pretend I didn't say that part out loud.

BOSS: Perhaps if we can't make the full increase, we could discuss flexible working hours or another perk such as a company car, transferring to the New York office or this signed DVD edition of *Twins*. I'll get back to you by the end of the day.

STEVIE: I'd be interested in flexible working hours and the signed DVD of *Twins*.

TESSA: Good! Not just nodding at everything like a little nodding dog, but letting them know which perks would genuinely help, and which would not mitigate less of a raise.

STEVIE: Thank you, Mr DeVito.

BOSS: Thank you, Stevie.

Exeunt. End of scene. Rapturous applause.

How to Ask for a Pay Rise

TESSA: Amazing work! You did so well in there.

STEVIE: Thank you! I got my pay rise AND a selfie with Danny
DeVito! What a day!

They high-five.

How to Make a Rental House a Home

Congratulations! You've made the big move and you're renting your first place! You did it! You're officially on the lease! We know the magic of having your own keys and a room of one's own, because before we started properly renting, we lived around London like tiny nomadic snails.

> TESSA: I spent a whole year sofa-hopping, sleeping anywhere anyone had any spare room for me. For a while I slept in an airing cupboard.
> STEVIE: I used to share a one-bed flat with my friend Tom and we took turns sleeping underneath a table in the kitchen.

We know you're chomping at the bit to get stuck in, but we've got to do some boring admin first. Before you do anything, read the inventory and check it against what's actually there. Any scuffs, cracks or weird old chairs not mentioned? Put them in an email with pictures and get the inventory updated before you sign it. Landlords rely on you being too excited to host a flat-warming party to do this, and will take anything 'extra' (i.e. not on the inventory) off your deposit.

STEVIE: I moved into a flat once and all of the drawers had dead maggots in them. I did not take pictures or put this in the inventory, but told the landlord in person who said, 'It's bits of rice.' Not wanting to make a fuss, I kept my clothes in a suitcase for the whole year and when we moved out he claimed I'd put dead maggots in his drawers and charged me a £50 'disposal fee'.

TESSA: I moved into a house once before they did the inventory, and discovered it was crammed with the landlady's questionable tribal masks and chicken figurines. We made them come back and do the inventory, and in listing everything they wrote, 'Horrible antique stool that is also an elephant,' which was actually mine.

Get permission from your landlord in writing before you replace anything. ANYTHING.

STEVIE: I got charged a fee for replacing a broken chair the landlord insisted was fine, despite it being described in the inventory as 'broken'. It had one functioning leg.

A few more boring bits: register with your new GP; register to vote; cut a spare pair of keys and hide them really well somewhere outside; find the stopcock (it's a tap that turns off the mains water and will be somewhere baffling, like on the ceiling) – you don't want to be hunting for it while the house is flooding; get the names and numbers of the plumber and the electrician from the landlord and stick them to the fridge.

That's it! Now we've done the boring stuff and we're ready to decorate! Let's go! . . . OK! On closer inspection, it's not that nice here!

When you really look closely, you might notice that the walls look more yellow than white. That the skirting boards don't meet the floor and the windows are caked in grime. Meanwhile, over on Instagram, @TuppyCoutts-Meadow just put up a picture of the flat she's bought and it's got exposed brickwork, exposed beams and a fully stocked exposed bar in the corner of the vast exposed living room.

When you unglue your eyes from Tuppy's dream home and stare up at the nude bulb swinging from the ceiling in your bedroom (which has been converted from the living room so the landlord could flog a two-bed as a five-bed on Zoopla), it's understandable you'd want to save your decorating skills for when you've got somewhere nicer. You'll probably have to leave in a year anyway, so what's the point?

Stop.

It's really easy to get into a 'When this/Then that' spiral. In fancy grammar terms it's called the future perfect conditional. When I get my own home then I'll make it nice. When I have more time then I'll write my novel.

But we say NO. This is when decorating is at its most effective. Don't waste a year of your life feeling bleak whenever you put the key in the door. If nothing else, when you finally do get an all-right rental you won't know how to make it nice because you haven't learnt from your questionable decorating choices.

'I can barely afford the rent,' you may be thinking. 'If you tell me to go to Anthropologie and "get a couple of bits", I will body-slam you into this grungy mattress I can't sleep on because it looks like someone died there and wasn't found for several weeks.'

You're in luck: this is all about low-budget decoration. If you are very rich and looking to furnish your £4,000-a-month rental flat (and we suspect you're not because you are, after all, reading a book called *Nobody Panic*), this is not the chapter for you. Good luck and go with God. Everyone else, find the least broken chair to perch on and gather round.

Before we start, these are our credentials, just so you know you're in safe hands:

TESSA: I only really like things that are other things. I own an octopus that is also a candle holder, a bird that is also a pair of scissors, a duck that is also a jug, a carrot that is also a pen, a snail that is also a bottle opener and a cowboy hat that is also a vase.

STEVIE: I thought Blu-Tacking loose coins into a big swirl on my wall was the height of sophistication and lost my deposit when removing them revealed loads of marks. I also tried to sew a pair of curtains out of very old socks. You're speaking to the real deal here.

TESSA: I always thought your coin piece was very creative.

STEVIE: Thanks, friend.

eBay, car-boot sales, charity shops (especially ones in posh areas), Depop, Gumtree and Freecycle are your friends. Go round IKEA, choose what you want and type that exact name into Gumtree,

Shpock or any other second-hand site. You'll be amazed how many people are selling the exact Hemnes chest of drawers you wanted for a fraction of the price.

Everyone's doing their best to shop as ethically and environmentally as possible, but don't beat yourself up if you find yourself in the Primark home department. Try for second-hand where you can, but if you need a throw to cover that rancid sofa and Zara have one on offer – just get it.

Colour-wise, pick a few shades and have them repeating throughout the flat to make it immediately classy. If you are very bad at matching colours, don't go for grey and black like Stevie tried, because it only works if the house is already extremely nice, and will reduce a sad rental flat to looking like a sad rental prison.

Behold the colour wheel:

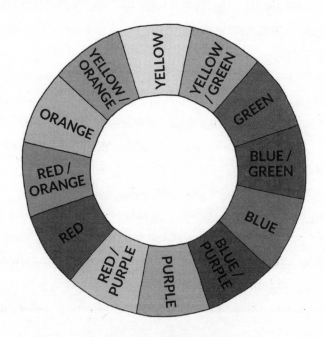

Sure. We regret publishing the book in black and white. Just try to imagine it. You pick a colour and the opposite colour on the wheel is complementary. Come on, this is a fantastic visual representation.

You will spill things on everything you own, so trust that white will look like a science project after three days and choose forgiving darker colours.

FRONT DOOR

When you go to someone's flat and think, 'Good lord,' (in a positive way) it's always because of the Little Things. And that's what we're going to do right from the off. Get yourself a cheap-and-cheerful welcome mat – replace whatever piece of shit (or actual shit) the landlord has shoved in front of the door and pop your own clean mat down. The rule of thumb for buying cheap but hiding the fact that you bought cheap is to opt for a few choice, minimal pieces.

HALLWAY

This is where the nude bulb doth swing, the badly cut carpet doth lie and the bare walls doth stare. If you do have a lampshade on the hall light, it will probably be full of dead moths.

When you move in, get new, cheap, clean lampshades for every room – including the hall. When you take the old ones down they will crumble to dust in your hands, but sail through it by pretending you're Indiana Jones carefully handling an ancient relic. Then put it straight in the bin.

The hallway is absolutely begging for someone to cover up its worst bits. Somewhere in the house, possibly in the cupboard under the sink, or tucked in whatever weird corner the boiler is in, there is probably a half-full tin of paint that is the colour of the walls. If you're confident you have indeed found The Paint (try it out in a very small corner), you can go to town covering up weird hand-prints, red-wine stains and the evidence of where someone dragged their bike through the hallway. It's free, quick and will make the world of difference.

If you can't find any paint, cover those holes and suspicious stains with pictures. Now we can really separate the wheat from the chaff – the wheat being people who put things in frames, and the chaff being everyone else.

Poundland do terribly made frames that crumble at the merest touch – but who will be touching them? Charity shops are always selling horrible paintings in decent frames. Cover up that bleak oil on canvas of a fruit bowl with your own picture and suddenly you're someone who frames things. You're the wheat!

STEVIE: Crucially, you don't need nails to hang things. Get your-self some Command strips; they work perfectly and when you take the pictures down they leave no marks. If you don't have anything nice to frame, I love arranging cards from friends, ticket stubs and scrapbook-type things in old frames like a little collage. Feels like art, but isn't art.

Get a scented candle or those sticks in pots of oil to cover the damp and place it close to the door so a nice smell greets you every time you come home.

We could tell you to buy a rug runner for the hallway if the floor is terrible, but if you're on a budget you'll have to decide which rooms get the rug – not everyone can buy rugs for all rooms. What are you? Royalty!? If you can – and thank you for reading our book, Your Majesty – then of course a rug runner that matches the lampshade (very important) can work wonders. Failing that, your pictures and your new lampshade look MARVELLOUS. Well done.

BATHROOM

It has a toilet and possibly a wall-mounted cabinet over the sink, positioned just low enough so it's impossible to splash your face with water without wedging your head in the space between the taps and the bottom of the cabinet, like you're trying to post yourself through the wall.

There may be a shower, or there may be a bath with a shower attachment. It might be freezing, or mouldy, or there's a broken vent resulting in it being both freezing and mouldy. Loo roll is jammed next to the toilet still in its packaging. A sad mug holds your toothbrushes, and the bath is littered with Alberto Balsam shampoo and one much-coveted bottle of Aussie, bought by the one housemate with a proper job.

While you can't change the cold or the type of shampoo you can afford, the sadness of the bathroom doesn't mean it should be abandoned. For starters, do not use the gross shower curtain that was there when you moved in. Replace it with a new one. A really cheap one, sure, but a PLAIN one – patterns always look naff.

TESSA: I disagree here and think patterns can be 'a bit of fun'. I also once had a very humorous shower curtain, which was the shadow of a unicorn taking a shower.

STEVIE: I stand by my point.

Get cheap towels that complement the shower curtain colour if you're feeling super fancy. (See? The colour wheel is very helpful.) And a matching mat so you don't do yourself a mischief getting out of the bath. And one really soft 'show towel' that you never use but just keep for display.

Yes, it makes sense to use your saddest mug for toothbrushes. But wouldn't it be nicer to buy a sleek-looking pot? And maybe a second pot for the toothpaste so your toothbrushes don't get covered in paste when your flatmate leaves the top off again?

STEVIE: This is me – I am that flatmate and I am sorry to everyone I have ever lived with.

While you're at it, get a soap dish or a cheap hand-soap dispenser that you can pour your Palmolive into.

TESSA: Keep an eye out in case you're ever in a bar when they finish off a bottle of Hendrik's Gin, which you can then turn into a soap dispenser. Everyone said, 'Why are we carrying this empty bottle of gin around with us?' when I got it, but then they said, 'Ooooooooh,' when they saw it had become a soap dispenser.

While you might not be able to keep your towels in the bathroom for mould reasons, a good trick is to buy a plastic hook that sticks to the back of the door, and a cheap hanging basket from Poundland (plastic, not metal, or it will immediately and very forlornly rust) so you don't have to bring all of your toiletries into the bathroom with you each time like you're staying in a hostel. A cheap crate can sit on the bath or even next to the bath to contain all of your various shampoos. And using a wicker basket for all the toilet roll, and then stacking them up like a log pile, will make it look like this is a bathroom where people *care*.

KITCHEN

Oh to have an island. An island where tall, sleek stools can be pulled up and breakfast can be enjoyed at the 'breakfast bar'.

> STEVIE: I pay £800 a month and I can touch the oven while sitting on the sofa, which, to be honest, isn't something I do regularly, but the point is, I shouldn't be able to, should I?

Rental kitchens are tricky because everyone will have brought bits and bobs from their previous flats with them, plus there's always some tat left over from the previous tenants, which means you end up with a weirdly high number of spatulas and only one fork. There will be two glass tumblers and 27 mugs, including the massive one from Sports Direct, which no one's ever bought, but every rental property must have by law. Everyone brought a chopping board.

Ignore Pinterest and mute everyone on Instagram who has a nice kitchen, because there really isn't any way to transform a shitty kitchen into a good one without ripping it out and starting again. Sorry. However, there are ways to make it a little bit less frustrating. Most importantly, don't struggle for a year with shit pans. Not only will you have Teflon flaking into your food, but it'll make you feel like a shit cook.

TESSA: What's wrong with Teflon?

STEVIE: I have done a lot of 4 a.m. googling about Teflon and it either causes cancer, leads to dementia or turns you into a lizard. And no, I will not be referencing my sources for this information. It's generally agreed that eating Teflon off old pans isn't a good thing to be doing.

TESSA: That's a terrible shame. I always liked the Teflon pan because it had a T for Tessa in the middle and I always felt very supported every time I cooked.

Either way, get some decent pans. Even if you're a fantastic chef, the crooked pan covered in flaking bits of black that looks like something a cowboy cooked his beans on in the Old West is not helping.

TK Maxx has a weird deal with Le Creuset, so you can always get very discounted, end-of-season, excellent-quality pans in there as long as you can tolerate them all being in the shades that didn't sell, like puce.

Flying Tiger Copenhagen has so many cheap Little Things for kitchens: salt shakers, chopping boards, oven gloves, mug trees – stuff that will add a bit of personality without taking up valuable cooking space.

Cutlery and glasses are alarmingly expensive to buy new, but you can get the family silver and some crystal tumblers for a pound if you're prepared to go second-hand and mismatched.

Buy big pots from Poundland for your utensils, and a medium one for your sponges and washing-up stuff. If you've run out of surface area, try using the walls. Can you put up some hooks and hang your utensils?

STEVIE: I once put hooks on the ceiling to try to hang onions like you see in Italian restaurants, but the kitchen was horrible and I could only afford one onion, so it just looked like someone had put an onion on a ceiling. Sometimes less is more.

Avoid googling 'Kitchen storage hacks'.

TESSA: I once attempted to make magnetic spice jars by putting spices in those little jam jars you get in hotels, sticking a magnet to the underside of the lid and then sticking the jar to the fridge. I went round collecting empty jam jars from breakfast tables after my grandparents' sixtieth wedding anniversary. I was trying to be quite covert about the whole thing and then a lady sidled up with a whole handful and slid them over to me. She whispered, 'I don't know what we're doing, but these are for you.' God bless you if that was you in the Portmeirion Inn, April 2016. I got home, cleaned them out, filled them with spices and then accidentally ordered weapons-grade magnets off the internet. I opened the box in the kitchen, where the magnets promptly leapt out of the box and stuck to the fridge, where they remained, unmoving, until we moved out. They're probably still there.

BEDROOM

The fun bit. Tempted to say, 'Who cares how you decorate this? Do whatever you like!' But if, like us, you fear you have no taste and wish to curate a classy-looking room like Tuppy might have, there are some things we've learnt while decorating our many rented bedrooms.

Get your colour wheel, Command strips, cheap frames – and go hell-for-leather. No bedside table? Get a crate or an old wooden wine box and cover it with some cheap material in a colour that matches the rug, or paint it using a £1 sample pot. Get a bedside lamp to create ambience. If you can't afford a bedside lamp, get some fairy lights that you can wind around the headboard and if anyone has anything to say about fairy lights looking tasteless, they can just shut up.

TESSA: For a while last year, I lived in a basement underneath an amateur drummer and was deeply miserable. I refused to listen to my own advice about not waiting to make things nice because I was convinced I was about to move out. Then I eventually bought one (1) string of fairy lights for the bedroom and texted Stevie in tears because I'd started crying about how nice it looked. Get some fairy lights.

Put cheap scented candles from Poundland on the windowsill. Obviously not bald – go for the ones in glass holders or use an old

66

jar with the label washed off. This is the kind of advice you only give after you've scraped wax off a windowsill for an hour.

Get some nice-looking fake flowers and arrange them in a cheap vase or an old jar. Apparently we are obsessed with old jars.

Cover your bed in a nice duvet (or an old jar??). We know we just said you weren't allowed white because you'll get it covered in stains, but the duvet is the exception. A crisp, white duvet immediately says, 'I'm a grown-up taking myself seriously.' Decorate your bed with colourful blankets and cushions that will mainly live on the floor and only be replaced when you are receiving visitors or Instagramming yourself lying in bed with the caption 'Cosy nights in'.

Storage is possibly the most boring thing to buy, but the most overlooked element in making a bedroom look nice. It doesn't need to be expensive; just simple, clean and big enough to cram weird shit into it when someone comes round and you want to bone them.

Shoes are a nightmare because you need to get to them quickly and they look terrible clumped along the walls. It's customary to shove them on the floor of your wardrobe, but then the doors never close properly and the bottom of your long dresses smell of shoe. If you can fit things under your bed, get some pull-out drawers on wheels and throw them all in there.

We are absolutely desperate to force you to buy a new mattress, but it's often impossible to budget for, so the most important thing you can do is buy a mattress protector. This means that when you wake up after a restless night and the sheet has been wrenched free, you will be protected, instead of coming face to face with a stained old mattress that 400 people have also slept on and my God what is that do you think it's blood?

LIVING ROOM

Sorry . . . you've got a separate living room? Wow. OK. Just, like, use it to store YOUR JEWELS AND GOLD INGOTS, why don't you?

The biggest and most fundamental change you can make to a living room is a sofa cover. The difference between a throw and a cover is as follows: when you sit on the sofa, a throw will flop down and appear to vanish up your bum. A cover remains where it is, almost like it's not a cover but the sofa itself, which is especially important if you have one of those faux-leather sofas landlords are obsessed with. They look all right until you spend the summer sticking to them and the winter freezing on them. A cover will make your sofa 100% more inviting.

Use lamps instead of the Big Light to create a homely atmos. Cover chairs and sofas with as many cushions as you can – but make sure they vaguely match the general colour scheme.

TESSA: I went through a long period of buying throw cushions, but only if they had animals on them that were also sigils from *Game of Thrones*. It was largely ill-received by the rest of the house.

There's a weird rental obsession with grimy lace curtains that go halfway up the window. Hide them under the sink and put them back up when you leave.

STEVIE: Tessa means you should replace them, obviously, rather than have no curtains.

TESSA: No, I don't.

STEVIE: Only take the horrible lace curtains down when you have the replacement curtains ready, otherwise you'll waltz in from a shower while home alone, forget you have no curtains, accidentally drop your towel in front of the family across the road who are eating their dinner and be forced to crawl out of the room like a naked mole rat.

TESSA: I advocate for no curtains. I'll take the natural light over the nude risk.

If you're sharing with a load of friends, the living room can become a dumping ground for all the stuff people don't want in their bedrooms. Splitting the cost of some boring storage boxes to put behind the sofa or somewhere out of the way can help stop that, as can getting one of those coffee tables that open up so you can shove things inside. Obviously that's not a necessity so don't worry if you've already blown the budget on 400 fairy lights for your bedroom.

Getting a bookcase is a nice touch – you can split the cost if it's for a communal area – and maybe look at getting a rug or, if you're feeling really fancy, a pouffe. Charity shops are good for pouffe hunting. Bonus points, by the way, if your pouffe has storage. Imagine a pouffe that opens up to reveal things inside. Imagine!

CONSERVATORY
Get out.

How to Listen

Humans are very bad listeners. Most of us passively nod and smile and don't take in a single piece of information because the whole time they're talking we're thinking about what we're going to say next.

We're all guilty of talking instead of listening. A friend tells a story about a terrible date, or a bad boss, and to try to help we talk about our own experiences and how we dealt with the situation. There's a place for these stories – they can make people feel much less alone – but they can't be the first thing you go to. When someone is having a tough time and wants to talk, we need to practise *active listening*. Not just being quiet while they're talking, but truly listening to what they're saying, and picking up on the clues to what they're *not* saying.

We've come up with the very catchy slogan:

There's no 'I' in listen.

Unfortunately there is, but we stand by it.

From now on, when you're properly listening to someone, you must remove the 'I' from the conversation.

That isn't to say you're not still an active part. Once you've removed the I sentences, there'll be so much more room for questions, allowing you to actually work out what's going on and what you can do about it. Oh! Oh! Wait, we've got one:

Only when we close our Is, can we truly open our ears.

Powerful stuff, right?!

It's not 'I think' and 'I feel', it's 'you seem' and 'that sounds'.

All anybody wants in this life is for someone to say, 'I see you,' like in *Avatar*. And that's what active listening provides. Except there's no I in listen, so maybe they should say, 'You are seen.' For God's sake, somebody wire these notes to James Cameron.

We learnt all this at the knee of lead FBI hostage negotiator Chris Voss, from his book *Never Split the Difference: Negotiating as if your life depended on it*, and to be fair some of what we've learnt is very specific to an actual hostage situation.

The FBI's Crisis Negotiation Unit developed this behavioural-change five-step plan:

1. *Active Listening: Listen to their side and make them aware you're listening.*
2. *Empathy: You get an understanding of where they're coming from and how they feel.*
3. *Rapport: Empathy is what you feel. Rapport is when they feel it back. They start to trust you.*
4. *Influence: Now that they trust you, you've earned the right to work on problem-solving with them and recommend a course of action.*
5. *Behavioural Change: They act. (And release the hostages.)*

So quuuuuite specific there to hostage negotiation. But if we can use these five steps to get a warlord to release his hostages from his stronghold in the Philippines, then we can use them to make our friend feel heard.

STEVIE: You're really using 'we' very liberally here. I assume you don't actually mean we.
TESSA: I'll tell you something else I learnt at the Academy: when you ASSUME, you make an ASS out of U and ME.
STEVIE: Oh my God.
TESSA: I actually learnt that from reading *Silence of the Lambs* when I was eleven, which we can all agree was Too. Young.

STEP 1: ACTIVE LISTENING

The first part of active listening is to let them get everything out without you wading in with your ideas. It's so easy and tempting when someone is upset to get straight to problem-solving, but problem-solving is Step 4 on the FBI checklist, so slow down there, bucko, and let them talk. Sometimes it'll all be coming out of them like a volcano and you've just got to get out of the way of the lava and let it run its course, or maybe it's all buried deep and you need to draw it out.

You can help this by not interrupting them when they're speaking and acknowledging that you've heard what they're saying with helpful little phrases like 'mm-hmm' and 'OK' and 'go on'.

STEVIE: Those phrases are so important. When people don't make them I feel like they have died of boredom or aren't listening.

But when people make a noise after every single thing you say they sound like they're malfunctioning, so find a happy medium. A liberal sprinkle of 'mm-hmm'.

When they've made a point, summarise it back to them to communicate that you've got the gist of what they're saying. Not like a robot, but in a 'OK, so you feel like your new colleagues haven't got used to having a new person in the office yet?' kind of way.

STEP 1A: MIRRORING

A great technique for drawing out information if the person is struggling to make sense of their feelings is the exquisitely named isopraxism, otherwise known as mirroring. (From the Greek *iso*, meaning 'same', and *praxis*, meaning 'behaviour', for any etymology fans out there.) We unconsciously mirror each other all the time, in conversation, in vocal tone, in body language. Even a tiny baby will raise their eyebrows if you raise yours. Humans love to mirror. It's why everyone in the theatre will start clapping without thinking if one person starts.

Chris Voss writes: 'For the FBI, a "mirror" is when you repeat the last three words of what someone has just said. Of the entirety of the FBI's hostage negotiation skill set, mirroring is the closest one can get to a Jedi mind trick. Simple, and yet uncannily effective.'

A Jedi mind trick? Yes, please. It sounds absurd but you just curiously, naturally say the last few words back to the person, then you wait.

STEVIE: I don't know about this. If you just repeat words back, it'll just sound like you're parroting them.

TESSA: Parroting them?

STEVIE: Yeah, you know, like an annoying parrot, like something you'd do at primary school.

TESSA: At primary school?

STEVIE: Yeah, if someone did that to me I'd just think they were teasing me.

TESSA: Teasing you?

STEVIE: I guess my instinct is to always – oh shit.

By mirroring, you're basically asking people what they mean, but saying, 'What do you mean?' can make people feel defensive. Mirroring gets the same results, but in an entirely non-defensive way.

STEPS 2 AND 3: EMPATHY AND RAPPORT

If this is your good friend, you should already have a pretty solid basis of empathy and rapport, but keep showing, not telling, them that you understand what they're going through and how they feel. You can share a choice story here if you like about a similar thing you went through. Then step up getting to the heart of the problem by bringing in another FBI technique called 'emotional labelling'.

STEP 3A: LABELLING

Chris Voss explains: 'When people are shown photos of faces expressing strong emotion, the brain shows greater activity in the amygdala, the part that generates fear. But when they are asked to label the emotion, the activity moves to the areas that govern rational thinking. In other words, labelling an emotion – applying rational words to a fear – disrupts its raw intensity.'

Once you can label an emotion, you take away all its power. If you can name something as pain or anger or betrayal or jealousy, then it's out in the open and you can start working through it.

When you're encouraging someone to talk, help them to label their emotions by offering suggestions. Even if you're wrong, it'll help them get closer to the right answer. You might say, 'It sounds like you're really upset,' and they'll be able to say, 'No, I'm not upset, I think I'm actually angry.'

STEP 4: INFLUENCE

Now that they've got everything out, they understand how they feel, they've labelled it and they feel fully seen and listened to, they might be ready to do some problem-solving and make some changes. They also – and this is crucial – might not. Maybe they don't have any demands. Maybe they don't have any hostages. Maybe they just needed someone to listen.

If, and only if, they ask you for advice by specifically looking into your face and saying, 'What do you think I should do?' then you may offer your advice.

STEP 5: BEHAVIOURAL CHANGE

Again, you might never make it this far, but if you do, you're only going to get behavioural change if the person comes up with this solution *on their own*.

Keep saying, 'It sounds like . . .' rather than, 'I think . . .' to point them in the right direction. They should be enthusiastically saying, 'That's right!' when you correctly label an emotion or make them feel seen and heard. They shouldn't be miserably hanging their head and saying, 'You're right,' when you've shouted at them about the crystal-clear solution.

Don't just go waddling in with the solutions, even when – and especially when – the solution is obvious.

Good luck out there, kids. Fidelity, Bravery, Integrity.

How to Drink More Water

GO TO THE TAP.
DRINK THE WATER.

Having tried many different techniques, including buying fancy water bottles, making a little chart, downloading a phone app, following a Twitter account that just tweets 'drink more water', squeezing lemons into it, adding squash to it and setting regular phone alarms, we regret to inform you that the only way you can drink more water is to drink more water. Sorry.

How to Handle Job Rejection

Listen. There's nothing for it, you will apply for jobs and you will get rejected. You'll convince yourself it was the poor quality of your application or your general personality when, more often than not, the job you were applying for had already been given to the account manager's nephew Quentin and they only advertised the job for show.

When we were young, back in the Old West, the internet was only just kicking off. You had to 'dial in' on the family computer to get online, which made an insanely loud and long noise, and then you had to get off the internet because your parents needed to use the phone. It was WILD. But now the internet lives in your pocket, and every day you have to see hundreds of people shouting about their once-in-a-lifetime opportunities, while you're faced with yet another 'due to the volume of applicants we cannot provide feedback' email.

TESSA: I once saw a girl write, 'Went for a job interview today and didn't get the job . . .'
STEVIE: Oh wow. That's so refreshing and—
TESSA: Wait for it. The sentence finished: '. . . instead they said

I was so perfect they offered me a totally new role, with a bigger salary!'

STEVIE: Stop it.

TESSA: True story. I include it here verbatim as a form of revenge.

People never post 'OMG! Got rejected again!' but if we saw the jobs people didn't get, rather than only the ones they did, we'd feel a lot more confident to keep on applying and a lot better about taking rejection in our stride. The average person is rejected 24 times before they get a yes,[6] but if you're trying to work in a particularly competitive field, we're fairly sure that number inflates to 24,000.

To level the playing field, and make you feel less alone when the inevitable happens, we've compiled a list of every job we've been rejected from.

THE JOB REJECTIONS OF STEVIE MARTIN (BA HONS 2:1) (LEVEL 5 BARRACUDA SWIMMING CLUB)

Cashier at Argos

Had an interview. The manager said I was 'very cold'.

What it taught me: In order to appear friendly, I have to smile a lot more than other people.

---

6 Pierson, O., *Highly Effective Networking: Meet the right people and get a great job* (Career Press, 2009).

Nobody Panic

Silver-service waitress at now-defunct restaurant The Curious Orange

Was devastated about this because I wanted to be a fancy waitress so much.

What it taught me: That silver service is a specific skill you have to learn. It doesn't just mean 'this restaurant has silver cutlery' and it's more involved than just putting one hand behind your back like a butler.

Copywriter at a production company

I got invited to a trial day where I wrote press releases for comedy shows. They said I was brilliant and I was never asked back.

What it taught me: Sometimes, you'll never know why you didn't get a job. There are so many reasons someone can reject you – they may be looking for something specific you could never know about; you might have the same name as someone they didn't like at school; they might have read the application on a Friday when they were tired and hungry. The point is: it's so far out of your control, it often has nothing to do with you, and you are not getting rejected because you are a small poo on the bottom of life's shoe. Look, I just made up that rhyme and I've been rejected hundreds of times – if I, a multifaceted poet, can be rejected, anyone can.

Internship at *Woman* magazine, internship at *Good Housekeeping*, internship at *Vogue*, internship at *Grazia*, internship at the *Daily Mail* (sorry), internship at the *Sunday Times*, internship at a

80

What it taught me: You never know what good things are just around the corner. I sat on the pavement outside the office for an hour before my interview, and I remember thinking I didn't know if I could face another rejection. And then that job changed my life. Not because of the money (it was laughably badly paid), but because someone believed in me when I had stopped believing in myself. Sometimes I find myself supporting people unwaveringly, almost aggressively hard. If you have even the inkling of a dream, I will shake you until you start pursuing it. If you are good at something, I will chant it from the sidelines until you listen. No one likes this technique and I have been asked to stop. And that is all John. He gave me all of that support and belief and now that I need it a little less, it's there for me to pass on. Keep putting one foot in front of the other and hang in there, because if you are sitting on life's pavement right now, you have no idea what good things are coming.

How to Understand Wine

Wine is such an unbearable and snobby subject that we thought the only way round it was to present this fun poster of WINE FACTS! We used to only buy wine with animals on the label and whisper, 'How can it be dry when it's literally wet?' but *then* qualified wine expert (and school friend of Tessa) Phoebe O'Donnell came on the podcast and our minds were blown. So we hope we can pass some of our new-found wine confidence onto you.

FACT!

The first rule of wine is that it's for everyone! If you like Blossom Hill, drink Blossom Hill! If you only like dessert wine, drink dessert wine! If you like Blue Nun, drink Blue Nun! There are no good wines and bad wines – if you like it, then it's a fantastic wine for you. No one is allowed to make you feel bad about what wine you like.

FACT!

What you might think of as types of wines are actually types of grapes. Merlot, Malbec, Chardonnay, Pinot Grigio, Sauvignon

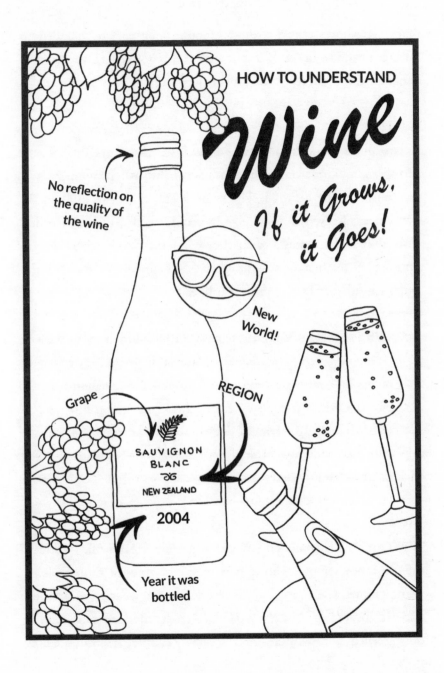

Blanc, Riesling – these are all grapes. They can be blended in different ways to make different wines and they will taste different depending on where in the world they were grown.

FACT!

A Sauvignon Blanc from New Zealand will taste very different to a Sauvignon Blanc from France because of the soil, the temperature, the sunshine, the altitude. The same grape can taste different in two vineyards even if they're only a mile away from each other. How they're harvested, when they're picked, how much they're squashed – it all makes a difference. Remember to look for the grape you like *and* the region you like.

> STEVIE: I always thought I hated Malbec and then after the wine episode, I bought a Malbec from Argentina and it nearly blew my mouth and brain away. I also hate French Sauvignon Blanc but ADORE it from New Zealand and can't express how cool I feel breezily specifying a grape's country of origin in bars. 'Oh, have you only got the French Sauvignon? No worries, I'll take the Pinot Grigio then.' Marry me.

FACT!

Wines are divided into Old World and New World. Old World is the old fancy regions who've been making wine for thousands of years: France, Germany, Italy. These wines are wearing a monocle and are covered in dust. New World are the modern gang who've only recently got involved: the US, New Zealand, Australia, Chile.

These wines have recently taken up base-jumping and are just happy to be here.

FACT!

If it grows, it goes! The correct phrase is actually, 'If it grows together, it goes together,' but we like ours better. If you ever spiral into a panic because someone asks you for an appropriate wine for dinner, just ask what's cooking, and pick a wine from that country. Spaghetti? Get a hearty Italian wine. Lamb? Try one from New Zealand. Steak? Something from Argentina. That's why wine tastes so delicious on holiday, because you're eating the region and drinking the region (also, you're on holiday). If you've ever brought a bottle you loved home from holiday, try to eat the same sort of food, or drink it all on its own.

FACT!

Wine is kept on its side so that the cork doesn't dry out and shrink, which would let oxygen in, which would ruin the wine. You don't need to store a screw-top on its side, but even if you've got a cork, you're not trying to preserve it for a hundred years, so it really won't matter where you keep it while it's waiting to be opened, as long as it stays somewhere with a constant temperature.

FACT!

If you go into a wine shop and say, 'I have a budget of £10 and I'm looking for a white wine that goes *whoosh* in your mouth,' or

'I'm looking for a red wine that tastes like log fires and Christmas,' they will not laugh and will help you. You're as entitled to be there as that man with the moustache looking for six crates of the 1907 Heidsieck that was meant for Tsar Nicholas II but was torpedoed by a German submarine during the First World War and then lay at the bottom of the ocean where it was preserved in perfect condition until it was rescued from the shipwreck in 1998. Actually, maybe let him go ahead of you.

FACT!

The grapes in champagne are Chardonnay, Pinot Noir and Pinot Meunier. We include this one because it always comes up in pub quizzes and now you can lean in with authority and whisper, 'It's Chardonnay, Pinot Noir and I've forgotten the last one – maybe Pinot Moomin?'

FACT!

Dry white wine just means the opposite of sweet. Brut means very not sweet. So brut champagne is a dry, dry boy and the opposite is sec or demi-sec. Sometimes it's hard to tell if you like brut or sec, dry or sweet – if you sort of shudder after you've sipped it, it's probably just too dry for you.

And remember, anyone who tries to make you feel stupid for liking a particular wine is an arsehole! Happy drinking.

How to Be More Assertive

Assertiveness isn't yelling, 'GET IT DONE!' at people in a board meeting. It can be as simple as being able to answer the question, 'What would you like to eat tonight?' without having a meltdown.

> TESSA: This has been a huge revelation to me. I realised that responding with, 'Oh, whatever you want, I'm easy!' was not, in fact, me being easy, but me being worried about making decisions that the other person would secretly hate. I only ever did what everyone else wanted to do, the whole time thinking I was being breezy. But a breeze knows which direction it's blowing in and whether that direction is Wagamama or not.
>
> STEVIE: I constantly offer Wagamama when people ask where I want to go for dinner. Which is strange, considering I barely go there.
>
> TESSA: And why is that?
>
> STEVIE: Because everyone else always wants to – oh, I see what I did there.

There is a huge difference between being assertive and being an arsehole. Assertive is being forthright about what you want or what you need, while being mindful of what other people might want or need. You ask questions and are willing to compromise. Arseholery is being forthright about what you want or need while ignoring everyone else. You don't ask, you don't compromise, and you walk all over people. It's a fine line, but fear of being an arsehole can keep you firmly in the passive camp. If you listen to others and try to be balanced and fair, you'll always stay safely assertive.

Assertiveness comes from self-respect. If you are a person, your thoughts and opinions are valid, and you deserve the option of Wagamama being thrown into the hat, and then that hat being thrown into the ring. Notice we didn't say you deserve to go to Wagamama – that's arsehole territory. But you deserve the chance to at least express your desire for katsu curry with a side of salted edamame beans. Everyone deserves that.

TESSA: If someone asked me where I wanted to go for dinner, the thought of choosing sent me into a white-hot panic. And it wasn't that I had a desperate restaurant desire and was keeping it secret. I would look inside myself to see what I wanted and honestly it was just tumbleweed in there. Nothing. So I had to really practise asking myself what I wanted, pretending it was only me going to dinner. It took quite a long time to get good at it, which, now I'm writing it down, is quite embarrassing.

STEVIE: Don't feel embarrassed. In order to truly know what I want, I do a thing where I pretend I'm going to get shot if I make the wrong choice. What even is that?! I'll be trying your method from now on.

TESSA: God, there's so much to unpack there.

Here are some scenarios and situations to show you the difference between arseholery and assertiveness. You might be passive for some, and arsehole for others, and that's OK! As long as you're aware of it, you can tone it down or build it up. Start slowly with low-pressure, low-stakes situations and soon enough you'll be able to do it in the boardroom. Or any room. There'll be no stopping you!

Where would you like to go for dinner?		
PASSIVE	ARSEHOLE	ASSERTIVE
Wherever you guys want to eat! I don't mind!	We're going to Wagamama. I've booked a table. I don't care that nobody else likes Asian fusion.	I quite fancy Wagamama if anyone else does too? But if not, just glad to be hanging out!

How do you celebrate your birthday?		
PASSIVE	ARSEHOLE	ASSERTIVE
The idea of people making a fuss makes me feel sick so I tell everyone I don't care, but then on the day when nothing happens I get a bit sad. TESSA: This is me. STEVIE: I didn't know we could chat in boxes! TESSA: We can chat anywhere![7]	However I want and wherever I want. Last year I organised a parade where I forced people to carry me in a sedan chair. Everyone complained and some people got hurt, but I don't care. It's MY day.	Whatever I fancy! I've had small dinners and big parties. If I get nervous about being the centre of attention, I always remember to let myself be celebrated! If people want to sing and make a cake, of course it's embarrassing, but I let it happen!

What did you think of that film we just watched?		
PASSIVE	ARSEHOLE	ASSERTIVE
I don't know, what did you think?	I hated it. It is irrelevant to me what you think because the only correct opinion is my opinion, which is that it was a literal piece of garbage and if you think otherwise then you are a piece of garbage.	Yeah, I thought some bits were really fun – very weird when the Joker showed up because I thought it was a romantic comedy, and I didn't get the bit when we went back in time, but I loved that big musical number. What did you think?

---

7 STEVIE: Good to know.

Do you find it difficult to say no?		
PASSIVE	ARSEHOLE	ASSERTIVE
Yes.	No. Never. I never do anything I don't want to do, regardless of the other person's feelings.	If it's really important to the other person, I'll do things I would prefer to say no to, but in general I know it's not healthy to be a people pleaser. I know my boundaries and I'm comfortable setting them.

How do you tell your boss you're booking a holiday?		
PASSIVE	ARSEHOLE	ASSERTIVE
I leave it until the very last minute, then whisper, 'I was wondering if I could take off two weeks in August? I've saved up my holiday, but no worries if not!' Then spend the whole holiday worrying I've let work down.	I say, 'I'll be taking a holiday in August despite the fact that I have no holiday left over. Someone will just have to cover for me.'	'I will be using my holiday up in August – just wanted to let you know in advance so we can all prepare accordingly!'

How often do you say 'sorry'?		
PASSIVE	ARSEHOLE	ASSERTIVE
40–60 times a day. Today I walked into a tree and said sorry to the tree.	Never. Never, ever. No matter what I've done.	It's instinctive to say sorry, but I make sure I catch myself. I say 'excuse me' instead of 'sorry to bother you' and make sure I say 'thank you' afterwards instead of apologising for asking for help.

How to Be More Assertive

How do you feel about changing the music at a house party to your own playlist?		
PASSIVE	**ARSEHOLE**	**ASSERTIVE**
That is my hell.	I do it the moment I walk in. No one ever has the right music on and I cannot relax without my superior beats.	If the vibe really needed it, or the party had really lost morale, I might step up and help out. But otherwise, if the host is happy, I'm happy.
How would you give back a coffee that was cold?		
PASSIVE	**ARSEHOLE**	**ASSERTIVE**
I wouldn't. I would rather die.	A cold coffee?! Fuck you. I would throw it in their face and demand an apology, two new coffees and a cake.	'Hi, I know it's not your fault – this coffee is delicious, but it's cold. Do you mind if I have a new one?'

How to Spot Relationship Red Flags

Hey, you! Want to know if they're The One? Remember those magazines that reduced complex psychological issues into a cute multiple-choice quiz? No? Well done for being so young, babe! And welcome to this fab format, which will mostly consist of reducing a complex psychological issue into a cute multiple-choice quiz!

Just keep a tally of what you get and we'll tell you if your One is right for you, or whether you should get out quicker than you can say, 'I think that flag looks more pinkish than red, but it could be the light.'

Now, listen, obviously red flags within a relationship are more nuanced than a quiz (or even a whole book) can cover, because every person and every relationship is different. Unlike *J-17* magazine, we can't tell you if someone is The One or not, but we can help open your eyes to some bad behaviours, and maybe plant the seed of the idea that this One might be Actually Quite a Bad One. And we say this as two people who have been with Actually Quite a Bad One, seen the red flags and lovingly made a quilt out of them.

THE BIG RED-FLAG RELATIONSHIP QUIZ

1. What do people you love and respect say about them?

A Your pals and rents (Nineties abbreviation of parents, not various rental payments) LOVE THEM.

B Yeah, they seem to like them. Sometimes when you chat to them about arguments, your friends will jump to defend you, but that's because they're your friends. Overall, everyone is happy for you.

C They either actively dislike them, and have said so, or things feel awkward whenever you bring them up. So you've stopped talking about them. If you're honest, not everybody knows you're in a relationship. They just wouldn't understand so it's easier not to mention it.

2. Do you find yourself lying to excuse their behaviour?

A No! Why would you do that??

B Only very occasionally when they've been a real dick. But you can be a real dick too. Either way, you always sort it out between you so there's often no point getting your friends involved.

C Yeah, but that's only because it looks worse than it is – your mates and your family wouldn't understand. It's just the ups and downs of a relationship, and everyone has those! Plus, they said it won't happen again!

3. Do you ever want to check their phone?

A For what? They're always leaving their phone lying around and it's all just work stuff and memes.

B Well, there was that one time you considered it, but that was just idle curiosity – and you stopped yourself because you know they'd never do anything. You trust them.

99

C You either have or you really want to – whether it's because of A Feeling or because of a particular incident, like that weekend they were totally non-contactable and you had no idea where they were.

> STEVIE: Or perhaps it's how they don't let you come to a particular annual party because 'it's not really for girlfriends' and then you find out their friends bring their girlfriends and it's actually so they can flirt and get off with other people. FOR EXAMPLE.

4. They have an opinion and you vehemently disagree. What do you say?

A You say . . . you disagree and then you talk about it? Is this a trick question?

B Sometimes you'll keep an opinion to yourself if you can't be bothered getting into a discussion right now, but when it comes up again you always talk about it. Also, some things are best left unsaid, like, 'That's the wrong way to cook pasta,' or 'Your haircut makes you look like Rod Stewart.'

C If you disagree, it often turns into an argument so you tend to keep things to yourself.

5. How do they talk about their exes?

A Gross subject alert! But whenever it comes up, they've always been fair and kind.

B They're sometimes reluctant to talk about it, but they're never unduly cruel or mean. Apart from that one ex who cheated on them – they're sometimes snarky about them, but it's always jokey and barely ever comes up.

C They either never mention their exes at all and shut it down if you bring them up, or, if they do, the only thing you know for sure is that all their exes were crazy psychopaths and terrible, terrible people.

6. Do you hang out with their friends?

A Yes – they're great!

B Yes, but not always. Sometimes you skip it, but you show up to everything that's important. You like their friends; they seem like good people. They take an interest in you, and you don't feel like a third wheel, which is nice.

C They prefer to keep friends and relationships separate. You've gone to some things, but you don't feel like you fit in. But that's your fault, really – maybe you're too uptight and not fun enough. You always seem to say stupid or boring things at just the wrong time!

7. Do they take an interest in your work?

A Absolutely – you always know each other's ups and downs and are there with advice when things go wrong. You know the names of their colleagues and have even joined work drinks a few times.

B Sure. There are times when you're both absorbed in your own little worlds, but they seem genuinely interested in what you do. It's helpful to talk to them about work problems; they like to try to solve them with you – and you hope they feel that you do the same for them.

C A bit. Well, not hugely. They ask how your day was but don't really know a lot about it. Your job is boring, so you don't blame them too much! You don't completely understand their job; there's a lot of characters involved, and when you try to ask questions they always roll their eyes because you don't get it, but that's your fault for not being smart enough!

8. How's the rumpy pumpy? (We can't remember how Nineties magazines referred to sex so have opted for this.)

A No complaints lmao rofl! (Text speak was quite big among the youth as we crested into the early 2000s.)

B It goes through stages – sometimes you're all over each other, sometimes you're not. Sometimes they want it more than you, sometimes you want it more than them. You address problems as they arise and you both fancy each other, so on the whole you're happy with your life re: rump and/or pump.

C It's wild! And you're not always steering the ship; they're in charge. That's exciting, though! Well. You have to fake enthusiasm sometimes – well, all right, a bit more than sometimes – and you always wait for them to initiate. Whenever you try to talk about your sex life, they get a bit defensive or shut the conversation down. It's hard to talk about, though – so many people struggle with talking openly about this stuff so you're not too worried.

9. Do they push you to do things you don't want to do?

A Never! Why would they do that?

B Only if you're self-sabotaging and pushing yourself would really help. Like that time they said, 'Maybe try getting out of bed before 11 a.m. every morning if you're struggling to get all your work done.' That was useful. Or pushing you to be braver at work. Actually, they push you all the time. They're always really cheering you on and believing in you.

C Yes, and sometimes it can make you feel anxious, but you know they just want you to improve. If only you could get a handle on it, be a better partner to them. You always seem to be messing it up.

10. Do they ever put you down?

A Put you down? They're too busy picking you up and swinging you round like a basket of muffins!

B Like teasing? Yeah, you tease each other, but only about silly things. They'd never say something cruel.

C Well, they tease you about your weight and your appearance and a couple of other things they know you're insecure about. And they compare you to an ex a lot, and say all the things the ex did better, but it's just a way to help you improve! You do need to improve!

11. Do they ever call you crazy?

A What? Lord, no. Well, once you were both running along the dunes on the beach at midnight and they shouted to the starlit sky, 'This is crazy!' Does that count?

B Sometimes you do things that are a bit left field and then you talk about it, have a laugh about it and you feel loads better. Like once you got upset about how lonely the golf balls at the bottom of the pond on the golf course must be, and then you agreed that they're probably doing OK down there and have a new life and if anything they're thriving.

C Well, yeah, but only when you are being crazy. Like if you ask too many questions, or accuse them of something. And you can't accuse your partner of anything, right? Ever.

12. BONUS QUESTION: Are they your best friend?

A Yes! Of course! And did you mention they are DREAMY?

B What sets apart your SO (we are abbreviating 'significant other' here, not yelling the word 'so') is that it's not just a Serious Relationship. You're best pals who bone. You tell each other stuff you wouldn't tell other people, you have each other's backs and for the first time in your life it feels like you're part of a real, equal team.

C You get lots of different things from different people – you two prefer to separate friends and relationships. There are things you do with friends, and things you do with a partner. So no, but that's not a bad thing!

OK, READY FOR THE RESULTS, BABE?

MOSTLY As

You have either just started going out with this person, or you are both fictional characters. Crack on, king. Just be aware that when something isn't perfect that doesn't mean the relationship is in crisis, so don't worry if there are bumps in the road ahead. Sounds like you've got great communication skills and you're going to be just fine.

MOSTLY Bs

There's the odd flag because you're two individuals trying to work things out – but it seems very balanced on the whole. It seems like you're able to point at the flag and discuss it openly, rather than wilfully ignoring it, or being made to feel crazy for pointing it out. If you're communicating about those ups and downs and always trying to improve as a couple, then there's no need for flag poles.

MOSTLY Cs

We're not relationship experts and we're not going to tell you to freak out because your relationship is toxic. However, if you answered C for more than a couple of questions then it's time to tackle that flag. Talk to your partner and make suggestions as to how you can put the flag back in the flag shed. Think about what you would want if you weren't worried about upsetting them, and how you can communicate that in a clear, friendly way without laying blame at their feet. Use a lot of 'I feel . . .' sentences rather than 'You do this . . .' Be honest with yourself, and if the response is negative, or the issue is shut down and flipped back around as entirely your fault or remains unchanged, then ask yourself if you want to be in a relationship where your feelings are readily pushed aside like that.

The thing about love is that all the stories are about it being wild and passionate, so when drama comes along, you think, 'Ah, yes, THIS is love.' You stop listening to your gut, because shut up, gut, this is LOVE. But it's not love. It's lust and passion and chaos and drama and lies and it makes you feel alive, but after a while it also makes you feel dead inside.

Love is calm and easy and it never crosses your mind to look at their phone because their phone looks boring. Love is coming home on a cold night and finding they put a hot-water bottle in your bed.

Always remember that you're never in any relationship too deep for you to call time. If there's a feeling in your gut, or a voice in your head telling you to cut and run, that voice needs to speak out. You can always walk away, and at the very least you'll take with you a healthier and better understanding of what you do and don't want in life. If you manage to leave a toxic relationship, you should be incredibly proud of yourself. Don't feel silly for being in denial for so long, you walk in the footsteps of some extremely fine people who've ignored some really big and extremely red flags. The flags look like bunting when you think you're in love.

We're sending you a lot of love, and if things are physical, frightening or you feel scared for any reason, then there are some resources at the back of the book that can help you better than we ever could.

How to Make Friends

When you are small, making friends consists of going up to somebody in the playground and showing them a nice rock. And sure, some of us (Tessa) still use this technique today, but in general, the older you get, the more your social circles decrease and the harder you have to actively try to make friends.

And try as you might – and we can see you're really giving it a go – you won't make friends sitting in your room being sad about not having any friends. Maybe you've just moved to a different city or your old friends have recently moved away. Whatever the situation, you're going to have to go outside and do things. Shoes on, kids, we're going out friend-hunting.

The key thing is to pretend you're more confident than you are, and be ready to make the first move. No wallflowers at this party.

If you're thinking, 'I could never!' may we direct you to questionable James Cameron extravaganza *Avatar*? US Marine Jake Sully, in the body of an avatar he's never used before, having been taken hostage by an alien race, sits down in an extremely hostile circle and turns to the alien next to him and says, 'Hey, man, how's it going?' If he can do it *on another planet*, you can do it. Be Jake Sully.

So, where are we heading on our hunt? Where are the best places to find friends?

AT WORK

By the law of averages, there must be someone at work you like a bit. If everyone at work bores you to death and you've got no friends, genuinely consider moving jobs. Sure, don't mention that in the job interview, but lots of people move jobs because they've got no friends – it's just nobody ADMITS it. Like getting up late. Or eating disgusting food combinations standing up in the kitchen at 3 a.m. (say, cold baked beans and mayonnaise. SAY). Or stalking ex-boyfriends you don't even like any more but must keep tabs on.

> TESSA: Stevie, that is absolutely disgusting.
>
> STEVIE: Which one?
>
> TESSA: The beans and mayonnaise! I don't care who you stalk. May I tell you all, we once took part in this comedy game show at the Edinburgh Fringe where I had to put a duvet cover on a duvet and Stevie had to eat a can of cold baked beans. She finished them with such speed and such gusto that the organisers and the audiences were genuinely taken aback. Even from inside my duvet cover I could tell there was real discomfort in the room.

If you don't work in an office or in a big group, getting a part-time job in a bar or volunteering somewhere is an excellent way to boost your social life. Worth thinking about if you spend your weekends upset and lonely and wishing someone would invite you to the pub.

Why not spend your weekends with people in the pub and be paid to be there?

The approach: Is there a fun person who sits by the printer that you've never spoken to but wears fun hats? Zone in on them. Say, 'That's a cool hat, where did you get it from?' Compliment + question = friendship. Never solo compliment because then they might just say, 'Thanks,' and go back to using the  printer. If they haven't got a fun hat, compliment any other item of clothing. If you work in a nudist colony, ask them about the book they're reading, then say, 'Weird how we work in a nudist colony, eh?'

If you're working remotely, you'll have to try extra hard to keep the friendship vibe alive. Call people instead of sending emails (this is also just excellent advice for life; you get things done so much quicker and there's no weird passive-aggressive misinterpretation. Plus, no one can say 'as per' on the phone).

Office bonding gets a terrible rap, but people will surprise you time and again when they shed their weird work persona and you realise they actually just have an extremely left-field sense of humour. Consider it blanket policy that if *anybody* in the office suggests *anything*, you're in. At least for a bit, while you figure out if you want to be friends with them or not.

AT AN IMPROV WORKSHOP

STEVIE: Improv isn't – no, don't roll your eyes. STOP THOSE
ROLLING EYES AT ONCE. Look at me. Improv isn't for

everyone, but I was trying to write a comedy show and was too frightened to go on stage, so I thought this would help and – COME BACK! I'm not saying take up improv. Maybe it's netball. Maybe it's archery. Maybe it's creative writing. Maybe it's welding. Maybe it's creative welding. Go do something you like and you'll meet people who like the same things as you. Essentially, this is saying 'find a hobby' without saying 'find a hobby' because finding a hobby is lame.

You've found a location where you both have to be every Tuesday night *and* you know everybody there has at least a passing interest in the thing you're interested in. And guaranteed somebody in your class will out themselves very early as being the absolute tool of the group, so you can bond over discussing how annoying they are.

The approach: Say, 'Anyone want to go for a drink after this?' You might feel white hot with fear, but we promise, promise, promise someone will want to come for a drink. If not, because they genuinely need to head off, say, 'Next time then,' and do not think this has anything to do with you. People have lives and next week they will be more prepared to drink after class because the idea will have taken root.

If people are hanging out at lunch, say, 'Do you mind if I sit with you guys?' even if it seems as though they're already in a friendship group. It's not weird that you're asking. It would be weirder if you sat three metres away from them, desperate for them to invite you over, which they never will because they think you want to be alone.

STEVIE: I used to do this all the time in the pub I worked at until a friend was like, 'Stevie, you need to stop sitting on your own at lunch and then being upset when people presume you don't want to hang out with them because you've literally chosen to sit on your own.' It was revelatory.

If you're a shy soul and your instinct is to go straight home or to sit by yourself, force yourself along for one drink. Force yourself to ask questions and chat to people in the break instead of going on your phone. You don't have to be the life and soul of the party, but the basic foundation of friendship is showing up. WWJSD? What would Jake Sully do? If in doubt, say, 'Hey, man, how's it going?' and see where that gets you.

If you're one of nature's cynics, keep showing up even though the group seems too gung-ho for your liking. Force yourself to join in.

TESSA: I should say here that, despite appearances, when it comes to new groups, I am a grower, not a shower (an expression I thought referred to perennial plants and which I used constantly about myself until about three years ago). In 2012, I danced in the opening ceremony of the Olympic Games and we rehearsed in a car park in Dagenham for nine months. I didn't make a single friend. We used to rehearse all weekend, they'd give us lunch, and I didn't speak to a single soul. I just used to sit by myself reading *Game of Thrones*. I think I thought that everybody was already in a gang, even though we all started out as strangers. Eventually, about eight months in, I started talking to the people on either side of me in the formation and slowly,

slowly came out of my shell. On the night of the ceremony, we were waiting to go on and I remember I had everybody laughing and somebody said, 'You're so funny. When did you move into our group?' and I had to pretend I'd recently moved sections and that I hadn't been there, completely silent, for nine months.

Anyway, the point is, sometimes you've just got to be very brave and say, 'Do you mind if I sit with you guys?'

AT A FRIEND'S BIRTHDAY

If you want friends, just steal your friend's friends! A party is a prime potential friendship gateway. If you're getting on like billy-o (Stevie is trying to bring this phrase back, please be respectful), you can literally say, 'You're excellent, let's be friends, please!' and exchange numbers. It's that simple.

The approach: Break the ice by asking people about their favourite unsolved mystery. If they haven't got a favourite unsolved mystery, don't bother being friends with them.

> TESSA: Mine is the Dyatlov Pass, thank you for asking.
> STEVIE: Mine is Tessa talking about the Dyatlov Pass, thank you for asking.

THE FRIEND OF A FRIEND OF A BOY WHO WENT TO SCHOOL WITH YOUR COUSIN

When you move to a new city you need to be absolutely shameless about friend-hunting. When you first get there the only characteristics these 'friends' need is that they are living, breathing humans who are willing to spend some time with you.

The approach: Zero subtlety, zero mercy. Let everyone you've ever met know you're going to be in a new place and you are down to clown. Stick it all over the internet. Be very clear that you will accept absolutely anyone who wants to hang out with you. Grill your extended family for anyone they may know in the area. Get the word out long before your arrival so you don't find yourself walking all alone around a new city and having yourself a little existential spiral. Get a chilled-out part-time job somewhere fun, like a games café or a vintage clothes store or an ice rink (trying to cover all the interests here) or, more likely, a bar. If you work in the week (and the friend-making potential at your day job is limited), you might not fancy also working the weekend, but it could just be a trial until you find some pals to hang out with on a Saturday.

ON HOLIDAY

While you're probably not going to be making BFFs on holiday (though it's been done), holidays are a fine time to flex that friend-making muscle. It's bold of you to assume you can bring anything to that 15-strong hen party, or the out-of-their-minds-in-love new couple, but most families, small groups of friends and long-term couples are always keen to have someone new to talk to, even if it's only so they will have something else to talk about afterwards.

The approach: Starting holiday friendships is easy because you just point at literally anything and ask questions about it. 'Is that a piña colada?' 'Are you guys from the UK?' and 'Isn't the sunset amazing?' Are you pointing and talking? Great. Now you're Holiday Friends.

STEVIE: I have never once made a friend on holiday. One time a girl started a sort of volleyball thing in the communal pool at a resort in Portugal and I played for a bit but then was like, 'You live in Surrey, I live in Cheshire, this can never work.'

TESSA: Couldn't you just be friends with her on holiday and then go your separate ways?

STEVIE: I would find that too difficult. Can't cope with the lack-lustre 'Hey, you should totally come to Surrey' messages that will inevitably dwindle to nothing months later.

TESSA: If I may, I think you are confusing 'temporary holiday friend' with soulmate. Holiday Friends are meant to last for the duration of the holiday and then no more. Like holiday romances. Love your new friend very intensely and then let them go. Maybe consider it a friendship-making exercise and accept you'll never see them again?

STEVIE: Can't bear it.

TESSA: I see. I think this is where we differ, you and I. I make friends every day. I consider the man in the Post Office to be my friend, even though I don't know his name and he is a conspiracy theorist.

STEVIE: Well, so are you.

TESSA: That's why we're friends. Maybe there are friends, and then there are Friends with a capital F. And you're absolutely right, you're probably not going to find a Capital-F friend in the hotel pool. But I think you've got to take the pressure off and keep making friends, in the hope that some of them become Friends.

STEVIE: I only want Friends with capital Fs.

TESSA: And I acknowledge I can't convince you otherwise.

So there you have it! It's scary making the approach, but it's worth it! You can't sit on the sidelines hoping someone will ask you to dance. You've got to get out there and do the asking! Practise saying, 'Hey, man, how's it going?' and, 'Do you mind if I sit with you guys?' until they're effortless. Now get out there and bag yourself some friends.

How to Bleed a Radiator

TESSA: Stevie, do you want to guess what bleeding a radiator involves?

STEVIE: I think it's when your radiator gets too full of water. So full that it can't circulate the water properly. So you have to unscrew a little hidden knob around the back and then water falls out of a pipe like a tap. You collect the water until you feel like your radiator is a little less full, screw the knob back on and boom. Done.

TESSA: Extremely reasonable guess, and also my guess. The logical guess.

Bleed. A. Radiator. *Bleed*. Has there ever been a more misjudged name for an actually quite simple household task?

People say, 'You need to bleed your radiators there, mate,' and you think, 'Oh, right. I'll obviously never do that.' But if they said, 'Have you considered letting some air out of your radiators so they work more efficiently?' you'd think, 'That sounds very achievable, sign me up.'

STEVIE: Oh, it's air. Well, that makes more sense.

How to Bleed a Radiator

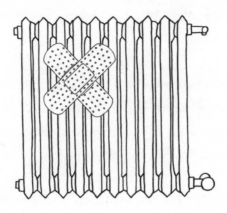

In the UK we're extremely bad at heating our homes. Every house has its own unique and absurd heating system with its own set of rules, and a boiler that has survived two world wars, thank you very much.

> TESSA: In my house at university we had electric storage heaters, which are square white boxes *filled with bricks*! They're illegal now, but the idea was that the bricks – which were made of clay or a ceramic material called 'grog' – heated up during the night when the electricity was cheaper, and then the heat was given off during the day. We obviously didn't understand how they worked, nor did we grasp that they can only give out the heat they've stored through the night, so if you didn't turn them on the night before, you didn't get any heat. It was luck of the draw whether the room was a sweltering Bikram yoga experience or freezing cold. Plus, we were just guessing what all the settings did, turning the dial at will, so occasionally we'd be making sure it was storing electricity when it was at the highest price it could

be. Basically it would have been warmer and cheaper to set fire to piles of cash.

The point is, you've got your own thing going on, but if, when your boiler turns on, it clangs and whistles like the engine room on the *Titanic*, and your radiators are only hot at the bottom rather than the top, it's time to call in the big guns and bleed these mother-fuckers.

STEVIE: How did that feel?
TESSA: I was just trying it out and I REGRET IT.

You've got pockets of air trapped in your radiators, which are stopping the hot water from getting round and are creating cold spots. Since you've already paid for the heating once you've turned the boiler on, it's costing you money to only get half the heat you paid for.

You'll need a radiator key, which looks like this, and can be found at any hardware store for about £1. It's also possible that you've seen one kicking about in a drawer and thought it was the wind-up mechanism for a clockwork mouse.

Turn on the heating and give it a chance to get going. Clang, clang, clang, off it goes.

Then get an old tea towel and loudly proclaim that you're off to bleed the radiators. If no one is in the house, wait until they're back and they definitely hear what you're doing, otherwise what's the point?

Touch all the radiators in the house (carefully) and see which ones have cold spots. Say, 'This one needs bleeding,' when you find one. Shout a bit louder if no one hears you.

Turn the heating back off and let everything cool down. Otherwise, when you open the valve with the radiator key, burning-hot air or boiling water will spray out. Safety first.

STEVIE: I would be so scalded right now if I had not read this chapter.

At the end of the radiator, there's a little stud-like hole, which is both square and not square: this is the radiator bleed valve. It definitely has a bleed valve; it might be somewhere odd, like facing the wall or at the bottom, but it will be there. When you put the key in it will lock in a satisfying way.

Put your tea towel on the floor to catch any drips of water, put the key in the valve and *slowly* turn it anti-clockwise. You should hear a hiss of air. Let this hissing air escape, which could take anything from a few seconds to a whole minute, and keep the valve open until water starts to drip out. As soon as the water is dripping – job done! You've bled all the trapped air from your radiator. All right, Rambo! Now turn the key back clockwise to close the valve.

119

Repeat that performance with all the radiators in the house. Maybe keep your key on you at all times in case your very special set of skills is called upon. We recommend turning it into a fetching necklace or sellotaping it to a hat.

How to Get into Ethical Fashion

For the ultimate guide on this, we recommend the brilliant book *How to Break Up with Fast Fashion,* by author, journalist and friend of the podcast Lauren Bravo, who goes deeper and further than we could hope to here.

Also, this one's quite stressful, so Stevie's peppered it with clock facts to keep the mood LIGHT.

> STEVIE: Did you know the term 'o-clock' is a contraction of the term 'of the clock'?

When we were young, the only available 'ethical fashion' was hand-woven hemp smocks that cost hundreds of pounds and made you look like you'd joined a cult and at any moment might be chosen as the next wife.

But now the tides they are a-turning and everybody nods in agreement when you start talking about organic cotton, instead of asking you to leave the party.

'Fast fashion' is the relentless churning of cheap textiles to the mass market, where the focus is no longer on making good-quality things to wear, but on always making something new to sell. Fifty

121

years ago you had two fashion seasons, summer and winter, and now we have 52, one for every week of the year. It's Primark, and ASOS, and H&M, and Boohoo and TeeHee and OohBoy and Pretty Little Boobs and other legitimate outlets. But it's also the entire garment industry.

We all know it would be better to buy a sustainable £200 cardigan, handmade in the UK, with a solid supply chain where everybody is paid a living wage and a tree is planted for every purchase. But you're never going to do that when you're living off your waitressing tips, can't afford to eat and Primark have one for £4.99.

It's true that if you buy cheap, you buy twice, but it's also true that if you're not rich, you can't buy a £200 cardigan. Of course, one beautiful pair of £100 jeans that last forever would be better than ten pairs of £10 jeans bought in succession one after another as each pair splits down the middle on the night bus. But if you haven't got £100 in your pocket, and you can't save up because you're once again mooning the night bus and you need those trousers right now, it's completely irrelevant.

We're also both very guilty of 'maybe this'll fix it' purchasing. Stevie went through a concerning spate of buying detachable collars off the internet, and Tessa has purchased the entire Hogwarts-themed collection from Primark.

Regardless of how and why we got here, the uncomfortable reality is that at the time of writing fast fashion is the second-biggest polluter of the planet, tagging in just behind the oil industry. The fashion industry uses 1.5–2.5 trillion gallons of water a year, five times more carbon than the aviation industry and – just a shade more horror and then we're done – because they're made with a plastic called EVA (ethylene vinyl acetate), it takes the average pair of trainers 1,000 years to decompose.

> STEVIE: Pennies are used to adjust the time in London's Big Ben clock tower. Each penny added to the weight of the pendulum speeds up the clock by 0.4 seconds per day.

The truth is, we are doing damage to the planet, and we're also doing terrible damage to the people at the other end of the supply chain. But! Think positive! How can we be better?

BUY SECOND-HAND ONLINE

Depop, eBay, Vinted, Shpock and any number of new apps are a wonderful place to buy yourself treasures. If you've found something you like on a high-street website, type in the full name and chances are it'll be there. Probably cheaper and, at the very least, better for the world.

Here are the three main rules of second-hand online shopping:

1. If a designer product is being sold at an absurdly low price, it's probably too good to be true.
2. Ask for measurements or more pictures if you can't be sure of the sizing. Who among us has not bought a rug that turned out to be a mouse mat in the shape of a rug? If the write-up says things like, 'I'm an incredibly petite darling little imp, and it's massive on me! It says size 8 but it would definitely fit a size 14!' err on the side of caution.
3. Do not ever remove the buyer's protection.

BUYING FROM CHARITY SHOPS, VINTAGE SHOPS AND CAR-BOOT SALES

TESSA: When I was growing up, absolutely everything we owned was second-hand and we lived like kings. Sure, I didn't own a pair of shoes that fit until I was 24, but that's a small price to pay for having the best toys and the best clothes, and all the bestselling books, just exactly one year behind everybody else.

STEVIE: Can you tell everybody about what happened with the trousers?

TESSA: Stevie was at my house one summer, and there was a big bag of clothes in the living room that was going to charity and my mum said, 'Oh, yes, have a rummage, have anything you want.' Stevie finds this pair of trousers, which my mum had thrown away without asking my dad. She sits down at the dinner table and my dad watches her for a while, and then just gently leans over and says, 'Stevie, are those my trousers?'

STEVIE: I was mortified.

TESSA: I laugh every time I think about it. He thinks this girl has shown up at his house and then gone into his room and taken his trousers! Anyway, get yourself to a car-boot sale. I've been to a few of these fancy London ones and that's not what I'm talking about. I'm talking about a massive field in the middle of nowhere with every treasure under the sun. Roller skates, fur coats, wedding dresses for a pound. Once, I bought an L.K. Bennett dress and then Kate Middleton wore it and I sold it on eBay for £300. Once, I nearly bought a full medical-school skeleton, but then the police were called and it was established that it's actually illegal to sell human remains in a field on a Sunday morning. The car-boot sale Holy Grail is a very rich and classy woman who's just gone through a divorce and is now throwing out all her cheating husband's things and all the things he bought her. 'That's a pound,' she'll say, dragging on a cigarette as you gather up priceless designer treasures. 'Fucked the nanny, you know.' She is out there – keep looking for her.

RETURNS AND WHAT TO DO WITH UNWANTED CLOTHES

The terrible, genuinely harrowing truth is that a huge number of stores put returns straight into landfill. Currently 300,000 tonnes of clothing go into landfill a year in the UK, many of them brand new and unworn.[8]

> STEVIE: In 1793, France tried to introduce the ten-hour day to make time-based maths easier. It was a fantastic idea except everybody hated it and noon was at 5 p.m.

Independent, smaller brands are more likely to resell returns, but they're also likely to be more expensive, so it's best to cut it off at the source and only buy what you think you'll actually wear.

eBaying or Depopping old clothes that you no longer want is the perfect way to close the loop and make some sweet Benjamins (money).

---

8 https://clothesaid.co.uk/about-us/facts-on-clothes-recycling

When you post your listing don't scrimp on the picture. Clothes being worn by somebody sell better than clothes spread out on your bed. Get in front of a bare or brick wall and have someone take some photos of you or a friend wearing the item and then crop your head out.

If you'd rather donate than sell them, clothes that are beyond repair can go to textile donation. Office clothes can go to projects like Smart Works, which provides clothes for women who can't afford a new outfit for job interviews, and old bras can go to Smalls for All.

IDENTIFYING ECO-FRIENDLY CLOTHING BRANDS

Thankfully, if a brand is eco-friendly and sustainable, it will shout about it on its website. If they say vague things like, 'We are committed to sustainable fashion,' look a bit harder and see if they've actually done anything about it. We can all be committed, mate, but what actual concrete improvements have you made? Buying from a small, independent company is automatically more environmentally friendly than buying from a huge brand, because they will be making a smaller amount, or producing to order, rather than churning out more than they need.

Sizeism is an issue here, as it is everywhere, with independent brands less likely to stock anything over a size 14. Every time you notice a nice little brand that doesn't stock larger sizes, drop them a polite message online asking when they'll have larger sizes in stock. If we all did this (which takes about 30 seconds), they'd get so bored of the messages they'd be forced into thinking about dressing all different types of bodies.

RENTING, SWAPPING AND REPAIRING

Instead of buying anything new, can you borrow something off a friend, rent or fix something you already own? The rental market for fancy outfits is booming, and for a fraction of the price, you could rent a designer dress, either as a one-off or as part of a subscription. Environmentally friendly, ethical, cheap – and suddenly you'll be rocking up everywhere in high couture.

Level up your coats and cardigans by swapping the buttons. Put massive gold vintage buttons on a boring cardigan and everyone will start asking where it's from. Swapping the dirty laces of your trainers for new bright-white ones is a minimum-skills, maximum-improvement shoe hack.

If it's a simple tear, you'll be surprised how far you can get by turning it inside out and doing a classic stitch with a needle and thread. For many years, due in large part to Meryl Streep getting a different coat cleaned every night in *The Devil Wears Prada*, we thought dry cleaners were a decadent and unfathomable luxury. But not only are they actually much more reasonably priced than we thought, they also do a tailoring and repair service and will work wonders when you've exhausted your Year 9 Textiles skills. If it's worth wearing, it's worth repairing!

Please follow Stevie on Depop @5tevieM, and follow Tessa to a car-boot sale so you can stop her from trying to buy another skeleton.

How to Be More Organised

by Stevie Martin, a Former Disorganised Person

STEVIE MARTIN'S DISORGANISATION CREDENTIALS

Number of phones lost between 2008–2017: 12
Additional notes: In 2011 I lost four phones in one year. The fifth I dropped while in a self-service independent burrito café and then left at the café. My flatmate got a call and a man said, 'Hello, I found your friend's phone in some salad.'

Average number of new house keys cut a year: 5
Additional notes: I used to regularly climb through the bathroom window in my parents' house and slide into the bath because I'd lost my keys. One time I slid in when the bath was full of water and nearly drowned.

Number of debit cards reissued between 2008–2017: 23
Additional notes: I once took my debit card out of my bag a little too flamboyantly while walking across the Hungerford Bridge and threw it into the Thames.

Number of purses bought: 15

Additional notes: While retracing my steps after a night out in 2012 I found one of my purses in a tree. It was too high up to retrieve. I had no idea how it got there and didn't know what to do so just . . . left it. It might still be there.

Number of missed appointments: countless
Additional notes: There was a good decade or so where I had a diary but never had it on me and so never wrote anything in it. Then I had a phone diary, but as you can see from the above, I was quite often without a phone, so that didn't help either. Also, I would type things like 'THE THING' in the wrong time slot.

Being disorganised felt, to me, like being cursed by a warlock at birth. Other people didn't know the lost/stolen card helpline by heart. Was there a training course everyone else went on that I'd missed? It got to the point where I went to the doctor – which took months because I was too disorganised to book a doctor's appointment – convinced there had to be a neurological reason behind why my friends called losing something 'doing a Stevie', but everything came back negative. I cried so hard when that happened, because then it *really* felt like I was cursed, and then I started therapy.

'Do you think I'm organised?' said my therapist, who never misses an appointment, knows exactly when I've paid her, how much I owe and has a large and incredibly complex-looking diary that she keeps on her knee throughout the sessions. I had been crying because I'd left my purse on the bus again and said that yes, of course I thought she was organised. She was the most organised person I knew.

She told me she was incredibly disorganised. That when she was younger she would lose everything all the time and forget where she was supposed to be, and that's why she has this massive diary by her side at all times. 'How can you possibly remember everything or keep hold of things without helping yourself? You've got to give yourself a chance, rather than throwing your hands up and saying, "Oh well, that's just me!" It doesn't have to be. I'd be a mess without this diary.'

Four years later, and I have just handed in the keys my landlord gave me three and a half years ago. I've lost no phones. I haven't called the lost/stolen card helpline once. To be honest, I'm quite emotional just writing this, considering how much being disorganised ruined my life for so long. Here's everything that helped me fool-proof my life:

1. **Have one main bag that functions, closes and has compartments.**
   When I think of my twenties, I think of crouching in a crowded train station rifling through a bag with a broken zip, looking for my debit card. This doesn't happen if you have a functioning bag with compartments and you know where everything goes. Mine has pockets and a little mini bag attached on a bungee cord where I keep my phone. My keys always go in my coat pocket. My diary always goes in the zip-up compartment, and my make-up always goes together in a make-up bag (not loose!). If you keep your debit card loose in your bag, you might as well throw it into the Thames. You need to know where everything lives, and stick to one bag, rather than 700 different ones of varying sizes and twelve rotating tote bags. Find one you love and stick to it.

2. **Do a verbal check before you leave the house.** Name the things (keys, wallet, phone) out loud while touching them. I used to just say the things without touching them and, unsurprisingly, this technique did not work.

3. **Always, always, always look behind you when you're leaving somewhere.** A train, a bus, a restaurant, the bathroom of a restaurant. Even if you haven't taken anything out and so couldn't possibly have dropped anything. Even if you're in a rush. It takes a nanosecond to look over your shoulder and it'll save so much crying.

4. **Sort out a diary system and stick to it.** Go for something simple rather than, you know, bullet journaling. You need something you can fill in quickly and with minimum fuss the moment you learn about the new event. Never tell yourself you'll pop it in later. You will not pop it in later.

5. **Set alarms for things you're worried you'll forget.** Got a call at 2 p.m.? Set an alarm for 1.55 p.m. Name the alarm 'Call with Janet at 2 p.m. about accounts', so when the alarm goes off you're not trying to decode what 'J' means.

6. **Have somewhere you put your keys every night.** Like a beautiful set of key hooks in the hallway (well away from the letterbox, if you have one, just in case you get burgled) or a key bowl like in the films. You know, when the detective comes home and drops their keys into a nice little bowl.

7. **Put things you forget with things you remember.** The day I started keeping my pill packet in front of my toothbrush is the day I cut down my panicked pregnancy-test purchases by 80% (the other 20% is entirely down to forgetting that I just ate).

8. **Use the starred emails function.** For online train tickets, booking passes, invoice reminders – anything that you need to get done – star it and organise your inbox so the starred emails appear at the top. This has changed my life.

9. **Attach stuff to other stuff.** I lose a lot of reusable water bottles, so I've attached the top of my new one to my bag and now it's not going anywhere. Unfortunately the attachment is quite short, so when I hydrate it looks like I'm trying to eat my backpack, but that's on me and my inability to differentiate 'cm' from 'mm' when reading product dimensions online.

Remember, it's a learning curve! So don't beat yourself up if it takes a while to bed in. I'm not there yet – last week I left my phone in the yoghurt section of Tesco because I needed both hands to pick up an especially large Onken – but as long as you're improving, it's working. Just be careful when taking your debit card out next to fast-flowing rivers.

How to Cope with Grief

We haven't, at the time of writing this book, suffered the kind of smash-you-in-the-face, world-overturned, never-be-the-same-again grief that we know a lot of podcast listeners who have written to us have experienced. Not a mum, a dad, a friend or a person you thought could never leave you. With that in mind, we asked Rachel Wilson, founder of the Grief Network – a community for people bereaved in their late teens to early thirties, which runs meet-ups and events in London that give young people a space to share their stories – for her top-five pieces of advice for those suffering after losing someone. Rachel lost her mum to cancer the day after her twenty-sixth birthday. Below Rachel's excellent tips, we've included some advice for friends of people struggling with grief (spoiler alert: reach in; don't expect them to reach out).

Other excellent resources if you're grieving include Cariad Lloyd's *Griefcast* podcast, which features guests talking about how they sank and swam after suffering bereavement, TheDinnerParty.org – an international community where you can join virtual tables to talk about grief and loss (the site also has bereavement resources) – and LetsTalkAboutLoss.org, which has a wealth of book recommendations, resources and chances to talk to others about what you're going through. Big hugs to you from us, and five pieces of great advice from Rachel:

1. Look after yourself

Grief has a sneaky way of making you beat yourself up. God knows why your brain does this – as if it isn't already in enough pain. But, as clichéd as the concept of 'self-care' has become, this is the time for it. Be gentle with yourself and really try to listen to your body and your mind about what feels good and what doesn't. Don't beat yourself up for feeling low or sad; acknowledge that this is a really difficult time and it's completely legitimate to feel crap for a long time. Allow yourself to feel what you're feeling.

2. Communicate with your friends

In a perfect world, your friends would be mind-readers brought up in a death-positive society where we openly embraced public grieving. More likely, they have received some unhelpful ideas about how to deal with a grieving person – like not asking about it in case they upset you more, or being afraid to speak about it because it makes them confront the mortality of their own loved ones. Some friends will be shit, and it might be time to reconsider your friendships (which is painful when you've already lost enough). But many others will really want to help and not know how. You may not be used to having to ask for help and you probably have no idea what you need, but if there are things you think will make you feel better, ask your friends and tell them how much it means to you. You shouldn't have to do this, but it's better than not asking and spiralling deeper into the sense that no one understands or cares about you. So communicate your needs as much as you're able, and point them towards any grief literature or media that has helped you so they might be able to understand what you're going through more.

3. Find your community
With social media and podcasts and a push to openly talk about death, more support communities are emerging. The Grief Network is great (I'm biased – I'm the founder), but there is also the New Normal, which runs groups for those who've experienced complex grief, those in BAME communities and the Queer communities. There's the *Bereavement Room* podcast, which focuses on diaspora experiences of grief, and *The Grief Gang* and *Dead Parents Podcast* too. Dive in and find the community that speaks to you. Reading books like *Grief Works* by Julia Samuel or *The AfterGrief* by Hope Edelman really help too.

4. All your feelings are valid
There's no right way to do grief. You might feel grateful or livid or bitter or connected; you might have your faith tested or restored; you might feel a weird relief if the person was ill for a long time, or you might feel like life can't possibly carry on. Grief is a whole spectrum of emotions that weave a thread through your entire life. This isn't to say it will be as painful forever, but sometimes it will spike and surge and other days it will be an inaudible murmur. Know that it is the most normal thing in the world to continue to feel grief on significant days, random days and huge milestones. A lot of people come to see their grief as a lasting connection to the love you feel for the deceased, and in some ways, though it's

still painful many years on, it can also be a strangely comforting reminder of the relationship you had and will continue to have with the deceased.

5. Find as many ways to express it as possible

You might be someone who balks at the idea of art therapy or anything 'New Agey', but it's time to find a way to physically express your grief, as well as talking about it. If you bottle up grief it will come out at one point or another and be wayyy more painful when it does. Support comes in all different forms, so find what suits you, but something that includes movement (exercise, dancing, travelling, if you're able), and something that involves creation (take up pottery! Do some art! Sing in the shower!) – these things will all help you to release the tension in your body that grief creates. Remember that support exists in different pillars – friends, family, professional therapy, exercise, etc. – so create your own toolbox of what helps you to continue to give expression to your grief.

A huge thanks to Rachel for her wonderful advice.

Here are a few tips from us on how to help a friend going through the grieving process.

1. Reach in

People always say you should reach out if you're struggling. And you should, of course, if you can, but it can be so, so hard to reach out. If your friend has fallen through the leaves into a hole in the earth, your job is not to call down and shout, 'I'm here if you need me! Do reach out!' and then sit beside the hole waiting for them. Your job is to find a ladder and climb down into the hole.

Don't know what to say? No one does, but something is better than nothing. Don't withdraw, even though that's the natural instinct. If you're writing them a message, use the person's name and don't use words like 'heartbroken' and 'devastated'; you might well be feeling those things, but not as much as they are. If you're really struggling to put the words together, just be honest. Say you don't know what to say, but you're sending them all the love in the world.

If you want to send them a gift, hampers of food, frozen meals they can microwave or Deliveroo vouchers are always helpful, as going to the shops and cooking can often be overwhelming when the bottom has fallen out of your world. Grieving friends told us they've been touched by cookies left on the doorstep, theatre vouchers for when the family is feeling better, books, subscriptions to Disney+, doughnut deliveries – basically, the point is, don't hold back. Just show up and keep showing up.

2. Listen without trying to solve the problem

If they want to talk, let them speak uninterrupted and without trying to make them feel better. They won't feel better, but just being able to speak about it, and get it out, will help them. You don't need to offer advice. Just keep nodding and asking questions and letting them talk it out.

3. If they don't want to talk, don't make them

Don't demand that they start expressing themselves and telling you everything; people deal with things in different ways. They might want to vent or they might want to be distracted, and it's up to you to follow their lead. If you ask, 'How are you doing?' the answer is probably, 'Bad,' but 'How are you doing today?' is more manageable. Just keep asking. Don't let there be a huge, bereaved elephant in the room.

4. Keep inviting them to normal stuff

They might not be able to come to the pub for a while, but don't stop asking them; one day they'll fancy it. The onus is often put on the grieving person to announce when they're ready. A sort of 'Well, they'll tell me when they fancy a drink' thing, but it's hard to do this. People who've struggled with loss can feel isolated in their sadness as it is, and worried that others won't want them there, bringing down the mood. Don't let them feel like this. Keep inviting them with a 'No pressure at all!' vibe and one day it might just be the lifeline they need.

5. Never criticise the way they are grieving

Think they should have got over it by now? Reckon their decision to self isolate is only going to extend the grief? Think taking better care of their appearance, maybe getting a haircut, could help them feel better? Keep your mouth shut. As Rachel says, there isn't a right way to grieve. It can take many forms, and some of those forms won't even look like grief.

STEVIE: When my boyfriend lost his parents, he became completely obsessed with baseball, to the extent that during the World Series he decided to get on a plane at 5 a.m. after the sixth game finished and watch the seventh game from the actual stadium in Houston. He then spent five days wandering around Houston having a nice time. His parents weren't baseball players, but this was a way of coping and escaping and feeling a little closer to them (they did live in America for a bit and his dad loved American sport, so we think maybe this had something to do with it). Anyway, imagine if I'd had a go at him for spending all that money and said he was mad. Sure, it was mad. But he had the money, it was what he needed and I'm so glad he did it (the Houston Astros lost and were outed for cheating, plus one of the pitchers was accused of beating up his wife – look, he picked a terrible team to support).

6. Recommend some resources

While in the eye of the storm, it's hard to go about researching good places to connect with other people who are having similar shitty experiences. Pointing friends in the direction of any of the resources listed in this chapter might be helpful in the future if they feel ready. At the very least, it shows them someone is thinking about them. A lot of this is just trying to show the other person that they aren't alone and that you care – often that's all you can do right now.

7. Grief doesn't go away after a week

Send regular messages saying you're thinking of them or funny memes to cheer them up. Grief lingers and it'll really help them to know you're still there. They're going to be a bit up and down for a while, so in six months' time, when they bail on you with an excuse that doesn't sound right, it's not the time to go off at them. Remember also that the birthday week of the person they lost, as well as the anniversary of their death, could very well be tough for them. They'll appreciate a bit of extra love and support.

How to Be Impressive in the Kitchen

Adapted from our New York Times *bestselling cookbook,* Oh Good, It's on Fire Again

Everyone longs to be a domestic goddess, god or gender-neutral deity. To effortlessly whip things up for unexpected guests, to bring delicious meals to the table with minimal fuss and no tears, and to be confident in the kitchen instead of paralysed by fear. We are not nature's chefs; for many years our signature dish was carrots *à la* hummus. Tessa didn't know that mashed potatoes had to be boiled first and Stevie once blew up a can of beans in the microwave, thought it was an anomaly and put in a second can of beans.

If you, too, fear the kitchen, here are some tips that will make all the difference:

You cannot cheat the system by doing things faster and hotter.
The secret to cooking is to slow down. Gently and lovingly cooking carefully chopped onions on a very low heat for 20 minutes is not the same as throwing broken shards of onion that you've ripped open with your bare hands into a pan and scalding them for 30 seconds like you're on some sort of reality show called *Xxtreme*

141

Onions. You cannot cheat the recipe by doing things hotter and faster, otherwise everything you bring to the table will be simultaneously tasteless, raw and burnt.

If you are a hobsman and like to see what you're doing instead of putting things into the deceitful oven, then always err on the side of less heat, increasing it gently if you need to. You are not a professional flaming-wok chef; everything should not be engulfed in fire. A 'low heat' is so much lower than you think.

This is how everything gets out of control, pans boil over, fingers get burnt, tea towels catch on fire. If you find yourself getting flustered and the muscles in your neck standing up with the sheer fraught-ness of it all, take a breath and pretend you are Nigella Lawson. Never hurried, never overwhelmed, just gently and erotically adding more butter. Slow down. Turn the heat down. Drop those shoulders. Carry on.

Preheating the oven is not 'for wimps'.
When you're in a rush, preheating is boring and seems pointless. But alas, you cannot mess around with the oven instructions, especially for baking. If it says 183 degrees, it does need to be 183 degrees exactly. When you turn the oven on, some parts get scalding hot before the whole thing settles at the right temperature. If you go in cold, parts of your pizza will be gluey and damp while other bits will be burnt to a crisp, and no amount of garlic-and-herb dip is going to save the situation. Think of it like having a bath: you don't just get into cold water and sit there forlornly while it heats up, feet under the tap so some parts are scalding and some parts are freezing.

STEVIE: Oh.

You make it exactly the right temperature, then you hop in. Same for your pizza.

Drawing the flavour out of ingredients takes time.
The difference between a nice pasta sauce and a delicious one is about an hour. If you leave things to gently simmer, they will transform themselves. That's why lots of things taste even more delicious the next day. 'Reduce' means to evaporate, so your sauce needs to look worryingly watery, and then be left on a very low heat for as long as it takes for all the flavours to merge. If you're adding curry or pasta sauce from a jar, tip the whole thing in, then fill the jar up with water, put the lid back on, shake it up and pour the water into the pan as well. This simultaneously ensures all the sauce is used up, gets some extra water in there ready to reduce and cleans the jar ready to be recycled. Thank you very much.

But what if you don't have an extra hour, because you're starving?

A good point, and one of the main things standing in everyone's way. When you're exhausted and hungry, you don't have the energy for this simmering bullshit. Throw some fish fingers in the oven and some potato waffles in the toaster. On the days when you do feel inspired to simmer, make double and put some of it in the freezer or keep in the fridge to come home to tomorrow. Good LORD, who are you, Martha Stewart?

Have the right stuff.

You think it's not important, but then you end up trying to cut an avocado in half with your keys and then there's avocado in your keys for a year. Get a really good-quality sharp knife, and a decent pan, ideally something deep and cast iron, with a detachable handle, so as well as using it for frying on the hob, you can also put it in the oven and then bring it straight to the table like a homesteader on the prairies. Make sure you have proper oven gloves. There's only so many times you'll try to get something out of the oven using your sleeve before you realise it's a very bad idea, and the number of times is 'once'. Ask for good-quality kitchen equipment for birthday presents, or get things second-hand.

Measurements are not suggestions.

One day, when you're a pro, you can throw things in while saying, 'Bosh!' but right now you need to stick to the instructions. It doesn't help that measurements are really tough. A woman on Gumtree recently advertised a chest of drawers and when people messaged to ask how high it was, she sent a picture of her holding her cat next to it and replied, 'It's about as tall as a stretched-out cat.' A kindred soul.

Measurements are hard, and in our opinion the almost identical 'tsp' and 'tbsp' is an act of domestic terrorism. Tsp = teaspoon. Tbsp = tablespoon. Remember that extra 'b' is in there for 'better not forget this is a tablespoon and not a teaspoon'.

If you want to get into baking, you need those fancy nesting measuring cups that look like saucepans for dolls. If you're following an American recipe it will give you insane instructions like add a

144

stick of butter – a *stick* of butter? What is this? The war? – to a cup of sugar. A cup?! Whose cup? This tiny china cup? This Sports Direct mug? With your special doll's pans, you'll get these measurements exactly right.

Know the secret to at least one dish.
For us, it's spaghetti. Here are two pasta game-changers, one from Gino D'Acampo (he of shouting 'If my grandmother had wheels she would be a bicycle' at Holly Willoughby on *This Morning* fame) and the other from Ella Risbridger of the excellent cookbook *Midnight Chicken*.

Your water needs to be not just boiling before your pasta goes in, but, as Nigella says, 'as salty and rolling as the Mediterranean Sea'. Throw loads of salt in there – the cheap red-tube salt; no need to waste the flaky stuff. Add your pasta when the water's really aggressively boiling, and then (and here's the game-changer) add a chicken stock cube. What? Yes. Welcome to the future. If you're a vegetarian, a vegetable stock cube will do nicely.

Let your pasta cook, throw it at the wall to see if it's ready, which isn't helpful or accurate but is fun. Then put down that sieve. Your days of draining the pasta water are behind you. Add your pasta directly to the sauce, using tongs if you have them, but a fork will do. Get it all in there, and then add several generous spoonfuls of your beautiful, thick, salty, flavour-filled pasta water.

Swirl all this around in the pan for a bit; let the sauce and pasta become one. Serve into a fancy bowl, rip some basil and sprinkle on the top, crack some black pepper, grate some Parmesan, eat in a candlelit alley with a dog well below your social class but with whom you are increasingly falling in love.

Don't let a dinner party freak you out.
If people make you feel bad about the calibre of your dinner parties, stop inviting those people to your dinner parties. All you need is nice friends, something to drink, candles and music. The fact that there was no actual dinner is irrelevant. The only rule of having people round for dinner is that you Chill Out.

> TESSA: I once threw a Halloween party and tried to bake Richard O'Brien's face into a lasagne. I'd also made a macaroni cheese that was a graveyard with bits of spring-onion leaves sticking out as grass and Malted Milk Biscuits as gravestones. I'd carved a pumpkin to be a punchbowl, then lined it with a plastic bag, but the pumpkin seeped into the punch. I filled a surgical glove with water and froze it so the ice looked like a spooky hand. I dropped it in the pumpkin punchbowl and it looked incredible for exactly one second, and then all the fingers fell off, reducing it to a too-big ball of ice in an undrinkable drink that tasted of binbag inside a colossal pumpkin. That's what happens if you don't just CHILL OUT.

If you're going to pass off shop-bought food as homemade, the key is to dispose of all the evidence. Burn the packaging ideally and dispose of the ashes in several separate locations. Smear sauce on your forehead, pop some pans on the draining board, throw a chopping board in the sink, dust the room with flour and toss a tea towel over your shoulder. Add swirls of yoghurt or shake herbs over ready meals that already have that herb in them (i.e. more coriander to the coriander-based takeaway curry and keep saying, 'Did I put too much coriander in it?' with a concerned expression throughout the meal). Put too many lemons into a massive bowl on the table. When the guests sit down say, 'Sorry, let me just get this out of your way.' Get a basil plant from the supermarket, put it in a pot and pretend you've grown it. Keep spritzing it with water throughout the meal to keep the illusion alive.

Cook vegetable sides – it confuses people, like CGI dogs in films. What's real? Difficult to tell. If you can cook your own rice, the jury will be so overwhelmed they'll have to discount this suspiciously fantastic lasagne on the grounds of reasonable doubt. Also because they'll be so distracted that you're serving lasagne with rice.

For pudding (or dessert/afters depending on your socio-economic background/location of birth) just lob some Häagen-Dazs onto the table. Or Viennetta – the fanciest yet cheapest pudding in the world. Put frozen berries in a pan on a very low heat with loads of sugar and watch them transform into a jus! A JUS!

If you like cheese, serve cheese. Put it on something nice to display it – a chopping board or big plate will do, but your imagination is the limit.

TESSA: I once served cheese on an antique trouser press.
STEVIE: I've got to step in here because sometimes your imagination doesn't have to be the limit and it's absolutely fine to serve cheese on an ordinary plate.

And that's it! You got there! You did it! Calm down, slow down, less heat. Sit around the table and soak up the glow of candlelight and nice friends and revel in being the host/hostess with the most/mostess.

How to Write a CV

The Curriculum Vitae. We all hate writing them, but there will come a day when you need one and there's simply no way around it. CVs need to be RELEVANT, SUCCINCT, CLEAR and TAILORED TO EACH JOB. Ideally one page, no more than two pages.

To make this easier, we've put together a top notch CV example on the next page. In it, Bruce Wayne is applying to be a superhero in a new city. The role specifies that the right candidate needs to 'work well alone and in a team, have their own transport and be ready for a challenging and fast-paced role'.

The presentation is professional and simple, clearly laid out, with no spelling mistakes. One page is ideal and full marks to Bruce for not making it the shape of a bat, which would have been very tempting.

BRUCE WAYNE

Philanthropist, entrepreneur, vigilante

Location: Gotham City   668-5775

b.wayne@normalguynotbatman.com

Vigilante who has fought scarecrows, cats, penguins and a man who thought he was the concept of a riddle. Highly trained by Ra's al Ghul. Co-founder and active member of the Justice League. Now looking for an exciting and challenging new superhero position.

- Wide skill set including philanthropy, durable costume wear (with nipples and without), hand-to-hand combat and inventor of the 'batarang' – a boomerang shaped like a bat.
- Created a youth outreach programme that produced at least one very competent sidekick.
- Graduate from Yale, with first-class law degree.
- Full driver's licence and own heavily armoured tactical assault vehicle.

2005–PRESENT: WAYNE EMPIRE, CFO
Worked closely with CEO Lucius Fox to ensure smooth running of the Wayne Empire.
Key responsibilities: sitting on board meetings, voting and holding large parties for clients.

2008: GOTHAM POLICE FORCE, Consultant
Consulted for the police on an ad-hoc basis for a publicity campaign against Batman.
Key responsibilities: workshopped tactics to venerate District Attorney Harvey Dent, fought clowns.

2017–2019: JUSTICE LEAGUE, Co-founder/project manager
Co-founded a think tank with Diana Prince.
Key responsibilities: fought Steppenwolf and his legions of Parademons by locating the final Mother Box, oversaw the recruitment drive.

150

He also hasn't titled each section 'Personal Statement' and 'Contact Details' and 'Employment History' because we need as much space for the good stuff as possible.

The short personal statement includes reference to the key demands of the job. This is where you put your most impressive and relevant information. 'Recent [your university] graduate with numerous work placements, including [impressive one], looking for entry-level [job title]'.

What's very nice is how he upscaled coercing Robin into being a sidekick into 'created a youth outreach programme'. The more of this sort of thing you can do, the better. Once helped your mate's band set up a Twitter account? You managed and maintained the social media profile of an emerging musician. Helped serve drinks at your neighbour's party? You've got experience catering for large events. Wrote one small article for the uni newspaper? You wrote for the uni newspaper. Don't outright lie, but certainly fluff stuff up so it sounds more important than it is.

In the 'key responsibilities' bit of your employment history, don't list things like 'creative thinking' and 'problem-solving'. They mean nothing. What did you actually do? What problems did you solve? What did you think creatively about? Did you help customers with complaints about their tariffs in a call centre? Did you co-create the menu at the restaurant? Did you assist the project management team across various portfolios? Think specific.

If you get stuck, always come back to the demands of the job.

What exactly are they looking for? How can you prove that? Keep it simple, relevant and clear and you'll be golden. And good luck to Bruce!

How to Get Over a Broken Heart

Welcome to your Winter of Discontent.

TESSA: The Winter of Discontent is something we invented (well, Shakespeare gave me the tip-off, but I embellished the idea). My friend Tom and I were both dumped at the same time, fresh out of university, and we spent a lot of time on his sofa, me weeping, him sitting very upright, staring stoically into space. It was the first time our hearts had been broken and we took it *hard*. We found some solace in discussing how no one had ever been in as much pain as we currently were, and creating the extremely elaborate WoD, which it feels only right to share with you now.

The Winter of Discontent is where you fall the moment someone breaks up with you. You fall out of the sky, as in the opening of the film *Predators* (the third and least popular instalment in the *Predator* franchise), and into the freezing tundra of a forest. The wind is howling, the snow is falling, the night is black and you're all alone.

Through the darkness you see the glowing lights of a small wooden cabin, smoke pouring from the chimney, and you bravely put one foot in front of the other through the snow until you use the last of your strength to hammer on the door. We open it. Two hooded figures: benevolent yet mysterious women. Tom used to run this trail stop, but he's happily married now and living in New Zealand where he's frankly *thriving*, so we're in charge. Once you've stepped across the threshold, we wrap you in your official broken-heart foil blanket and guide you to the fire.

As you sit by the crackling flames, you notice that this cabin-tavern hybrid we're running is much bigger than you thought, and it's full. There are so many people here, shivering under their blankets. There's weirdly no comfort in that; your pain is greater than theirs, your love was greater, they do not feel what you feel. They don't deserve the heartbreak blanket, only you.

Everyone around you is in shock. Some are being sick. Some of them are delirious with madness, muttering how their love is coming back for them. You will never be like them, you mutter to yourself.

'How do I get out of here?' you ask, but all the crying you're doing is making you quite hard to understand, so to be polite we just nod wisely. You repeat your question. 'We'll show you,' we reply, the lights in the cabin growing dim. 'But first, we will tell you our stories . . .'

TESSA: My first great heartbreak was my university boyfriend. After we graduated, on the hottest day of the year, he broke up with me in a canoe. In. A. Canoe. He said, 'I think we should break up,' and I laughed because I thought he was joking. Then I turned around, because I was paddling at the front, and could see that he wasn't joking. I was so surprised and so panicked by the feeling of freefall that I took the only logical option and jumped in the water. Then I lacked the upper-body strength to get back in the canoe so he had to paddle me to the bank. We sat on the river bank crying while I was dripping with river water until eventually I drove him to the train station, went home and fell hard and fast into the Winter of Discontent. I remember we talked on the phone about a week later and it was all right actually. We had a good laugh, and then at the end he said, 'Well, have a good week then,' where he used to say, 'I love you,' and my legs just crumbled in the street. Also, I wrote a desperately indulgent poem called 'At the End, the Weighing of the Heart'. Can you imagine?

STEVIE: The first time I got dumped I carefully explained that, sure, he'd cheated on me, but that was no reason to break up! I was cool with it! He broke up with me twice more and on the third and final time I left his flat in tears and got drunk for a year. Once, I ended up in the same club as him and he left with another girl so I went home and cried so hard I was sick out of my bedroom window. I left garbled voicemails and sent him long emails for about two months before embarking upon the Great Drought of 2009–2012 when I didn't even kiss anyone. I wore my sadness like a shroud, and if anyone showed interest I would nod sadly like a Victorian widow. I got out of the Drought by getting into an incredibly toxic relationship with someone who didn't really know how to love anyone and who also cheated on me. I forgave him because it was what I deserved. I also wrote multiple poems; one of them was called 'The Girl Who Can't Let Her Heart Be Known'.

The candles in the fireplace gutter, burnt so low they're almost spent. There's a quiet hush in the tavern and we are ready to answer your question. 'The only way out of the forest is through,' we say. 'Only time can heal your withered, broken heart. Not today, not tomorrow, but one day, it will be summer, and this winter will be a distant memory.'

And into the silence, we start handing out worn leather saddle bags filled with supplies.

The first is the Knife of Severance, which you must use to cut all ties. Everything. Delete their number, block them online, burn every bridge, salt the earth. You cannot be friends. You cannot go back. Don't wait for them to do it first. Be the one who takes control. Free yourself of scrolling through everyone who watched your Instagram stories looking for their profile picture.

> STEVIE: A friend decided to look at her ex's new fiancée – just to see, you understand, nothing more! Anyway, she ended up tagging herself in their engagement photo.

The second is a glass ball of pearlescent light, no bigger than a stone, and this is the Orb of Imminent Danger. It glows red after three white wines and the sudden desire to send them a voice note at 4 a.m. There is not one example in all of human history of someone being dumped and winning their lover back with the majesty of a drunken, incoherent voice note. Obey the orb.

The third is a vial of Remembrance, so that you may always remember that you are a total babe and they are a piece of shit. Sup from the vial and do things that confirm this. Dress up and go out. Dress up and stay in. Get off with people. Don't get off with people, but wear that really great hat. Dye your hair so you feel like a new person. Listen to the angry songs on Beyoncé's *Lemonade* and scream-shout the lyrics in the shower. Really give vocal weight to that bit where she talks about plugging up her menses with pages from the Bible. Make playlists. Have baths. Lie in bed all day. Do whatever feels good.

Fourth is a scroll of parchment with the names of the people around you who will put up with your bullshit, care for you and respond when you message them to say you have seen a good dog. For nothing will bring you to your knees quicker than seeing a good dog and having no one to tell.

And fifth is the Tinderbox of Fury. By the light of your own anger must you see your way through the forest. Use it to do all the things they never thought you could. Make great career strides as a form of revenge. Write down all the things about them that pissed you off, then use the Tinderbox to ceremoniously burn the list.

Otherwise the bag is empty. One day, years from now, you will look inside and see a coin at the bottom that you never saw before. You will tip it out, hold it in your hand and realise that they were just a person all along. Just a flawed human being who was careless with your heart, for this is the Coin of Forgiveness. If you look for it, you won't find it. It'll be there when you least expect it.

How to Leave a WhatsApp Group

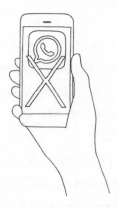

EXIT 1: THE MIDNIGHT DASH

Attempting to disappear into the night without anyone knowing. Effective, but also anxiety-inducing and will never produce the results you actually crave (closure, relief, euphoria).

GROUP NAME: BOOZY SLUTS (Employees of a career advisory website you worked at, 2012–2014.)

Aimee

Omg remember that time we photocopied our boobs?

Katie

Hahahhhahahahaha LOLLLLLL 😂😂😂 (You haven't spoken to Aimee since the last work Christmas party when she told you she was worried about you because you didn't have children and then photocopied her own boobs. Nobody joined her. You had to hold the photocopier lid open for her. It was weird. You have no idea who Katie is.)

Hannah

Crazy times! (Hannah was your line manager and the times were not crazy. They were, as already noted, weird.)

Stevie

Hahaha memories! (The primary sign of a dying WhatsApp group is people resorting to commenting on the past.)

4.01 a.m.

Stevie has left the group

(The time stamp raises alarm bells. Apart from revealing you care so much about leaving this group that it has created anxiety-induced insomnia, it's rude to leave without a reason. What's worse, it could be viewed as a drunken mistake, resulting in a separate WhatsApp from Aimee asking if you'd like to be invited back and you, not knowing what else to do, saying yes and remaining there until you die. Or they die. Or everyone dies because of climate change.)

EXIT 2: DURING THE IDEAL WINDOW (THE IW)

Leaving a group swiftly and cleanly is possible, but it's all about timing. In this case, when the event for which the group was created is over. Depending on the situation, the IW lasts for about 24–48 hours from the moment the last activity is over and closes irreparably after that.

GROUP NAME: BOOZY SLUTS

Aimee

Now THAT was a leaving bash! (We have gone back to 2014 after you've just left your job and when you should have left this WhatsApp group in the first place.)

Katie

We're going to miss having you in the office!!!! (So Katie works in the office? Fascinating. Still getting nothing.)

Stevie

Aw me too, guys! What a time. (Nice, vague and accurate. It was, in fact, a period of time.)

Aimee

Stevie

Righty-ho! (You can be forgiven for the odd, insane phrase – leaving WhatsApp groups is hard.) I'll leave this group so you guys can keep it for work stuff. (Very powerful. 'I'll leave this group' – decisive, clean – 'so you guys can keep it for work stuff' – selfless, noble, professional, dedicated to the company.) Drop me a WhatsApp if you're ever out for drinks! (This is an empty gesture; you are planning on gradually drifting apart over the next six months.)

Stevie has left the group. (Nothing like a woman who is swift, decisive and in control of her own WhatsApp groups. One can do nothing but stan.)

EXIT 2: VERSION A – THE CLASSY DUCHESS (ONLY POSSIBLE DURING THE IW)

The IW also works for birthdays, hen dos, work events. Once the function of the group is over, you are well within your rights to make a calm and collected exit.

Stevie

Amazing hen do, guys! Thank you so much to Laura for organising!

Stevie has left the group. (Not even saying you're leaving – just thanking the hostess and walking out the door – makes you look like an elderly heiress who has decided her own rules for social etiquette and perhaps doesn't even know you aren't supposed to leave WhatsApp groups. An air of quiet awe will be left in your wake.)

EXIT 3: THE OPPORTUNISTIC DEPARTURE, ALSO KNOWN AS THE COWARD'S WAY OUT, OR ON THE COAT-TAILS OF THE BRAVE

In this risky variation, another participant has found their own IW, and you have an extremely limited time frame – in this case, exactly five minutes – in which to make the most of this opportunity.

GROUP NAME: HANNAH'S BDAY BASH

Hannah

Last week was sooo much fun! Have just been looking at the photos!

Lauren

I LOVED IT! (Lauren spent the evening talking about herself, apart from when she referred to your job as 'a hobby'.)

Jo

Yayyyyyyy!

Katya

Amazinnng! (No idea who Katya is either.)

Stevie

Hahahaha! (You've picked a reaction here and hoped for the best, rather than scroll up and read the original message. Nobody will notice this time, because it's close enough.)

Jaz

🖤 🖤 🖤

Inez

Freya

So great! If ok with you all I'm gonna leave the group just cos my WhatsApp is FULL of groups 😂 but can't wait for the next birthday bash!

Freya has left the group. (Not a Classy Duchess, but still very strong. Freya did not wait to see 'if ok with you all'. Very good, Freya.)

Stevie

Me too – love you all! 🖤🖤🖤🖤🖤🖤🖤🖤🖤 🗿 (In your haste to leave you jabbed at the emojis too quickly, accidentally including a rogue Easter Island Head. However, the multiple emojis have helped distract people from your questionable moral fibre.)

Stevie has left the group. (You must jump on the mass exit IMMEDIATELY before someone has time to say, 'Wow, can't believe Freya left,' and you lose your nerve.)

EXIT 4: THE HERO'S WAY OUT

Aim for this exit where you can – it's civil, to the point, knows what it wants and is sure as hell going to get it. It sounds like I fancy this exit. Hahaha, imagine. But is it single?

GROUP NAME: BOYZ IN DA HOOD (Comprised of five white people – male and female – who you met on holiday a year ago. You have met up twice since then and it was awkward. You did not name this group.)

Tom

This is wild. [A link to a YouTube video of a man making a guitar out of cans.]

Liv

LOVE IT. (Liv has not opened the link.)

SJ

Guys, I've only just gone and HAD A BABY. [A picture of a baby] (Last time you saw SJ was on the holiday. She was high on mushrooms and screamed, 'CHILDREN ARE SHACKLES!' at the moon.)

Stevie

Amazing! (You are referring to SJ's baby news, not the guitar video. You have not opened the link either.)

Sam

I've got a discount on Ray-Ban sunglasses. If anyone's interested hmu. (This arrives three months after the previous message.)

Stevie

Heyyy so I'm trying to stop staring at my phone all the time (self-deprecation softens most blows) and am coming off pretty much all WhatsApp groups. (The 'pretty much' legally covers you in case you're caught being part of another WhatsApp group.) Love you all loads (say this even if you don't) and you know where to find me! (They probably won't find you, but good to throw it in there.) ♥ ♥ ♥

Stevie has left the group. (Like a break-up, or an exit from a party way past its peak, you must be swift and decisive. No hanging around waiting for people to go, 'Ohhhhh nooooo, stayyyyyy,' because you will, indeed, stay. Or, nobody will go, 'Ohhhhh nooo, stayyyyyy,' and you'll be so outraged you'll end up staying in the group until somebody does. By which time the window for leaving the group will have closed and you're stuck there with everyone knowing you actually wanted to leave.)

EXITS TO AVOID

1. The Spoken-word Poet, aka the overly long explanation that draws way more attention to it than necessary

Stevie
Hey guys – just a little note from me, and I guess an update, to say that I just think it's time for me to maybe try and stop going on WhatsApp so much – and while I absolutely really do think that this group has been a useful and illuminating and frankly wonderful addition to my life, both practically and indeed spiritually, in this current climate of phone usage I'm aware of my attention span getting worse and worse, and of my heart and butt palpitating every time I receive a notification. So it is time, and with a heavy

heart, that I must exit stage right from the play that is this group. I hope you find it in your hearts to forgive me, and to reach out individually if ever you wish to wave hello to an old friend who once sailed within the boat of your heart ⛵

Stevie has left the group.

2. The Enigma, aka the overly blunt goodbye that renders the exit incomprehensible

Stevie
goodbye.

Stevie has left the group. (Unless these people have done you wrong, they deserve a bit of courtesy before you get up and leave. You wouldn't leave the bar mid-chat; don't do it in a WhatsApp group.)

3. The Magician, aka leaving in a puff of smoke with no comment at all

Tom
More like CHANG CHANG on the door baby!

Lucy
hahahahahahhha!

Jack

Stevie has left the group. (Powerful and, in its way, extremely comedically effective, but also brutal.)

The WhatsApp Exit is an artform that many have tried and failed to master. But no matter how difficult it may be, life is truly too short to read updates from people you don't care about. Go forth and leave that group, friend.

How to Read Tarot

Please note, this chapter is very much intended for recreational tarot readers rather than those who take it much more seriously as part of a wider faith. If you read this as a pagan, the flippancy of it might make you want to kick us right in the Two of Wands. Which is fair enough.

You will only read tarot when someone has dumped you, ghosted you, fired you, you've got into a confusing new relationship or an argument with a friend, or life has in some way made you feel like you're on an unmanned ship sailing through a storm with nothing but a few biscuits and an albatross for company. If life is going well, your tarot cards will sit in a corner gathering dust. If it is not, they will live on your kitchen table, wrapped in a velvet cloth, presiding over every decision as you draw your intention for the day and repeatedly get The Tower, or The Hermit, or Death.

STEVIE: I got heavily into horoscopes in the summer of 2012 when I became essentially homeless and jobless at the same time. It said I would have 'an interesting 2013'. I Pritt-sticked this onto the door of my next flat and then lost a portion of my deposit because I couldn't get it off without ripping the paint.

TESSA: I have a 100% track record of making people cry when I read their tarot. And 99% of that, I have to admit, is because they were already ready to cry. The remaining 1% is a mix of confidence, candles and me saying things like, 'The cards show you what you need to hear, not always what you want.'

With tarot, it's not the answers, but the questions that are important. Whether you believe in magic or not, there are multiple studies showing that the brain can have extraordinary control over physical changes in the body.[9] Once you've focused on something, you've strengthened a neural pathway and your behaviour will start to change. Like when you do a love spell for that boy in your art class and it emboldens you to share his paint pot. Or if you ask the tarot cards about whether you should leave your job. Whatever the cards say, the fact that you've admitted out loud that you're considering leaving your job could be enough to finally put those wheels in motion.

The point is, it becomes a self-fulfilling prophecy. If you are asking about whether your relationship will survive the coming year, the fact that you're asking is much more significant than drawing the Five of Pentacles or not. Why are you worried about your relationship? Just by bringing it up, you've admitted this is an area of your life that maybe needs work and attention. (Just looked it up – the Five of Pentacles means isolation, poverty and financial loss. So not looking great for the relationship.)

---

9 https://www.webmd.com/pain-management/what-is-the-placebo-effect#2

Unless you are gunning to be a full-time tarot card reader (in which case, put this book down, you're wasting valuable time), you're not going to be fannying around learning all the meanings by heart. A quick search of the internet will provide all the card intel you need.

Proper tarot card readers are supposed to build a relationship with each and every card, spending years working with the deck so that they can feel their way through each meaning. Recreational tarot card readers don't have the time for that, but if you don't want to break the vibe by searching for answers on your phone, find a pack of cards that come with a book, so you feel like a witch consulting an ancient tome. If you can't find a book, buy a beautiful notebook and copy down the meanings so you feel like a witch consulting an ancient tome. The point is: witch, ancient tome.

There are only two reasons why you'll ever want to read tarot: one, you're on a ship alone except for one albatross (please refer to introduction) or two, you have friends round and they say, 'OOOH, LET'S READ EACH OTHER'S TAROT!' and you're all, 'I have some tarot cards!' to which they say, 'Can you read them?' and you've, somewhat presumptuously, said, 'Yes.' This phase happens immediately after you've downed a cocktail somebody has just invented and immediately before you all start doing 'Light as a feather, stiff as a board'.

So, how do you read tarot?

Here is a simple spread to get you started.

PAST, PRESENT, FUTURE

Step 1
Before you begin, light some candles. It will help the mood, which in turn will help you focus. Plus, nobody wants to have their tarot read under strip lighting.

Step 2
Remove the instruction card. People have varying opinions on what deck you should use. Some say it has to be Rider-Waite or nothing. Others use Angel Cards. Some believe you should never buy a deck of tarot cards, but wait until you are given them. You can also use a normal deck of cards – there are loads of resources online for interpreting the usual hearts, clubs, spades and diamond deck. Tarot cards, after all, used to be simple playing cards that were used to tell the future – so you don't need to spend loads of money on a fancy deck!

> TESSA: I have the Byzantine Tarot collection, which is very reasonably priced and comes with a little book that has a potted history of each card so you can really impress people. This is the version my friend Caroline has, which is how I got into tarot in the first place, and which I hard-recommend as a starter pack. I also have the Rider-Waite set, Moon Tarot, *Game of Thrones* Tarot and the Tarot of Sexual Magic, which is so erotic I genuinely find it too stressful to use. But I do advocate very strongly choosing a pack where you love the pictures.
>
> STEVIE: I found my pack in one of those parts of London Tube

stations where people leave books for others to read. Exciting, you might think – and it is! – until you see the pictures. Tessa's Wheel card is many beautiful celestial beings on clouds looking down at the earth while a magical compass spins in the midst of it all. My Wheel card is two badly drawn hogs wearing dresses and a fish sitting on what looks like a roundabout, with one of the hogs holding a plank of wood. The other hog is hanging upside down, exposing his full arse. I'm not making this up.

Step 3

Either formulate your question or have the person you are reading for formulate their question and say it out loud. If it's their first time, people will ask fortune-telling questions like, 'Will my crush notice me and will we go out and will he stop fancying Hayley and choose me as his partner for our assignment in Design and Technology?' Perhaps try something a bit broader, like, 'What will happen with me and my crush?' (Also, we've made you sound 14 years old. If you are then hello! Thanks for reading this book! If you aren't then apologies, it was the use of 'crush'. When we were young, we had no faith or creed but the word 'crush'.)

Step 4

Have the person shuffle the cards while focusing all their attention on their question. By 'focusing all their attention on the question' we mean thinking about all elements of it. If you're reading alone, you shuffle the cards. If you've asked about your job this year, then think hard about every aspect of it, and how it makes you feel, then think about the question again. Keep thinking and shuffling until it feels right to stop.

Step 5

Deal three cards, face down. It's up to you whether you deal them for the person, or you spray them all out face down in a semi-circle and let them choose the three that call to them. Whatever feels right. If they're panicking about making a choice, say, 'The cards will tell you which one to choose,' in an authoritative yet mystical voice.

Lay the three cards out next to each other: these are the past, present and future.

Step 6

Overturn each one, consulting the meaning in your book (or on the infinite free wisdom of the internet). The past card refers to what the situation was like before. The present card is what it is now. The future card is what it will be like in the future.

You can turn them over all at once, or you can go one by one and talk through them. Ask the reader what they see in the picture, and generally they will find themselves there.

> STEVIE: Unless, of course, you are using my tarot cards.
> TESSA: I did this once, and my present card was a blonde girl in a large white nightie crying in bed next to a hanging display of swords. Someone might as well have taken a picture of me. But my future was a giant hand dropping gold coins into a vineyard, so you know, swings and roundabouts.

They will say, 'Oh my God, that's me on a ship trying to put all my jugs in the cupboard! That was exactly what it was like at work!' Or, 'That's me in a cave surrounded by swords!' Tarot works a lot like therapy; you're just giving people a chance to talk.

> TESSA: If the pictures are super descriptive, they'll do 90% of the work for you.
> STEVIE: This has only worked for me when I've done readings for hogs.

If you're reading the book out loud to them, skim-read ahead slightly just in case something really terrible is in there. If they're already crying, maybe skip that part.

The future card is a hard one because there's plenty of shining golden cards in the pack, filled with lovers and money and chariots, but there's also desolate and dark cards in there that are very hard to draw positive meanings from.

TESSA: I once did this reading for my housemate and we got El Diablo (the Devil). I was trying very hard to spin that into a positive meaning and then, on the stroke of midnight, a man started banging on our door and shouting in Spanish. Completely true story. Most I have ever screamed.

It is VERY IMPORTANT to remember that a bad card doesn't necessarily mean something awful. Even Death doesn't mean death; it signifies change and fresh starts. Don't ever get freaked out by a tarot card reading. A bad card might mean things will be bad in order to get good again. Or, you know, (whisper this very quietly) it might not mean anything at all. The only takeaway is that you're bothered by the subject of your question, and that's something that's 100% within your control.

TESSA: Hey, Stevie?

STEVIE: Yes?

TESSA: I just asked the cards how our book goes and we got The Star! 'The most hopeful and positive of the cards. We are in touch with a universal energy and there is hope and belief for the future!' It's a woman in a meadow and she looks thrilled with herself.

STEVIE: Tessa, my Star card is a nude woman weeing on her own foot. This is not a joke. I am crying laughing.

How to Change a Light Bulb

We were very excited for this chapter to finally provide definitive, clear advice about light bulbs, but having now researched them at length, if we attempted to include diagrams of every type of bulb and bulb base, this book would be 100% bulb pics and renamed *Nobody Bulbic*. We read an article called 'The Most Common Bulbs' and it included 56 different varieties. Also, the word 'Bulbic' has made us feel sick. Anyway, the take-home is that you are not stupid for being confused, but don't give up – you CAN change this light bulb.

Step 1

Switch the lights off so you don't kill yourself. If you can't tell if it's on or off because your only light bulb has blown and that's why you're here, switch the electrics off at the mains.

Step 2

Remove the old bulb carefully – don't just smash it out with a hammer – and keep it rather than chucking it away so you can see which kind you need to buy as a replacement. You can also try looking up the

normal people have if even the ones on the pedestals hate themselves?

First of all, the fight is long and hard and deeper than you imagine. Huge businesses can't sell you this cream, or that diet plan, or these hair extensions, if you don't find yourself lacking. Capitalism relies on you hating yourself. If you like, every time you find yourself thinking something negative, catch yourself and think, 'Woah there! Capitalism got me thinking that my magnificent body is lacking just so they can sell me something? Fuck you, capitalism.'

Maybe you read that and thought, '*My* body isn't magnificent,' and that's a totally normal response, but isn't it a sad one? To have one life and one body and be filled with hate for it. It tries so hard! It works when you're ASLEEP! It blinks without you asking it to. It tells you when you're too hot. The hairs on the back of your neck tell you when you're in danger! It's a miracle!

Of course, you weren't born hating your body –

STEVIE: As a child I would be constantly remonstrated for taking
    pictures of my own bum with the family camera.
TESSA: I once took all my clothes off at a christening.
STEVIE: Was it your christening?
TESSA: Oh very much no.

– you've learnt to hate it, so what practical steps can you take?

1. Diversify your social-media feed
This is the solution to so many issues, but especially with body positivity. If you're presented with a variety of different body shapes

whenever you scroll, you'll start to break down the mantra that the ultimate goal is to be a thin white woman laughing at a salad. Or, if it's winter, steamily aroused while cupping a broth. The main thing is to stop looking at aspirational (and usually doctored) content that makes you feel lesser. Anyone who makes you groan and think, 'I wish I looked like that,' needs to go.

2. Accept that you won't want to wear everything

If a cropped top, pencil skirt or assless chaps don't make you feel great, that's OK! There are so many other items of clothing you can wear instead! A lot of messaging around body positivity is all 'anyone can wear a bikini', and of course anyone CAN wear a bikini, but don't force yourself into one if it's going to make you feel shit on the one holiday you're taking all year. By all means bring one and wear it, but you haven't failed if you go get a wrap because you can't relax. They're just pieces of cloth.

If, in the list of Clothes That Make You Tense, you find yourself including such basics as 'all trousers', 'all skirts' and 'any top that doesn't completely hide me like a billowing circus tent' then this isn't a matter of clothing taste, but something deeper. This is taking over your whole life.

If it's 'all trousers', find a pair that fit (not that you hope will fit one day or you think should fit) and casually start wearing them around the house. Experiment with different styles. Nip to Tesco in them. Do not stand in front of a full-length mirror and stare at yourself for an hour because not even the *Mona Lisa* stands up to such scrutiny. Keep trying different shapes until you think, 'OK, these aren't so bad,' and eventually graduate to a drink in the pub in them. Add in a jazzy top or a fun necklace or excellent shoes so the trousers aren't the focus point. Remember that absolutely nobody is looking at your trousers. We are all a collection of swinging limbs, necks, hair, eyes, feet, legs and torsos. People aren't looking at the thing you hate about yourself; they're too busy thinking about the thing they hate about themselves. That and thinking, 'God, that's a fun necklace!'

3. Move yourself

Not to be thinner, not to be more toned, but to remind yourself that your body is so much more than how it looks. 'I want to be the strongest, most flexible, fastest version of myself' is so much healthier than 'I want to look like a different person'.

> STEVIE: My exercise aim last year was to 'get fit' and then Footgate happened, which showed how little progress I'd made with body positivity. So this year I changed my aim to 'do ten push-ups and touch my toes' (not concurrently, just, you know, when the mood strikes). It's been six months and I can still only manage two, but during this quest I have felt a change in my relationship with my body. I'm prouder of it. Sometimes, when I'm annoyed that I've eaten rubbish for the third day straight or I can't fit into something, I remember I can do two whole push-ups and touch my toes. It gives me a bit of respect for what it can do, rather than what it looks like.

'Move yourself' doesn't just mean boring running either – running isn't for everyone.

> STEVIE: I was once walking along the road and a bee started chasing me, so I ran away and the bee chased me down the hill. I outran him and then I thought, 'This is all right actually,' so kept up the pace. Unfortunately at that time I was smoking 20-a-day so when I arrived at my flat I was sick in the bath and didn't run again for 11 years.
>
> TESSA: One New Year's Day I ran very fast to the end of the road and thought, 'God, I feel fantastic!' before being sick in a shrubbery bush.

Getting into exercise can be daunting, especially if you start out joining places called SWEATBITCH with advertising slogans like, 'IF YOU'RE NOT SCREAMING, IT'S NOT WORKING, DICKHEAD.' Those places are for real gym enthusiasts who say things like, 'I've shredded too many gains.'

Join free taster classes that have the word 'beginner' in the title, and try out as many different things as you can. Try trampoline, cardio, spin, hydrospin, stand-up paddle-boarding, kickboxing, barre, anti-gravity yoga (where you get in a big silk sheet and spin upside down). Try a Park Run, where you run five kilometres around your nearest park every Saturday morning at 9 a.m. It sounds gross, but you're done by 9.30 a.m. and can go back to bed and the smug high lasts all week.

Give yourself a fighting chance by doing things with a friend, and by getting all of the gear. Even the best athlete struggles to feel good in their PE shorts and a shapeless old grey T-shirt. Invest in the best sports bra and the best trainers you can afford.

Try out the free personal trainer session at the gym and get them to explain exactly where you're going wrong with your plank, or whatever you've always thought you can't do. Sometimes just having someone slightly adjust you can make all the difference – a light will switch on and you'll go from thinking, 'This is impossible,' to 'Ah! This is hard but I *get* it.'

If all else fails and you've totally lost the will to do anything, put on the music video to Beyoncé's 'Move Your Body', join in for four minutes and imagine how embarrassed you'd be if she showed up to your school canteen and you didn't know the moves.

4. Get nude

Not to the Post Office, but around your house. When you're on your own take everything off and swan about. Hey, look, nothing happened. Just a person striding about in the nude. It's just a body! Do this regularly, and get used to the feeling.

> STEVIE: I once realised I had no towel in the changing room at the gym and had no choice but to burst open the shower door and stride confidently to the locker with my clothes over my shoulder and my faff out. Nobody blinked. I didn't get any applause. Still, it was a real nude breakthrough.
>
> TESSA: Until a couple of years ago, my motto was 'Cardigan or Death'. I was obsessed with my upper arms and how they were the very worst thing in the world and they must never, ever be exposed. One day I was so unbelievably hot at a party I had to

185

take my cardigan off, the whole time thinking, 'THE ARMS ARE OUT!' and then I just . . . forgot about them. As I was walking home I started to think what a waste it had been, worrying about my arms all this time, and from there it was a gradual unravelling of my strongest-held beliefs until my motto became 'The Right to Bare Arms' and I had gone full Nude Renaissance. Now you can barely keep me in my clothes. I whip them off at a moment's notice. I think it's my way of making up for lost time.

5. Get rid of body neggers

Whether it's a relationship or a friendship, cut out people who make comments about your body. If a partner makes anything that's even a hint of a negative comment, get up and walk straight out the door. Don't let them tell you it's a joke – you'll know it's a joke, because you'll be laughing.

> TESSA: A friend of mine says I walk downhill like someone whose kneecaps have been put on backwards. Which is technically a negative comment, but also an accurate and comedically excellent observation. I laughed! An ex-boyfriend said I was the fattest girl he'd ever been with. I did not laugh. I should have got my stuff and walked out the door without another word, but I didn't. I think my Nude Renaissance is to do with not letting anyone talk shit about my body, least of all me. Be with someone who shouts, 'Wayoooh!' every time you get out of the shower. Settle for nothing less.

If it's someone you can't cut off, like your family, sit them down and firmly tell them their comments are hurting your feelings and they need to stop. They might say, 'But I just want you to be happy!' and then you'll have to walk them through how being smaller doesn't equal being happy, and if they really wanted you to be happy, they would use their words to make sure your confidence and self-esteem were sky high, not rock bottom.

6. Get therapy

If this is taking over your life and actively stopping you from doing things, then it's a great idea to speak to a professional. Do you think many deathbed regrets include, 'I wish I had worried more about how I look?' No, exactly. Let's start taking those steps towards getting help. And remember, this is an ongoing thing; you won't finish reading this chapter and suddenly feel fantastic in your skin and whip your kecks off, because it's hard to retrain your brain from a lifetime of conditioning. It's going to take time, kindness and consistent, gentle effort to quit thinking negatively about your body, but if you accept that you're going to have good days and bad days, while taking little steps to minimise the latter and boost the former, you'll be well on your way to being nude all the time. Which can only be a good thing. Unless you're in a public place, in which case you will be arrested. (Unless you run really fast. Best of luck out there.)

How to Nail a Job Interview

Adapted from The Job Interview: Choose Your
Own Adventure *series*

1

Good lord! It's the week before that job interview – what are you up to?

a) Just going about your life. You can prepare for it the night before. (Turn to **2**)

b) You've researched the company and prepared some answers to the classic questions, such as why you want to work there, what you can bring to the company, what your strengths and weaknesses are. You're also going to look over your CV to make sure you can talk about everything you've put on there and try a few practice interviews with your housemate. (Turn to **3**)

2

a) You stay up very late cramming for the interview and don't get the job due to a vague aura of fatigued hysteria that lingers around you. Better luck next time!

3

It's the night before – what have you laid out to wear the next day?

a) You've asked around and found what people tend to wear in the industry you're looking to break into, but have erred on the smart side just to be safe. (Turn to 5)

b) You've got some brand-new smart shoes you're excited to wear and you've borrowed a few business-casual pieces. You haven't tried them on yet, but you're pretty confident. (Turn to 4)

4

a) You arrive wearing your dad's suit and your mum's blouse. This is the first time your shoes have been out of the house and your feet are bleeding. You're walking so tentatively while trying not to get blood on the carpet and are so taken aback by the sheer size of your mum's shoulder pads that you give off an extremely stressful energy. The interview is over very quickly and you do not get the job.

5

Your interview is scheduled for 9 a.m. What time do you plan to arrive?

a) 9 a.m.! (Turn to 6)

b) 8.50 a.m. (Turn to 7)

6

a) An undetonated bomb from the Second World War is discovered on the main road into the city, meaning you have to take a detour that adds ten minutes to your journey. You're late and sweaty upon arrival, which annoys (and dampens) the interviewer, who you're unable to impress adequately enough to overturn their initial bad impression. (The bomb is safely removed without any casualties and improves historical interest in the area.)

7

Just before you go in, you calm yourself down by . . .

a) Smoking a fat bifter. (Turn to **8**)

b) Planting your feet on the floor to ground yourself, breathing slowly, looking through any notes you've made and glancing at your CV to refresh your memory. You also take your coat off and place your bag on the floor to leave safely in the waiting area, so you don't have to faff about when you're called in. (Turn to **9**)

8

a) The CEO of the Fat Bifter Company, for which you are interviewing, suddenly appears and says, 'Can I smell a fat bifter?' and you say, 'Yeah, man!' and he hires you on the spot. Unfortunately this is a hallucination from the bifter – you have in reality been escorted out of the building and possibly arrested.

9

When you walk into the room you . . .

a) Shake the hand of everyone in the interview, make eye contact, keep your notes on your lap if you're worried about your hands shaking and request a glass of water to prevent your mouth from getting dry. (Turn to **10**)

b) Smoke a fat bifter. (Turn to **8**)

10

The interviewer asks you to explain a gap in your CV. The truth is, you spent that time travelling around Asia smoking fat bifters. You hadn't prepared for this as a question and aren't quite sure how to answer . . .

a) You take a pause, have a sip of water, say, 'Good question! Let me take a moment to think about that,' and remember that professional honesty and positively spun truth is always the best way. 'I took some time out to see the world and work out what it was I wanted to do,' you say. 'So I went travelling to give myself time to think. When I returned I went straight back to employment, first in catering, which I didn't include on the CV for space reasons – but which taught me how to manage people and work as part of a team.' (Turn to **12**)

b) You tell them you were smoking fat bifters. (Turn to **11**)

11

a) The interviewer is thrown by you and, despite your good qualifications and easy manner, you don't get the job because your energy confuses them. Better luck next time!

12

They ask you if you have any questions for them. You say . . .

a) 'How much money will you pay me, hombres?' (Turn to **11**)

b) 'How would you describe the company culture?' 'What would you say are the strengths and weaknesses of the department?' 'What are the most important things you'd like to see the successful applicant accomplish in this position in the first year?' 'What's the performance review process like?' (Turn to **13**)

13

At the end of the interview you . . .

a) Thank everybody and say your prepared goodbye line, which is: 'Thank you so much for meeting with me. Best of luck with the rest of the interviews!' before taking your glass of water outside with you, or asking, 'Where shall I put this?' because you read about the famous 'coffee cup test', where candidates who leave their cups behind are automatically crossed off the list. Even if your company isn't conducting very over-the-top psychological tests on interviewees, clearing it away yourself shows that even when you're nervous, you're still a good egg. (Turn to **15**)

b) Throw the glass of water out of the window. (Turn to **14**)

14

a) Why?

15

After the job interview you . . .

a) Do something nice to take your mind off it and send a professional, concise thank-you email. You don't ask if you got the job, because if you did they'll let you know. If you forgot to say some important things, or made any mistakes, you don't kick yourself; you just work on them for next time. Interviews are a real skill to master and regardless of the outcome you should be really proud of yourself that you showed up on time and did your best.

How to Sleep

(Rain sprinkles on a babbling brook in front of a waterfall in front of a stream in front of a river.)

Hello, and welcome to this sleep story on the *Nobody Panic* meditation and anti-insomnia app.

If you're listening and thinking, 'This is too heavy on the water sounds, I might need to wee in a bit,' don't hesitate to switch over to the non-water nature-sounds version.

(A fire crackles on a log.)

Do you struggle to sleep? You're not alone, even though it can sometimes feel that way when you're up at 4 a.m. with nothing but the whir of the refrigerator and the sound of your own thoughts for company. It's worse if you have a partner, because then you have to lie there staring at the ceiling, listening to someone else doing the thing you're supposed to be doing, and doing it really well. According to the NHS, over a third of the population have problems drifting off,[11] so it's not just you.

---

11 https://www.nhs.uk/news/lifestyle-and-exercise/sleep-problems-in-the-uk-highlighted/

How to Sleep

Settle down amid the bedding you have made as comfortable, clean and sleep-positive as possible, in your below-room-temperature bedroom (your core body temperature drops when you fall asleep and a cool room emulates this, which some scientists believe may help you drop off more quickly[12]), with your sleep mask and earplugs in and your feet out of the duvet . . .

> TESSA: Is this a joke? I'm not putting my feet nowhere, baby.
> They're staying IN. The second they're out they'll be stroked
> by a small dead Victorian ghost.

. . . and your feet firmly encased within the duvet, despite scientific studies showing that cooler feet help you sleep,[13] as they are crucial body-temperature regulators, and let's begin. Starting with this sleep story:

Once there was a girl called Stevie. There was also a girl called Tessa, but she falls asleep immediately every night and then lies completely motionless until the dawn so won't be participating in this sleep story. The girl called Stevie has struggled to sleep for as long as she can remember, lying awake reading Mills & Boon novels called things like *Untamed Billionaire, Undressed Virgin*, which she'd stolen from her nanna who was – once these books were banned from charity shops in the mid 2000s – the kingpin of an illegal Mills & Boon trading ring among the elderly population of Shrewsbury.

---

12 http://healthysleep.med.harvard.edu/healthy/science/what/characteristics
13 http://healthysleep.med.harvard.edu/healthy/science/what/characteristics

Anxiety, screen time, room temperature, worrying about not sleeping, warm feet, a later circadian rhythm, the street lamp shining on your face – any combination of factors could be stopping you sleeping.

There's a theory that the time you were born affects your sleeping patterns. It's largely unsubstantiated, but the next time you oversleep you can whimsically wave your hands and say, 'Well, of course, it's the time I was born.'

Stevie is what scientists call a Night Owl – someone who is naturally inclined to stay up and get up later. You might relate to this, or you might be a Morning Lark: someone who actually enjoys getting up in the morning and generally finds it easier to sleep, in which case, well done, good for you.

Or you might be a Sloth and take several hours to do a simple task and ideally like to sleep for 17 hours a day, or a Giraffe and prefer lots of short naps rather than a big sleep. Or a Spider, and just like to be awake all night staring into the abyss. But the Owl and the Lark are the only ones recognised by science.

The key to better sleep is to start committing to trying to sleep better from tonight. Promise that you won't turn your nose up at any suggestion, no matter how wanky.

(The fire crackles in a disapproving manner.)

Sorry, we meant pretentious. It took Stevie years to download the Calm app because it was 'for wankers', but unfortunately it helped immediately. Once, on a beach holiday, she fell asleep to the sound of the Calm app's seascape because the actual sea was keeping her awake.

If you can't afford the Calm app but do have a partner, get them to tell you about something objectively boring that they find interesting. Stevie gets her boyfriend to tell her about the sound quality in cinemas versus streaming platforms. If anyone asked her to return the favour, she would talk about how to get enough protein as a vegan or what happens to decommissioned oil rigs. Other sleep-story-esque suggestions: late-night Radio 4 programmes, the shipping forecast on a loop, those ASMR videos of people whispering (search for it on YouTube if you've never heard of ASMR, you're in for a real treat), natural soundscape videos that last for several hours (beware of the adverts that crop up around 4 a.m. and give you a heart attack).

If the sleep-story method isn't working – wait, you do remember that this is a sleep story, don't you?

(Fire crackles memorably.)

Good. If it isn't working, try playing image-association games with yourself, with images linking together to form absurd nonsense. It's recreating that weird between-worlds state where you start to doze and experience incredibly vivid, trippy, hyper dreams – how it felt when you started to fall asleep in class. You were trying to focus on what the teacher was saying, but all kinds of nonsensical half-dreams were happening instead. Allow your mind to run free with symbols and images willy-nilly.

STEVIE: Never said 'willy-nilly' before. From now on I will use the more formal 'William Nillsworth'.

If you're not a visual person, try the four-seven-eight breathing cycle: inhaling for four counts through your nose, holding for seven and exhaling out of your mouth for eight. You're supposed to make a whooshing sound on the exhale, which can sometimes wake your partner up. If they're cool with it or you don't have anyone in bed with you, start whooshing William Nillsworth. Or try it without the whoosh element. You're just relaxing yourself, yeah? You're not trying to sleep. That would be too much pressure. Just relax.

Now let's lean into a little reverse psychology. Sure, if you don't sleep you'll be a little tired tomorrow, but you can still function, so there's no need to clock-watch. Remember that time you did a 17-hour waitressing shift after an all-night bender? You've drunk 100% fewer Jägerbombs tonight.

After 20 minutes of relaxation techniques, try going somewhere that isn't your bed and doing something gentle like knitting, drawing, listening to a sleep story and absolutely not going on your phone and reading articles called 'Why Only Getting Four Hours Sleep a Night Is Killing You'. After an hour or so, try a relaxation technique. If you're still not tired, go back to the boring activity. Repeat this cycle until you're ready to go to bed.

Accept what's happening and don't beat yourself up about it. There are mathematical formulas for caffeine consumption, precise nap-timing and people swearing blind that silk pyjamas changed their sleep cycle forever. The truth is, everyone's different, and what works for one person won't necessarily work for you. Just be nice to yourself, try to relax rather than sleep and, if all else fails, have a listen to this crackling sound for a while. Even if you don't fall asleep, it's quite pleasant.

(Fire crackles pleasantly.)

How to Break Up with a Friend

PART ONE

This is a two-parter because there's lots to unpack here. When it comes to romantic relationships, we're inundated with information about spotting red flags and leaving bad lovers, but friendship is never discussed in the same way, and so it's never occurred to most of us that we might actually be in toxic relationships with a friend.

There's also no playbook for cutting ties. We've seen how terrible romantic relationships play out in films and cartoons and operas (throwing something in for the cultured folk), but the terrible friendships always survive.

The films and cartoons and operas continue to plough this 'Best Friends Forever Means Forever' narrative because the only film that ever attempted to address a friendship break-up was Disney's *The Fox and the Hound* and the whole experience was so mentally scarring they never attempted it again.

But say it with us: you are allowed to let these friendships go. Some people are destined to come into your life only for a short amount of time. You don't get an award for still being friends with people you knew at school; you're not the same person as you were five years ago, let alone aged five. That person you've known for a decade but who always makes you feel bad? You do not have to hang out with them. What a gift!

So do you have a toxic friend? Is there someone you need to set free? See if any of these people ring a bell.

'You've got a new job? That reminds me of a story about my new job . . .'

When was the last time they were interested in something you were doing? And how often do they twist the conversation back to themselves? Test this by bringing up something that has nothing to do with either of you. Like Dutch elm disease, or how musician Paul McCartney actually died in 1966 and was replaced by a look-alike. Does it turn into another monologue about them? Try it again, but this time with the Neolithic medicinal practice of trephination, and if you appear to be back discussing them within a few sentences, it's time to rethink things. Wouldn't it be nice to hang out with someone capable of a normal two-way conversation?

'I got that top too! And those trousers. And rented a flat in the same area. Could I live inside your skin, please?'

Imitation is the greatest form of flattery, but if it's driving you mad then bring it up in a jokey way ('Wow, it's like I've been cloned!' or 'How very Sam Rockwell in *Moon*,' if you want to go niche), which could be all that's needed. If they continue to morph into you, it's time to either have a less jokey word, get a more confident mutual friend to intervene or force them to go to boring meetings you can't be bothered with, presentations you're too nervous to deliver or parties you don't want to attend. If it's all too much then you're well within your rights to step away.

'You're a total *%$^ing £$$@%%&*^!'

The punctuation denotes shouting and swearing. If your friend is going through a tough time and they're lashing out, that's different. But anyone you constantly fight with, swear at, cry over or bitch about to other people is someone you don't need around. You're too old for drama. Even if you're reading this aged twelve. Drama is not necessary for any relationship to function. You're not on a reality TV show. You don't need to be leaving the audience gasping at the endless dramatic updates in the ongoing saga of your friendship.

'Well, no, I know I said that but I didn't mean that actually happened.'

Whether to impress you, deflect or cover up dodgy behaviour, if someone regularly lies to you – even if they're hilarious lies – that's toxic. If they're lying about stupid things, what else are they being untruthful about? If someone can't even tell an anecdote without spinning off into fantasy, how can you rely on them to be honest with you when you need advice, or you need them to keep something secret?

'Come on, it was a joke!'

Good, solid comedy joking is at the heart of any good friendship. You are weird and your friends need to be able to tease you about it, and you need to be able to tease them about how weird they are. Everyone is weird. But if you're not laughing then it's not a joke. If a 'friend' makes you feel bad, ugly, incompetent, stupid or sad, why are you sticking around? You can't choose your family, but you can choose your friends. So choose people who boost you, support you, and leave you feeling warm and glowing – even when they're rolling on the floor cackling that your favourite footwear looks like orthopaedic shoes or saying you dress like a lactose-intolerant steampunk.

Try saying, 'That's mean,' or, 'Bit harsh.' Rude people aren't expecting to be called out, and a simple, 'Whoah, OK,' delivered with the right amount of controlled spike, can be marvellously effective. If they don't stop, it's time to stop seeing them.

'You're a big twat. I can't stress this enough: I don't like you.'
Sometimes it can be pretty obvious they are putting you down, in which case, please refer to the previous section.

You have 27 missed calls.
There is a difference between trying to hang out and neediness. If they are calling you all the time and messaging you constantly, and you turned off your read receipts specifically because they kept sending '?' when you didn't reply immediately, that's not OK.

PART TWO: THE BREAK-UP
You've identified a friend as toxic, and now you're ready to distance yourself. It feels weird and over the top to follow the same rules for friendships as you do for relationships – taking a friend out for coffee and saying, 'I'm so sorry, it's not you, it's me. I think we

need to break up,' is technically the right thing to do but feels pretty melodramatic. So what's the alternative? Ghosting?

While we would never advocate ghosting in the suddenly-stops-messaging-never-to-be-heard-from-again sense, we do recommend a bit of Casper the Friendly Ghost-ing.

> STEVIE: I have a few people I had to Casper. I stopped reaching out to them when I needed help or advice, kept messages light and airy, and didn't go out of my way to arrange one-on-one dinner dates. Gradually the friendship changed and became much healthier; we now have fun if we see each other at parties and go for the odd drink here and there, but I don't cry as much. Casper is a friendly ghost, remember?

If you redraw the lines for yourself, you'll often find that nobody notices or minds. People drift apart and come together all the time – it's a necessary part of life – and it might be good for both of you to have a breather. If you've found them difficult, then chances are they've found the friendship hard work too.

If the Caspering works, great! If it doesn't, it's time to assess the situation. Are they clinging on even more tightly than before? Are they furious? If so, you need to Have A Talk.

The aim of The Talk is to try to deal with whatever elephant has decided to walk into the room and sit on both of you. You need to be very brave and point at the elephant and name him and acknowledge him. He might be named Babar, but more likely he is named Jealousy, Hurt Feelings, Left Out, Feeling Too Fragile at the Moment for Jokes, or any number of things that have caused him to walk in and crush your friendship. It is horrible to do, and your voice might sound quite muffled underneath his giant elephant bottom, but the moment you can name him together and acknowledge he's there, he'll wander off to bother some other unsuspecting friendship.

If you've had The Talk, things have not improved and you just need to go full steam ahead into the break-up, here are some potentially helpful sentences arranged in order of bluntness. Always opt for the lowest level possible; you can go up, but you certainly can't dial it back down once you've gone in too high.

Level 1: 'It's been quite chaotic with us recently, and I think we both need some space.'
Positives: It includes their feelings, rather than you just cutting and running. Doesn't lay any blame. Risk of defensiveness is low.

Negatives: They could respond with, 'I'm fine,' in which case you'll be forced to move to Level 2.

Level 2: 'I've been struggling with how we are with each other, and I think I need some space.'
Positives: Assertive. No room for disagreement because you're saying how you feel.

Negatives: Could hurt them. Possibility of defensiveness quite high.

204

Level 2a (if they are hurt): 'It says more about me than you. I'm emotionally all over the place at the moment and need time to sort my head out.'
Positives: Shifts the blame away from them, and offers some acknowledgement that it takes two for a friendship to get stuck on the rocks.

Negatives: You've suggested that in the future, once you've sorted things out, you will be prepared to come back to the friendship. This could well be the case, but it's worth noting in case it . . . isn't.

Level 3: 'I feel like you've hurt my feelings a lot recently, and I need some space.'
Positives: Direct but still using 'I feel' phrases so as to avoid being accusatory. Move to Level 3 when somebody has actively done something upsetting, using examples *only where necessary*. Listing a load of things they've done wrong is likely to get a terrible, defensive reaction even from the calmest of people.

Negatives: Likely to get something like '*I've* hurt *your* feelings?!' followed by really kicking off.

Level 4: 'For [insert reason] I don't think we can be friends any more.'
Positives: Cannot be misinterpreted. Very strong, very bold, only to be deployed when someone has done something inexcusable and you cannot fathom seeing them again.

Negatives: If you're absolutely sure that this is the end of the road and you have no interest in seeing them ever again, then it sounds like it would be a waste of tears to do this one face to face. Keep things quick and decisive and just send a text.

HELPFUL HINTS FOR THE ACTUAL BREAK-UP

- Be ready for this to be an unpleasant experience and remember that what you want is simply to get out, not to lay blame or score points.
- Be aware that you might learn you played a larger part in the friendship's demise than you thought.
- You can't control your friend's response. If they hate what you've said and think you're the devil incarnate, that is unfortunately the state of play. If the volcano is going to explode, you just need to stay out of range and keep your head down.
- Don't drag them on social media. Remember, we agreed you didn't need any drama? It will get screenshotted and it will get discussed in a WhatsApp group you're not in.
- Don't drag them in real life either. Ignore anyone who says, 'Honestly I won't tell her,' after a bottle of wine. They will voice-note her in the Uber home.

Above all, remember that friendships come and go; they are chapters in your life rather than the whole book. You haven't failed because you're not best mates with some girl born in the same hospital ward as you. Crappy toxic behaviour is crappy toxic behaviour, whether it's coming from someone you just met or someone you've known your whole life. Surround yourself with people who make you feel funny, cool and interesting. Casper everyone else.

How to Have a Smear Test, Colposcopy or Biopsy

Adapted from Stevie Martin's memoir, Life Among the Stirrups *('Confusingly titled'* – The Guardian*)*

I should begin by saying that the depth of my knowledge extends only as far as owning a cervix and going through the process. If you, too, have a cervix and have been terrified to attend your first smear, or have opened a letter, read the word 'abnormal' and started tearfully planning your own funeral, please put down the pamphlet on coffins and have a cup of tea or whatever calms you down. Drambuie?

Let's casually survey some facts I wish I'd casually surveyed when I got my first abnormal smear result and informed my boyfriend I 'probably have cancer'. Around 1 in 20 people will have an abnormal smear result, and only 1 in 2,000 will have cervical cancer.[14] You're looking at pretty good odds. If this was a horse at the Grand National, the bookies would be like, 'Why are you talking about cervical cancer? Could you bet on a horse, please?'

---

14 https://www.bsccp.org.uk/women/frequently-asked-questions

There are plenty of relatively benign options for an abnormal smear result. HPV, or Human Papillomavirus, often sparks abnormal tests and HPV infects around 80% of sexually active adults. If you've boned someone, you probably have it (I have it!). Today, everybody in UK schools gets the HPV vaccine in Year 8, which is pretty cool. If you left school before 2010 you missed it (I missed it), but if you're under 25 you can still get it directly from your GP. HPV shows no symptoms whatsoever and usually clears up by itself in a few years. It's not herpes and it's certainly not HIV; it's just an incredibly common and largely benign virus. Only in very rare cases does HPV cause cell abnormality that can develop into cancer. Not will, but CAN.

Abnormal test results are warnings rather than a diagnosis. If you'd care for a battle analogy, a smear test is one person looking out over the hills and saying, 'Oh, that's something – could be the enemy or it could be a moose.' A colposcopy is where they get the binoculars out to see definitively whether it's a moose or not, and a biopsy is firing a cannon at the now-clearly-enemy line that a) provides evidence as to how strong they are and b) kills some of them.

I have had all three – countless smear tests, three colposcopies, two biopsies – and I am here to tell the tale. I will not sugar-coat anything, but I also won't exaggerate. All I read online was 'THIS IS THE WORST THING THAT'S EVER HAPPENED' and, spoiler, it was not the worst thing that's ever happened. Once I did a handstand on a wasp and, while not as upsetting as I thought it might be, it was still worse than all my smear tests, colposcopies and biopsies put together. Certainly for the wasp.

THE SMEAR TEST

12 p.m.

My name is called. Sure, my appointment was meant to be half an hour ago, but the NHS is underfunded and luckily the show about a man learning to fish on the tiny TV set in the corner of the waiting room was more diverting than expected. My friend had a smear test and accidentally shot the speculum out of her vagina and into the doctor's face. What is a speculum? Why was the doctor's face so close to her vagina? I am 25 years old, this is my first smear test and I am terrified.

12.01 p.m.

I am asked to take off my trousers and underwear in a curtained-off section of the surgery, which is all very respectful and discreet given that they're about to look directly up my faff. Now my trousers are off, I realise my jumper is way too short and my whole butt is out like Winnie-the-Pooh. Luckily, I'm given a piece of paper to cover myself with. Not A4, but a giant paper thing the size of a bath towel. I then sit on a papered chair surrounded by lots of gadgets that wouldn't look out of place at a sex party, I think, having never been to a sex party.

12.02 p.m.

'Could you scoot your bottom down a little lower on the chair?' the doctor asks. I struggle to do this because I don't want to put my vagina in her face. Nobody needs that. What if I shove it way too close to her and she has to say, 'Can you take your vagina out of my face?' I move about two millimetres, she asks again, and this back and forth continues roughly six times. There's also another woman in the room, who might be a doctor or a nurse or a specialist; I have no idea about either of their job titles, only that they are two incredibly friendly West Indian women. I know this because they ask me where I'm from and I say, 'The North!' because I'm so frightened I've forgotten where I'm from, and then I ask them and they say, 'We are both from Barbados!' and then laugh riotously and I also laugh and they get out what looks like a large clear test tube and start lubing it up, so I stop laughing.

12.03 p.m.

The speculum goes in and I make a noise I've never made before. When people say they don't like smear tests, it's not the actual smear test, it's the speculum. The speculum is a plastic test tube that goes in and then opens up like a pair of bellows or a car jack. The thing you've got to remember is, this is like the first time you put a tampon up there. Or a penis. Or a dildo. Sorry, but no room for pussyfooting when you've got your legs in stirrups. If you are tense, your muscles will be tense and the speculum won't sit in comfortably. It doesn't hurt, provided you relax yourself, I promise. Just keep breathing and remembering that your vagina is built to accommodate a full baby's head, so this is all psychological.

It's cold, it's slimy and it just sort of sits in your vagina like a polite robot penis unsure what to do with itself. Then the doctor opens it up, which isn't uncomfortable but certainly feels like your vaginal canal has become a windsock. Again, it doesn't hurt! Honestly! It's just weird. So focus on relaxing those muscles and remembering that there's much worse that could be happening. Cystitis, for one.

12.05 p.m.

The doctor tells me she's going to do the smear test using what looks like a tiny toilet brush. It doesn't scrape. It brushes against my cervix gently, is over in seconds and I'm not confident anything has fully happened.

12.06 p.m.

That's it. We're done. Trousers back on. It was so fast I was taken aback. I was moved. It was poignant.

A COLPOSCOPY

2 p.m.

I'm 29 years old and I've just had my second smear test (wore a long T-shirt in preparation, remembered to breathe, absolutely breezed through it), but this time a week later I got a letter saying, 'ABNORMAL CELLS'. It said other things as well, but obviously I didn't read them because of the 'ABNORMAL CELLS' bit. What are abnormal cells? Are they cancerous? Are they multicoloured? I didn't read the letter, I just went on Mumsnet where everyone said it would be horrific and I'd be bedridden for days. Probably should have read the letter, but it's too late for that now. I try to scroll Instagram to distract myself because there's no TV in the waiting room this time. My hand is shaking and I see a girl I went to school with who now has 500k followers hanging out of a window in Paris. I bet she doesn't have a cancer-riddled multicoloured cervix.

2.15 p.m.

I am called through. It's two different but equally lovely women who are so friendly I want to cry. When I sit on the big chair, I remember to scoot my bottom down and wonder if they are both thinking, 'She is the best colposcopy patient we've ever had. What an excellent vaginal position.'

2.16 p.m.

A colposcopy begins. In my internet research, I was so busy trying to find out if they hurt that I failed to look up what actually happens. Turns out, they squirt dye onto your cervix and put a tiny camera up the speculum to have a closer look. You don't feel the dye, the camera doesn't touch you and while it's happening you field questions like, 'What do you do for a living?' and, 'Have you seen *Hamilton*?' which shouldn't be an effective distraction tactic but you've barely got through the second verse of 'The Room Where It Happens' before everything's up you and the assistant is watching your cervix on a monitor. I ask if there's anything good on, which gets a cracking response.

2.22 p.m.

They ask if I'd like to see my cervix and turn the monitor to reveal an image of a squashed, black, evil doughnut. Turns out, the dye they use is black and the evil doughnut is my cervix. 'You should use rainbow-coloured dye,' I say, unable to stop the relentless stone-cold bangers. 'Or maybe even gold. Like Goldfinger, but Goldcervix!'

They laugh, but I get the feeling the joke didn't land. Maybe they aren't big James Bond fans.

TESSA: After they showed me my cervix on the screen, I said, 'That's amazing!' And they agreed. And then I said, 'You should sell them on keyrings at the end!' By which I *meant*, you know, like after a rollercoaster when you get a picture of yourself. Absolute silence.

2.23 p.m.

A slightly lighter patch on my cervix is pointed out by one of the women. 'These are the abnormal cells,' she says. 'I'll just do a quick biopsy and see if we can get most of them out.' I am now no longer having a good time.

A BIOPSY

2.24 p.m.

I have burst into tears and the woman is saying, 'Oh, don't worry, you've done so well. It will be over in a couple of seconds,' while preparing an anaesthetic needle that she is hoping to inject into my cervix before cutting a bit of it out. I am dripping in sweat and so tense that it's surely a matter of time before I accidentally fire the speculum into her face.

2.25 p.m.

'I just need you to breathe out in one long, big breath,' she says, disappearing between my legs while I wait for the pain. She comes back out, having apparently already injected my cervix, and I am almost indignant at how little I felt. By the time she's explained that the needles are very fine and the thought of it is always much worse, she's cut a bit of my cervix off and I haven't felt a thing.

As with many things in life, the worry is far worse than the event. I almost wish she'd done it without telling me, but that would be, you know, illegal.

2.28 p.m.

When I am let down from the stirrups there is one moment where I feel the beginnings of a stomach cramp, but then the cramp doesn't arrive. On a scale of 1 to My Uterus Is Caving In, it was approximately a 1.3 (somewhere between 'OK' and 'I might be about to get my period but then again I might have eaten too many breadsticks').

2.29 pm.

I am given a big pad to put in my knickers in case the black dye leaks out. The pad is quite comforting, and oddly reminiscent of those early period days when I'd tried to insert a tampon and fainted, and so wore only sanitary towels until one shifted during a particularly vigorous netball match, the adhesive on the back of the pad inadvertently giving me an excruciating bikini wax. After that it was tampons all the way. Where was I? Oh yes, the biopsy is over.

2.31 p.m.

I'm told they didn't cut out all the cells, only enough to allow them to inspect further. I'm told I can come back in a year's time for another colposcopy to see whether my cervix has healed itself. If it hasn't, I will need another biopsy and perhaps they will have to cut out all the cells. I ask how I can help my cervix to heal. She says, 'Limit stress, eat well and get lots of sleep,' and I laugh hysterically for seven years. I am still laughing now. (Spoiler alert: it did not heal itself, I had another colposcopy, another biopsy, and the cells were deemed 'low grade' enough for me to continue my life with just the usual smears.)

3 p.m.

On the way home, I start to feel uncomfortable as the anaesthetic wears off. This is the worst part of the biopsy. You might get cramps for the rest of the day, so don't plan anything too strenuous like, say, potholing. I have a nap with a hot-water bottle and get an early night. Not that you'll be up for it, but having sex within 24 hours is not recommended.

And there we have it. The smear, the colposcopy, the biopsy. I have a smear test every time I'm told to, and whole-heartedly encourage you to do the same. No matter how scared you are of a biopsy, remember that it's so much worse in your head and that none of it is as bad as failing to catch something really worrying nice and early. And please don't steal my 'Anything good on?' gag. After the disappointing reception of 'Goldcervix', it's all I have.

How to DIY

Here are the two great commandments of DIY:

1. Yes, you can.
2. Gosh, OK, not to worry, you can definitely fix that.

TESSA: I am an extreme DIY enthusiast who, truth be told, doesn't really know what she's doing. I spend a lot of time drilling and then going, 'Ah yes, that appears to be brick, that's made a mess, hasn't it?'

STEVIE: Tessa will be taking the reins with this one because I've never even held a drill, let alone drilled it into a brick.

You will 100% make mistakes, think, 'Jesus, lord, there goes the deposit,' and then you will 100% be able to fix them. It's just about having a go, and then keeping on going. No matter what you're trying to achieve, there's a YouTube video out there of an earnest man walking you through it. Just keep pausing, and go as slowly as you need to.

DIY is mostly confidence, and confidence comes from knowing you can fix it if it all goes awry, which it will, so believe in yourself.

Or to clarify, believe in yourself up to a point and then stop. Don't piss about with electricals, pipes, plumbing or supporting walls. This book hasn't got any insurance, so please know your limits.

Then there's actually one more commandment which is:

3. Get the right tools for the job

Everyone bangs on about how 'a poor workman blames his tools', but the expression should be 'a good workman admits there's only so much you can do if your screwdriver came out of a cracker'.

Tools aren't as expensive as you think. The power tools, yes, of course, that's big money, but decent everyday tools are reasonably priced and boy, oh boy, will they make a difference. You'll transition from crying as you try to screw in a screw with a penny to thinking, 'Holy shit, that was easy!' Then walking round the house like Inspector Gadget, wondering what else you can fix (nothing – quit while you're ahead).

THE SEVEN TOOLS YOU NEED IN YOUR TOOLKIT

I'll present these in order of use, then you can slowly work your way through and build up your collection. If you're sending someone off to university or pondering a house-warming present, a toolkit makes for an amazing gift. Get the proper stuff, not the matching pink set from the petrol station (listen, I'm not throwing shade, I own them, and the matching Barbie-pink jump leads, and they Do Not Work) and not Tommy Walsh from *Ground*

Force's collection from Poundland because – and God bless you, Tommy – they will break.

1. A Stanley multibit ratchet screwdriver

At the time of going to press this thing costs £11. The best £11 you'll ever spend, I'd argue. It has all the different types of screwdriver heads you could need and they all fit in a little carousel, so you don't need lots of screwdrivers, you just need this one. I don't know how a ratchet works and I refuse to learn, but just know that it makes a very pleasing noise and twists back on itself so you feel like an absolute pro.

2. A retractable tape measure

Maybe you have one of those paper measuring tapes you get free in IKEA, or possibly a lovely seamstress one that, again, you got in a cracker (Big Cracker Industry really going head to head with the tool market here), but nothing compares to a retractable tape measure. I'm going to stop using this expression now but, hoooooo boy, will you feel powerful! Measuring is also an invaluable life skill and will stop you being constantly surprised by the size of things when they arrive in the post. I once walked to Homebase to get a piece of copper pipe I had measured with a piece of silk ribbon. Get a tape measure.

3. A spirit level

Another magnificent tool. Vital if you're putting up a shelf, but lovely just to go round checking if things are straight.

STEVIE: When I was a child and I heard my parents talk about spirit levels, I had got quite into *Pocahontas* and believed they were discussing the spirit of the wood and its level of intensity. Like a high blood-sugar level. A high spirit level. Very disappointed when I found out what it was.

4. A hammer

A decent claw hammer with a nice rubber grip on the handle. A claw hammer has the bit for hitting in the nail, and then the claw bit for levering the nail back out again when it inevitably goes in the wrong place.

5. WD-40 and duct tape

These two come as a team because the famous saying is that 'If it moves and it shouldn't, you need duct tape, and if it doesn't move and it should, you need WD-40'.

STEVIE: The toolkit of the gung-ho practical housekeeper is veeeery similar to the toolkit of a serial killer. Maybe pop it away if you've got guests.

6. Pliers

These will come in way handier than you think, like an extra bionic hand. Need to pull staples out of some wood? Loosen a nut or a bolt? Cut a zip tie? Remove paper out of the printer when it's jammed? Pliers.

7. A wood saw

Yes. OK. Very serial-killer vibes, but that's why it's number seven on the list, right down towards the bottom. Don't start with a saw, but once you've got a bit of confidence you can progress to cutting bits of wood to size.

> STEVIE: I was going to say nobody needs a saw, but I sleep on a bed that is missing a leg and propped up with books.
>
> TESSA: Exactly. Quick trip to the lumberyard, nice bit of scrap wood, retractable tape measure, cut it to exactly the right height, somebody's got themselves a new bed leg!

KNOW YOUR SCREWS

There are hundreds of different types and shapes of screw, varying in size from a colossal screw for a railway sleeper, all the way down to a tiny screw for the corner of your sunglasses, so we can't cover them all, but we can end with a little knowledge about the most common screws and screwdrivers, because the most regular thing you'll be doing with your toolkit is fixing wobbling drawers, tightening things that have come loose or putting together flat-pack furniture.

The older we get, the more we realise that people feel locked out of so many different industries, because the industry uses language that nobody understands. But if you fight through the panic where you think, 'Not for me!' and learn a couple of the words, then the world is your DIY oyster! Don't ever be afraid to explain what you're trying to do in the DIY shop and ask for help.

PHILLIPS SCREW

This is the Phillips screw, otherwise known as the Hot Cross Bun. A guy called John P. Thompson invented it in the 1930s, and then when no one was interested he sold the design to Henry Phillips. So if you ever lose confidence in the DIY store, you can say loudly, 'I actually call it a Thompson screwdriver!'

The Phillips screw needs the matching Phillips screwdriver.

SLOTTED SCREW

This is the slotted screw, also known as Not Pregnant. This OG godfather of screws has been around since the first century, so show him some respect, but also, the screwdriver does slip out easily so you can see why they had to invent something else.

He needs the matching slotted screwdriver, also known as a standard screwdriver – flat-blade, slot-head, straight, flat-tip, flat-head – or, the one we'll obviously be using, the Common Blade.

POZIDRIV SCREW

This one is the inexplicably named Pozidriv (an amalgamation of Positive Drive), otherwise known as the Union Jack, the Exploding Star or the Phillips That's Got Ideas Above its Station.

It looks like a Phillips but it's not, and the correct screwdriver is this one that looks like the Pope's hat. A Phillips screwdriver will just about work with this screw, and vice versa, but you'll damage the screw and the screwdriver. (Until literally just now I'd been using these two interchangeably and the fact that they are different screws explains a great deal.)

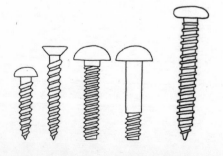

How to Care Less About Life's Milestones

Try as you might, it's impossible not to sometimes mark your life against the life you thought you were going to have. When you were tiny, you had all these dreams about things you would do by certain ages because life seemed impossibly long, and then those ages come and go and you realise you're never going to be the youngest person to climb Mount Everest, thirty seems to be coming in pretty hard and fast and you don't appear to have made your first million yet.

There's nothing like a birthday to make you come to terms with how many times you've shot around the sun on this giant rock we're all destroying.

TESSA: Really keeping the mood light I see.
STEVIE: I'm trying to make the point that age means nothing and
    humans have created milestones as a rod to beat ourselves with.
TESSA: I reckon just say that?

Age means nothing and humans have created milestones as a rod to beat ourselves with. We judge ourselves against the previous generation and we can't help but panic that we aren't our parents. But, say it with us, Age. Is. Meaningless. Your mum owned a Volvo and had three kids by the time she was 22? In the 1500s, your mum would have had three kids by the time she was 15 and thought migraines were ghosts living in her head. Best not to compare yourself to past generations unless you really are devastated not to be sold to a middle-aged landowner by your twelfth birthday.

Milestones are everywhere. The '30 Under 30' lists, 21 things you should have achieved by the time you're 21, so-and-so becomes the youngest millionaire ever to blah-blah-blah. The plot of *My Best Friend's Wedding* is that if they're not married by the time they're 28, they'll marry each other. The only time that would be a reasonable pact to make is if the film took place in the Middle Ages when life expectancy was 30 at best.

Humans invented the milestones, which means we can all just . . . stop caring about them. Once you accept that they don't actually exist, you'll see there's always time to live the life you want, no matter how old you are.

TESSA: Which is why I will not deviate from my belief that I can still be an Olympic gymnast.

You can live the life you want no matter how old you are, unless your ambition is to become an Olympic gymnast. But this shouldn't stop you from learning gymnastics! Maybe just drop the Olympic bit!

TESSA: I shan't.

We all had these lofty ambitions long before we knew what money was. Before we realised that being an adult means waking up and inexplicably spending £45 before you've even got out of bed. Life is hard, and becoming obsessed with milestones is at best pointless, and at worst a self-fulfilling prophecy.

STEVIE: A friend of mine believed the marker for success was 'making it' by 30. If he didn't, he was a failure. He would say it to me all the time, so when he turned 30 and wasn't where he wanted to be it absolutely floored him. He fully gave up, became horribly bitter and resentful and now does something completely different that he hates. There is absolutely no reason to give up because of some weird made-up deadline you implemented based on nothing. He fully orchestrated his own self-implosion and I shall not allow anyone reading this chapter to do the same.

OK, so you're not where you want to be. Whatever you've managed so far is fantastic. If you're not reading this book from an underground sewer tangled in a 36-part rat king then you've done incredibly well. Keep going.

Resentment and frustration will freeze you, so don't let it. Look at your situation, look at how you can improve it and keep moving forwards. Unless you're inside the rat king. In that case try to find a jutting pipe or something to grab onto and maybe you can jimmy yourself free.

If you dreamed of greater success then, as Britney says, you gotta work, bitch. But at the same time, don't beat yourself up for not yet achieving everything you want. It's not the be all and end all. Impossibly wealthy, incredibly successful people who seem to 'have it all' can often be the most miserable.

There are a million pathways to success. That's why there are so many books called things like *There Are a Million Pathways to Success* by people called Tony Goldwinner. This is not a real book or a real man, but go to the self-help section and you'll see how many books start with: 'At 40 I was going nowhere, and then I discovered The Goldwinner Way' (sorry, obsessed with Tony Goldwinner now. We've created a full and robust personality in our heads and feel like we know him intimately as a friend, a colleague and possibly a lover. Why not? The man wrote *There Are a Million Pathways to Success* for God's sake).

If you want to change careers, change careers. If you want to retrain, retrain. If your truth is that you want to be an ice skater, or make ice cream for a living, or design spaceships, then do it. Your time on this spinning rock is finite and short, so go get ice-skating lessons and live your truth.

The only thing stopping you is thinking that you can't.

STEVIE: My mum went to university and got a degree in interior design when she was 40, before embarking on a 20-year career in the industry and winning a bunch of awards. She had two teenage daughters (sorry, Mum) and my dad was away for most of the three years, meaning she did the whole thing largely by herself. I thought it was too late at 24 to become a journalist. If you're thinking, 'But it is too late in MY career and at MY age,' THIS IS EXACTLY THE POINT I AM MAKING. IT IS NOT TOO LATE.

This is the crux of the entire chapter:

You are not too old and it is not too late.

40 OVER 40

For your delectation, people who pivoted careers later on in life (there's not actually 40 because we ran out space)

- Kate Atkinson wrote her first novel when she was 43.
- Vera Wang didn't enter the fashion industry until she was 40, and is now worth $400 million.
- Donald Fisher opened the first Gap store with his wife Doris when he was 40.
- Alan Rickman quit a successful graphic-design career in his mid-twenties to become an actor, and didn't get his big break until he was 42 years old.

- Robin Chase founded Zipcar with just £52 aged 42 and is now, obviously, rolling in it.
- Julia Child worked in advertising and then wrote a cookbook at 49, which turned her into a super-famous celebrity chef.
- Arianna Huffington started *The Huffington Post* when she was 50.
- Colonel Sanders was 62 when he first franchised Kentucky Fried Chicken.
- Arwen was 2,700 years old when she married Aragorn, a 30-year-old man.
- Edward Cullen was 107 when he married Bella Swann, a 17-year-old girl.
- Noah was 950 when he transitioned away from carpentry and built his first arc.
- Dracula was 489 when he left Transylvania for the first time and sailed to Whitby to attempt world domination.

NB: If you're fine with metaphorical life milestones but find those chunks of stone along country paths engraved with things like 'STOCKPORT 10 MILES' difficult to cope with, we're afraid we can't help you.

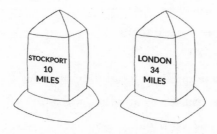

How to Respond to Catcalling

When someone leans out of a van, shouts across the road or, for example, pulls up in a car next to you, manually winds the window down (which takes ages), shouts, 'Minge!' then slowly winds the window back up and drives off, the shock can leave you reeling on the pavement, making noises like a carp before eventually gathering the wherewithal to shout '. . . Well, well, fuck you!' when they're already several miles up the road.

> STEVIE: I can still hear my carp sounds. They were like 'ughagghh hreeeg' – OK, I can't adequately express them written down. You'll have to buy the audiobook.

It's a horrible feeling to have your power wrestled away, and you'll want to put them in their place or embarrass them in front of their pals. Nothing worse than a perfect response dawning on you hours (or months) afterwards, so why not browse through these tried-and-tested comebacks for some inspiration?

And, of course, only use these for your run-of-the-mill wolf whistles and catcalls. You know the difference between someone shouting meaningless things just to feel powerful and a dangerous situation. If it's the latter, hotfoot yourself out of there and stay safe.

'ABSOLUTELY NOT!'

Rather than a direct riposte, this actually works better if it's not a grammatically accurate reply to their catcall, but rather a statement about them in general. 'OI, TITS!' 'Absolutely not!' Opting for something short, sweet and simple helps you regain control without the worry of rattling off a Pulitzer Prize-winning monologue.

A PULITZER PRIZE-WINNING MONOLOGUE

Write a book that wins a Pulitzer Prize and which, while being a gripping standalone narrative, could also work as a direct response within the context of a catcall or generic harassment, before memorising said book so you're ready to shout it at the perpetrator. It shouldn't take longer than three working days.

SAGE ADVICE

Similar to the Pulitzer Prize-winning monologue. To ensure said harasser hears the entirety of the advice, one must run after them. This is more difficult if they happen to be in a van travelling at 30 mph. If you can't keep up, they may only hear: 'IF YOU READ *BOYS WILL BE BOYS: POWER, PATRIARCHY AND TOXIC MASCULINITY* BY CLEMENTINE FORD YOU MIGHT SEE . . .' which isn't enough to educate.

Consider wearing roller blades at all times. This avoids incomplete advice that harms both the harasser (they cannot learn with only half the information) and stops you bellowing '. . . THAT

WHAT YOU ARE DOING COMES FROM DEEP-ROOTED INSECURITY!' at a passer-by who got caught in the crossfire.

'NOT TODAY, SIR'

They expected a reaction, but they didn't expect a Dickensian reaction. See also: 'A pox on you', and our personal favourite, 'GOOD GOD, MAN', elongating the words and imbibing them with the trembling power of Sir Christopher Lee or Sir Patrick Stewart. Or whichever old RSC actor you connect with the most.

'TAKE ME ON A DATE THEN'

We would not ordinarily suggest encouragement, but hear us out. You go on a date with said harasser, followed by a second, a third and a fourth. You are now in a relationship, memories of him shouting abuse at you long gone. Five years on comes an engagement followed by marriage with a house and, of course, children. The moment your daughter transitions from teenager to woman, you turn to him and say, 'Remember how you screamed at me in the street? Imagine what you'd do to a man who did that to your daughter,' and file for divorce. Totally worth it. 100%.

WHIP OUT SOME BAGPIPES AND START A-PIPING

It's certainly a choice.

'BY THE SEVENTH SON OF THE SEVENTH SON I LAY UPON YOU THE CURSE OF MY ANCESTORS'

Regain literal power by cursing the harasser. Retractable wizard's staffs aren't cheap but are worth it for the moment you whip one out in the Aldi car park following a wolf whistle or grotesque sexual comment. Nobody is ever anticipating a hex from a woman brandishing a staff, so you can always guarantee the element of surprise.

'. . .'

If you don't say or do anything, you haven't failed. You haven't lost points because you were unable to formulate a cutting witticism after being startled out of a daydream on your walk home. It's not up to you to single-handedly take down the patriarchy with one riposte. We often feel frustrated by our own silence, leading to the insane pressure to memorise, and have ready at all times, an articulate response to aggression.

Thing is, it doesn't matter what you say or don't say. The sort of person who screams something at a stranger on the street is not going to rethink their actions. They won't read the book you want them to read. They also won't be deterred if you shout, 'NO!' or give them the finger (but do it anyway because it's so satisfying). They will just continue until they find someone who gives them the reaction they want. You are freed from having to put them in their place, because they are getting put in their place every day, every night, at work or at home; that's the reason they need to scream things in the first place. They are desperately sad. You should not be responsible for a stunning oration when the person you're shouting it to isn't even responsible for basic etiquette and human decency. Feel intense disgust and pity for this person, go home, have your tea, have a good vent and banish the moment from your brain. That's a very important stage that should not be skipped. Unload that shit – don't let it fester away inside of you – and look after yourself, because it's unfair. You're right to be upset and you're allowed to respond however you want to respond. Whether that's with silence or with wizard paraphernalia.

How to Poo

This one is going to be a no-holds-barred discussion, so buckle up! We aren't doctors or scientists, but we fervently believe everyone should be able to talk about poo. If you don't, it becomes this embarrassing, shameful thing, and it might make you nervous to go to a doctor if something is wrong. Plus, recent studies have shown there's a huge connection between your brain and your gut, so if you're nervous talking about poo you're going to be nervous pooing. Also, it's poo. It's funny.

We care passionately about this topic because both of our digestive systems are an absolute state.

TESSA: I have to run to the toilet and stay in there for 45 minutes while I get so hot I have to take all my clothes off and put my wrists against something cold and put my head between my knees and make a noise like an injured manatee.

STEVIE: One time, we were all exchanging near-miss toilet anecdotes and Tessa said, 'Hahahaha, yeah, so I was going to the loo and I'd taken my clothes off—' and that wasn't the funny part of the anecdote, because she'd presumed everyone took their clothes off when going to the toilet. A real eye-opener. Oh, and I have stress-based IBS as well as being a highly strung person, so you can imagine how fun my toilet trips are. If you can't, just imagine something not fun.

Because of this weird culture of silence where we all pretend nobody poos, we're all desperately out of sync with our stomachs and what they're telling us. When we get sick we presume it's a particular food that's the problem, and it can be, but more often it's stress, lifestyle, dehydration or something going wrong inside. Blaming food leads to you ordering food tests off the internet late at night and sending off clumps of your own hair.

TESSA: I've done this and the report said I was allergic to mutton.

Instead, we should all be trotting down to the doctor, and not being ashamed to tell them what's going on because they've been to medical school for seven years and they've seen some *crazy* shit. Your embarrassing poo story is not going to impress them.

TESSA: The moment I decided to go to the doctor was when my harrowing farts got absolutely out of control. Once, driving home from a party, I was pretending to be asleep on the back seat and doing a terrible fart every seven minutes or so. My two friends in the front kept screaming and trying to work out where it was coming from. Eventually they pulled over on the hard shoulder of the M4 because they thought, and I quote, 'something had died in the exhaust'. Once I did a fart at a dinner party that I knew immediately was going to be terrible. Boys would be blamed, people would collapse. I chose the only available option. In the few seconds before it reached people, with the calm dignity of a newsreader announcing that we are at war, I said, 'Ladies and gentlemen, I have done an absolutely harrowing fart.' I am not exaggerating when I say that people took their plates and ran from the room. The hostess, unable to carry enough dishes to safety, was screaming, 'Get the bolognese! Get the bolognese!' lest any food be left in the room to curdle. We gathered in the hallway, holding our plates. One guest repeatedly shook his head and said, 'I can't believe that came from a human woman.'

STEVIE: To be fair, if I was a doctor I'd be impressed by this story.

To help you feel a little more in tune with your stools and what they're trying to tell you, behold, the Stool Chart!

		Bar
		Industrial
		Retro
		Mid-Century
		Antique

Just a little joke there, just a classic gag.

Behold, the Bristol Stool Chart!

Type 1		Separate hard lumps, like nuts (hard to pass)
Type 2		Sausage shaped (but lumpy)
Type 3		Like a sausage but with cracks on the surface
Type 4		Like a sausage or snake, smooth and soft
Type 5		Soft blobs with clear-cut edges (passed easily)
Type 6		Fluffy pieces with ragged edges, a mushy stool
Type 7		Watery, no solid pieces, entirely liquid

You want to be aiming for regular mid-table cables, so if you're languishing at either end of the spectrum, or finding yourself wildly oscillating between 1 and 7, then something's not right.

Type 1: Rabbit droppings or marbles. Very small, tight and hard to pass. You know when people have those weirdly glossy pebbles in bowls in their living rooms? Yeah.

Diagnosis: Extreme constipation. This one spent too long in your colon, where all the water got absorbed out, so you're getting these dehydrated pebbles of poo. Everything here has been in your digestive tract for about 100 hours.

Solution: Drink loads of water (actual water, not just a tea or a beer and claim that all liquid counts) and eat as many fruits and vegetables as you can. Make sure you're chewing as much as you can, and not surprising your stomach by wolfing down a sandwich at your desk. You need to give your body a bit of a heads-up by smelling your food beforehand and totally focusing on what you're eating. This one can happen when your gut hasn't moved around enough, so check if you're in a sedentary job or if you're getting enough exercise. Also – stress. It's always stress.

Type 2: Like a bunch of grapes, or many pebbles grouped together in a sock. Or a caterpillar.

Diagnosis: Constipation. This is a gang of Type 1 who all bunched together for safety and then stayed in the colon for ages because they were having such a good time. You're probably also bloated and uncomfortable like the lady in the advert who used to pour food into her handbag.

Solution: Stop putting any more food in your handbag for a bit. Try two days of just eating fruits and vegetables, pints of water and lemon. Just water, no alcohol or sugar. Remember when Augustus Gloop got stuck in the extraction pipe? That's what's happening in your colon. We need to gently move him out with lots of water and not just shove more food on top of him.

With this one, it doesn't help that the modern toilet situation is set up all wrong. Our gut is not designed to poo while seated; we're at the wrong angle, so it's like there's a kink in the garden hose. Squatting allows for a nice, straight, intestinal tract, but can be difficult and dangerous to do on a modern toilet. You could do yourself a real mischief up there. The compromise is to put your feet on a little stool, or to lean forward and go up onto your tiptoes.

Type 3: Not a bad one this – Types 3, 4 and 5 are all generally healthy. Like a corn on the cob, or a log with a few cracks on the surface. Easy to pass, no problems. Give yourself a sticker.
Diagnosis: A strong, healthy poo – everything in good working order. Keep it up!

Type 4: The Gold Standard. Nirvana. King of poos.
Diagnosis: You are the poop lord.

Type 5: Soft blobs like clouds. Comes out easily, perhaps with a sense of urgency.
Diagnosis: Generally fine, but you've got a hint of diarrhoea here. It's on the move pretty fast, so this once can be a nervous poo. A spike in blood pressure before an event can cause you to run to the

bathroom. It can also be caused by spices, so this one can be a post-curry poo, and dehydration, so it might be a hungover poo.
Solution: Drink plenty of water.

Type 6: Fluffy and mushy. Barely recognisable as a poo, more just bits. Probably yellow in colour because it hasn't been in your body very long. You had to rush to the toilet.
Diagnosis: Can be all the factors of Type 5 but ramped up a level. Extreme sense of panic and urgency running to the bathroom.
Solution: Drink as much water as you can, plus salt and electrolytes. Something you ate really didn't agree with you and your body flushed it out as quickly as possible. Try to work back through a food diary from the last few days and see what it might have been, or try an Elimination Diet and slowly reintroduce foods to see if you can find the culprit. It's possible you're very, very stressed, and obviously saying 'calm down' is meaningless, but be aware that it's physically affecting you.

Type 7: Weeing directly out of your bum.
Diagnosis: You have diarrhoea. Also known as pebble-dashing or the Jackson Pollock.
Solution: This will pass, but if it doesn't after a few days you need to see a doctor. Drink gallons of water and get some electrolytes in you because you're losing so much liquid.

Type 8: All of these, in order, starting with Type 1 and moving rapidly through to Type 7, while you take all your clothes off in the bathroom and think you might pass out. You have IBS.

Type 9: The Holy Shit! Otherwise known as 'Oh yes, I remember I just ate beetroot'. A beautiful but panic-inducing shade of red.

Type 10: The mushy peas. A poo the exact shade and consistency of mushy peas. Can sometimes be absolutely fine, perhaps caused by medication, green vegetables or green food dye, but can sometimes be an indicator that you're about to go down with extreme food poisoning.

The brown colour in poo is called bilirubin (a lovely name for a boy) and it's caused by the healthy breakdown of red blood cells. If your poo is yellow or green, it means it shot through the colon so fast it didn't have time to go through the Billy Rubin process. Work backwards and work out what you ate that caused your body to want to get rid of it as fast as possible.

Type 11: Black poo. Don't panic, but do trot yourself down to the doctor with this one. Black poo can be liquorice, but it can also be bleeding in the upper gastrointestinal tract, so it's better to be on the safe side if this has happened a couple of times.

And there we have it! You held onto your hat and got to the end of the poo chapter! Top marks. Enjoy working out which number on the chart you are, and absolutely never be ashamed to go to the doctor if things are out of control. Your body is just trying its best.

(If you're still considering a food test off the internet, you're allergic to dairy, gluten, alcohol, eggs, white meat, cane sugar, pomegranates, star anise, potatoes, red meat, turnips, salt, soil, mutton, asparagus and bracken. Hope that helps!)

How to Network

Even if you're super confident in social settings, networking is the worst. It could be an actual networking event your work has demanded you attend, where you speak to no one all evening while sweating in the corner, or it could be the office Christmas party. Or a large family gathering where you've lost sight of your immediate family and don't know who anyone is, or a friend's party where you've wildly misjudged the number of people you mutually know. Whatever is happening in the room, there's too many people, they all seem to know each other and you're dripping in sweat.

Thankfully we've come up with a pseudonym to help you through:

Not Everyone Thinks We ORK! (We came up with this at 2 a.m.)

Just kidding (not about it being 2 a.m.).

What are you going to do in a crisis networking situation? You're going to head to the **BAR!**

B – is for **Boat**. And everyone is in the same one.

Take a deep breath and remember that everyone in this room is flying down the Hudson without a paddle, praying someone strides up to them, claps them on the back and says, 'Well, howdy, partner, what is it you do?' or 'How do you know Carol?' even if there is no one called Carol here. No matter how well everyone's arranged themselves into tight-knit circles of white-toothed smiles, knowing guffaws and jovial back-slapping, you've got to remember that this is all a big performance. Nobody has noticed that you aren't talking to anybody; everybody is too busy freaking out about their own situation. If you saw a heat map of everybody's head at this point, it would just be white-hot panic.

STEVIE: Tessa, please tell everyone about the networking woman who turned up to your school and taught you an insane technique to enter a conversation.

TESSA: Yesssssssss. I'm loath to offer this up as advice, but once, in Year 10, we were all left in the hall for an afternoon called 'Working the Room'. A woman in a powder-blue three-piece suit with a matching powder-blue flower in her enormous hair, with an energy I have never encountered before or since, gave quite a manic talk on networking, which no one really grasped because we were 14. Her main suggestion was that to break into a circle of people that you wanted to be part of, you loitered on the edge of the group until somebody said something funny and then, when everybody laughed, you 'ducked and lunged' into the group, laughing maniacally as you went, and then bobbed up in the conversation as though you'd always been there. Then, when everyone looked at you, you were supposed to introduce yourself by saying your name, three things about you and then repeating your name. 'My name is Tessa Coates. My passions include free-diving, Murray Mints and traffic data analysis. That name again, Tessa Coates.' I think about her maybe once a week.

So don't do that. But do strike up a conversation with someone nearby, safe in the knowledge that everybody is desperate for someone to talk to. Not sure what to say? Allow us to take you to . . .

A is for **Ask Questions**

That's all it is – just keep asking questions. Don't open with, 'Hello, what's your biggest regret?' Ease yourself in with small talk. Do they know if there are any more canapés coming round? Networking events are so tricky, aren't they? What did you think of that speech? As ever, please insert relevant things to the event, and don't read these out loud from the book.

If you're a nervous soul in social situations, make sure you always pass the conversational tennis ball back across the net so it's their job to return it. That doesn't mean you have to be ready with a *Mastermind* set of rapid general-knowledge questions; just ask them questions and follow-ups. Observe Stevie's fantastic ball-passing skills . . .

STEVIE: How do you know Jeremy, the host of this bar mitzvah?

TESSA: We play competitive paintball together. How do you know him?

STEVIE: We worked together in the Antarctic on a penguin-breeding programme. Competitive paintball sounds fascinating – how long have you been doing that?

TESSA: I played for a long time at uni, but then I stopped for ages.

STEVIE: Oh, how come?

TESSA: I guess I lost all my confidence after the international capture-the-flag competition in Zurich. Also, I was sleeping with the captain.

Three questions in and a stranger is telling a fantastic story about a torrid love affair in Zurich! What a turn this bar mitzvah has taken! Keep passing those tennis balls.

It's a myth that networking is about reeling off your CV and asking people to give you a job. The aim of a networking event is to actively not do that, and then in about seven months' time, when you've completely forgotten about it, some guy you've completely forgotten meeting is asked who he'd like to hire and he will remember you telling a very funny story about Zurich. 'Hmm,' he thinks, 'we also discussed her interest in marketing, but I was too drunk to remember. She was a good laugh, though – maybe I'll give her a call!'

R is for **Relax!**
Fake it, fake it, fake it. Look like you're having a wonderful time and you've never felt more at ease. Keep your body language open, stand up tall, make eye contact. Imagine you're Barack and Michelle Obama combined. What would they be doing in this situation? They'd be smiling warmly, making eye contact, effortlessly writing autobiographies and catching flies with their bare hands or something.

The key is to approach the experience with curiosity, rather than blanket fear. It's just loads of people standing in a room pretending they wouldn't prefer to be doing literally anything else rather than standing in this room. It's absurd! Lean into it!

Don't start beating yourself up about your weird questions. There's a lot going on without adding a layer of 'Oh God, why did I say that?' to proceedings. It's fine to ask people what they do for a living. Also, it's a legitimately interesting question and people either love talking about their jobs, or they'll deflect by moving the conversation somewhere else – which opens it out for yet more top questions from your fine self.

Always remember that you can take a break any time you need. Ducking out to the loo, smoking an entire pack of cigarettes or having a little vacant stare at the refreshments table pretending to select a drink because you're too terrified to turn back around and face the room is not only expected, but encouraged. Nobody is watching you. Also, you're a grown-up and can leave whenever you want (depending on the event), which is why you should aim to arrive a bit late, so the awkward pre-party vibes are out of the way, and leave before the professional equivalent of somebody asking if their drug dealer can 'come hang'.

And there you have it! **BAR! B**oat (we're all in one), Ask Questions, Relax.

And what does that spell? Exactly, let's head to the free bar. The bar is the demilitarised safe zone in the networking minefield. You look like you're just alone here because you're getting drinks for your many, many friends. If you see someone getting a load of drinks for a cool group of smiling networkers, OFFER TO HELP THEM CARRY THE DRINKS. Capitals for emphasis. While you're walking over to the group, ask a casual question to get some form of conversation going and by the time you get there, you're part of the tight-knit circle.

STEVIE: Tessa, to finish, please tell everyone about the networking woman and her one incredible technique.

TESSA: She's back! This one, and credit to her, is actually a very good tip I've used at every party since. If there's a free bar, always get two drinks. It gives you something to hold and instantly makes you feel purposeful, instead of like a lemon. If you start talking to someone and you like them, you can say, 'Oh, I got this for my friend but I can't find them, do you want this?' If you get stuck talking to someone and they turn out to be awful, you can gesture apologetically at your drinks and say, 'Lovely to meet you, I just have to give this to my friend.' And then disappear! If you didn't manage to lose yourself in the crowd after your emergency exit and they're still watching you, go up to anyone and say, 'Please would you pretend to be my friend? I got stuck talking to someone terrible and had to pretend to leave.' I'd be your pal if I was on the receiving end of that. If all else fails, now you have two drinks.

STEVIE: Such a good idea.

TESSA: She also said you should say 'Bing!' right before you enter the room so that your face has a lovely smile.

STEVIE: That is a less good idea.

TESSA: Bing!

How to Understand Tax

A poem in eight cantos

STEVIE: I thought this was supposed to be a rap?
TESSA: Yes, well, I lost confidence. Plus, I think you *could* rap it.

Our story starts in Ancient Rome,
With Augustus on the throne,
Who said, 'Hey, chaps, hey, lads, come here,
I've had the most sublime idea.
You know I love to start a war,
I've got three on, I'll start one more,
But here's the thing, I know, it's funny,
But we're really running out of money.
So what if to stop me going broke,
We go and tax the common folk?
Now don't freak out, it won't be much,
I'm not completely out of touch.
So there's no fuss, it's my intent
To cap the income tax at 1%.
If you're wealthy you pay more,
You pay much less if you're poor.'

Nobody Panic

Fast forward several thousand years
To you at your computer, streaming tears,
So stressed you think your heart might burst,
It's midnight, January 31st.
In the UK, as you'll come to learn,
This is the day to file AND pay your tax return.

And just to keep things really weird,
The tax year has been engineered
To start itself on April 6th
And end again on April 5th.

What a baffling choice to make!
Surely there must be some mistake?
But no, back long ago and far away
The 25th March was New Year's Day!
'Lady Day' started the financial year,
And marked the moment Gabriel appeared,
To tell young Mary – this is wild –
'But you're carrying God's unborn child.'

'Lady Day' starts the year anew,
And stayed that way 'til 1752,
When England was forced to change its ways
And swap calendars, losing eleven days.
The Pope insisted on Gregorian,
And putting the Julian in the bin.
But to make sure they still got their tax,

How to Understand Tax

The Treasury pushed the tax year back,
And then, a Leap Year blunder,
In the year 1800,
Meant adding on one more day,
Which brings us to the April 6th we use today.

So what exactly do your taxes mean?
Why, when you've got your pile of beans,
Do you have to *give them back*,
And pay your awful income tax?
Well, museums, sports, financial aid,
Libraries, the police, the fire brigade,
The parks, some schools and, God bless,
Our very best thing, the NHS –
All these things we get for FREE!
Because we pay HMRC.
(And always will – don't vote Tory).

If you're safely on a salary,
Your boss will pay your PAYE,
This stands for Pay As You Earn,
And means you don't need to do a tax return.
If you're on somebody's staff,
They pay your tax on your behalf.
Nice and simple, nothing tricksy,
On April 5th, get your P60.
This is a list of every pound you've made,
And proof of all the tax you've paid.

Nobody Panic

When you leave a job, in shame or dignified,
You're handed a P45.
This is what you've paid, and some advice,
So your next job does not tax you twice.

The bit that makes your brain explode,
Is the Enigma team of secret codes.
The normal one is the letter L,
And everything else is tax-code hell.
S means Scotland is where you did your sales,
C means you did all your work in Wales.
A new job might send your paychecks
With W1, M1 or the letter X –
Emergency codes because you're new,
Until your official tax code comes through.
If you have a second job codes can frustrate,
But BR means the Basic Rate,
And the Ds as a general rule of thumb
Mean the higher rate on second income.

(If you think this is tricky and you're annoyed,
Now, God forbid, you're self-employed.)

There are three tax brackets as is traditional,
Basic, Higher and Additional.
The more you make, the more you pay,
The more tax you have to give away.
But here's something to help you sleep,

How to Understand Tax

About £12,000 is yours to keep!
That's your Personal Allowance, you pay no tax,
That's yours, you never give it back.

(This changes all the time,
So please, in court, don't use this rhyme.)

Up to £12,000 you pay not a dime,
Then after that it starts to climb,
12 to 50, you're on the Basic Rate,
You pay 20% on everything you make.

Then after 50 it's quite the jump,
And now you're going to need to stump
Up 40% that you now owe the state,
Because you're on the Higher Rate.

If you're making more than 150k,
And that is a serious amount of mon-ay,
Then you need to be content,
To pay back 45%.

Written down, you can see why
People always like to try
To get around the tragedy
Of giving half their money to Her Majesty.
These are your precious hard-earned beans,

And now you have to give them to the Queen.

Paying taxes is no fun,
But stay organised and get it done.
If you try to lie, then we ought
To tell you that you will get caught.

Tax avoidance is a *legal* way of finding cracks
To minimise your income tax.
And if you're of a more criminal persuasion,
That one's known as tax evasion.

Martha Stewart was a famous tax evader,
Though also a commercial insider trader.
So was Chuck Berry, Judy Garland, and Al Capone,
So if you go to jail, you're not alone.

STEVIE: I think we can agree that's the greatest chapter written
on tax in the history of light-touch comedy self-help books.
I'm putting it up for a Nobel Peace Prize.

How to Behave When Your Friend's New Partner Is Trash

It is very hard when your friend has chosen somebody absolutely dogshit to be their soulmate. You invite your friend somewhere, get a message saying, 'We're on our way!' and your heart just sinks. Oh great. The partner is coming too. But if this friendship is going to survive, then you are going to need to behave. So, what kind of trash are we talking?

A DULL WASTE-PAPER BASKET

There's nothing wrong with them as such, but they like to tell you the N in PIN stands for number, so when you say PIN number you're actually saying Personal Identification Number Number.

We're sorry, but you just have to let your friend live their life. Try to find the good in the partnership. Does the waste-paper basket provide stability? Do they allow your friend to flourish as the social butterfly of the pairing? Are they kind? Does your friend love being told facts about financial acronyms? If there's no bad behaviour, but you really can't handle being told the PIN thing again, work out a way for you and your friend to hang out without their partner. Make sure that when you invite them somewhere, you say casual things like, 'Just the two of us!' to make it clear it's a no-partner zone. When their partner is there, do your utmost to be nice, otherwise you'll run the risk of losing your friend.

A PHYSICAL BURNING TRASH FIRE INSIDE AN INDUSTRIAL SKIP

If this person is lying, cheating, making your friend cry, stopping them doing things they used to love, saying horrible things or in any way turning them into a shadow of their former self, then it can make you want to shriek, 'THE PERSON YOU HAVE CHOSEN IS A BURNING BINBAG AND I HATE THEM!' at regular intervals.

This will have the exact opposite effect of what you want. They will not down tools and say, 'I didn't realise, thank you so much. Two milkshakes to go, please!' before the two of you ride your bicycles into the sunset. Instead, they will get defensive and upset and shut down on you. In their heart of hearts they might know you're right, so they'll stop telling you things and ultimately your friendship will disintegrate. Or, at the very least, they'll buy a house with this person and you'll both end up having to pretend you didn't call their lover a 'piece of shit that's also done a shit on itself'.

Start raising things, in a calm and non-accusatory way, when the partner is not there. If they say something like, 'Jonty doesn't like me staying out late,' then calmly challenge this. Why do you think that is? How do you feel about it? Keep judgement out of it, and don't ask leading questions such as, 'Does Jonty know you're a fucking adult and not a toddler? Jesus CHRIST!' while crushing a wine glass with your bare fist.

If things continue to escalate, you may want to have A Talk. Your job is to be a steady rock and a safe space, with a touch of unpaid counsellor as a side hustle. Note: unpaid side hustle. Don't go in acting like a therapist, because it'll get weird.

> TESSA: I am the very worst at this. I want to immediately put on a pastel cardigan and say, 'How do you think your relationship with your mother has impacted your behaviour today?' which is breathtakingly annoying and I'm truly sorry to anyone on the receiving end of it.

Have they talked to Jonty about his problem with them staying out late? Don't label things they haven't labelled – for example, 'This sounds controlling' – but give them space to make conclusions on their own.

Explain that you worry about them because you love them, and some of the things they've told you feel a bit concerning. Tell them about your own dumb romantic decisions, especially if you got out and felt better afterwards. Now you're two people making messy choices, rather than one unhinged zealot who won't stop shouting at the other.

If your friend agrees that things with Jonty are bad, but says the thought of being single again is too much to bear, then remind them that a life alone is a thousand times more wonderful than a life with someone they don't love. There are nine billion people in the world. It's not Jonty or Death. It's Jonty or a period of sadness and loneliness, followed by recovery, strength and meeting someone who is better suited to you, especially now you know yourself better and Jonty has taught you some clear things you want to avoid.

They might take this advice, but they also might not. Or it might take them a long time. Being a friend is knowing when to stop pushing, and just be supportive.

> STEVIE: I've been on the receiving end of people straight up telling me my ex-boyfriend was trash, and I morphed into a small clam, too embarrassed to talk to those people about it again. Now, when I think a relationship might not be right for a friend, I know how it feels for them. So I start by saying I trust them and am really clear that I'm there if they ever need to talk. I will give them my honest opinion, but I won't judge them for not following it because I myself went out with a piece of binshit for ages.

A BIN BAG THAT'S TOO HEAVY AND LEAKING A BIT SO YOU HAVE TO RUN IT OUT OF THE HOUSE AT ARM'S LENGTH

Sometimes the partner is, to you, obviously temporary. Maybe your friend met them while taking ayahuasca before bonding on a beach over a shared love of shells. In which case, step back and let them ride it out. Who knows? Old Shell Face might be the one for them. If they're clearly happy, you don't need to be furrowing your brow and asking what they talk about since neither of them speak a single word of the other's language. If you think it's all going to end in tears, jovially and lightly raise that concern, then let them live their life and be ready to pick up the pieces. If this is something they do over and over again, try to find that line between saying

258

that you don't want to be the Official Shoulder to Cry On any more and not doing it so aggressively that they stop talking to you completely – or, worse, marry Shell Face despite the language barrier, just to prove a point.

ON CLOSER INSPECTION, NOT TRASH

It's also very possible that they're not trash at all and, if you're really honest, the truth is that you just hate that your friend likes somebody more than you. It's really tough when friends move on. When they fall in love, or get new jobs, or new friends, or move out, or get married, or have babies. It's a rite of passage to feel your friend's path diverge from yours, and to feel left behind. Be brave! Let them go, be happy for them and know that they always come back – and that friendships are supposed to evolve and grow.

Important Note: If the situation has gone beyond trash and you're worried a friend is in any danger whatsoever, there are some important resources at the back of the book (see page 402), with numbers you can call 24/7, and we're sending you and your friend all the love and luck in the world.

How to Move Back In with Your Parents

This can be a deeply unpleasant experience for everybody involved. You thought you'd made huge strides into adult life and now, for all kinds of reasons, you're back living in your childhood bedroom and people keep saying, 'Well, look who it is!' and 'Somebody decided to join us, I see!' and 'Good afternoon!' at 9 a.m.

Maybe your parents are thrilled to have you because they hated being empty-nesters. Maybe they're horrified because they thought you were long gone and they wanted to turn your room into a dance studio. Either way, the balance of power has shifted and nobody knows how to behave any more.

> TESSA: I moved back home after I graduated and it mostly consisted of me lying face down on the kitchen floor, wailing, while my dad strode over me to go to work and my mum asked why I didn't 'just say I was an engineer' and 'get on some kind of graduate scheme'. They didn't know what to do with me, and I didn't know what to do with myself, so I became a sort of live-in painter-decorator.

Attempt to keep things as harmonious as possible by following some ground rules:

1. How long are you going to be here?

You may not know the answer to this question, but it's helpful for everybody to have a time frame. Is the plan six months, and then hopefully you're back on your feet and you can move out? Great, that's workable. What's not workable is saying, 'Just one more week,' every week for six months.

2. What's expected of everybody?

Yes, you're a grown-up now, but you've also had to come home, so where's the line between what they can and can't tell you to do? Have a good chat about the boundaries. How a curfew is probably not cool, but also that you won't be throwing parties in the living room. Oh yes, and you smoke now. Sorry! But you'll keep it far away from the house and won't hang out of the bathroom window. Be clear with each other about what the new rules are and communicate that this situation isn't ideal and you're very grateful and you're going to try to make things work.

3. Can you pay rent, and if you can't, can you behave?

> TESSA: My bedroom is in the attic, and when I was ten I announced that no one was allowed to go in my room. My dad said, 'That's fine, you can buy the attic off us,' and then he wrote down how much he thought the attic cost, and I looked at the number and said, 'Actually, I'm very happy for people to come into my room.'

There has to be a trade-off somewhere, so either you pay some money and you get more of a free rein, or you don't pay anything and keep your shit together.

4. Be useful

If you're home because you're also unemployed, make sure you don't allow yourself to totally wallow in despair. Other people are trying to live here too. Your parents are from a totally different generation and you're up against things that literally didn't exist when they were your age. Of course you're going to get unhelpful advice like, 'What do you mean, they rejected you? Why don't you go down there and ask them why?' In their day, this actually worked and you could buy a house on your way home for half a crown and a bushel full of yams.

If you're struggling to cope, reaching out for help is so important. It's likely that you don't know what you need (well, you do: money, purpose, a job, a home of your own), but keep communicating with each other, so they can do their best to help you. Just be aware that everyone is trying to function here. If you're supposed to be looking for work and are patently not doing this, it's going to upset the other members of the household.

TESSA: Once, I drew a very elaborate owl at the kitchen table and then everybody came home from work and asked what I'd done that day and I showed them and my mum said, 'Tessa has drawn an owl.'

STEVIE: I'm only being quiet here because I've never moved back home, but I really enjoyed this owl anecdote.

5. Do the cooking

Nothing is going to make you feel more hopeless, and your parents more mad, than you falling back into a cycle of having your meals made and your clothes cleaned for you. Do your own laundry, for heaven's sake, and establish which days of the week you're going to cook for everybody. Take the bins out. If you've come home just for the weekend, then of course it's nice to be cared for and loved, but any longer than that and you'll need to be taking care of yourself. Otherwise, don't complain when your parents treat you like a child. Very harsh, but very true.

Think of this as the Dead Fish Rule. A dead fish is fine in the house – a novelty even – for about three days. After that it starts to smell. You are the dead fish.

STEVIE: When is a dead fish a novelty???

TESSA: I didn't make up that saying. It's Benjamin Franklin. 'Guests, like fish, begin to smell after three days.'

STEVIE: Yeah, but he doesn't say, 'A dead fish in the house is a bit of a novelty.'

TESSA: Listen, once, our neighbour came round with a four-foot-long trout and we all took turns saying, 'He's left the eyes in so it'll see you through the week!' which was a bit of fun.

STEVIE: Right.

TESSA: And once, my Canadian auntie sent us a wrapped Christmas present in September and we just left it in the living room by the fire and on Christmas Day it turned out to be a colossal salmon! I've got more of these if you want?

263

STEVIE: I could listen to you talk about fish all day, but I'm aware of the book's word count.

6. Take any old job as a stopgap

Even if you hate it, even if you've got a degree now and you're back doing the job you did when you were 15, just do it. Get some money in, stay busy, stay active – good things are coming.

7. Maybe keep politics out of it

The situation is already fraught enough. You don't need to be bellowing every night at the kitchen table because your parents disagree with the Transport Secretary. Just accept that everyone has a different opinion, and everyone is just going to have to grit their teeth and live in harmony. No politics at the table. Or near the table. Or anywhere.

8. Try to have a nice time?

They're your family, after all, and it's nice to have a home. Keep communicating, keep the peace, be honest with each other, don't let resentments get buried and then explode out of nowhere while you're all watching *The One Show*. Underneath it all, you love each other very much; this is just a difficult transition period and, regardless of how they're acting, they're doing you a big favour by putting you up like this. It's only temporary. Repeat this to yourself like a mantra before falling asleep in your too-small teenage bed.

How to Put Up a Shelf

PART ONE: STEVIE HAS A GO

I've never put up a shelf in my life. The closest I've ever come to DIY is putting up a flatpack bookcase with a pan as a hammer. But how hard can it be? I can do this.

Step 1
Get all your things together. We're talking nails, we're talking a hammer, we're talking your shelf. I think that's everything. Oh! Brackets? Two brackets. They are L things, like this:

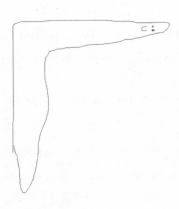

They don't usually have faces, but I thought it would be nice to make the bracket more friendly.

Step 2

Ask a friend to hold the brackets against the wall where you would like your shelf to go. Take your nail, place it in the little nail hole and bash the nail until it goes right through the bracket and into the wall. Then do the other one and balance the shelf on top of both of the brackets.

Step 3

Congratulations! You have put a shelf up.

PART TWO: STEVIE READS THE INSTRUCTIONS

Step 1

Get all your things together. Two brackets, your shelf, a drill (ah), a spirit level, your pencil, screws (not nails), a screwdriver (classic), rawlplugs (fuck).

Step 2

Place the brackets on the shelf, one far left and one far right, and fix the brackets onto the shelves with a screwdriver. Ah yes, brackets on first, very sensible.

Step 3

Hold the shelf against the wall and use the spirit level to make sure the shelf is straight. Pencil-mark onto the wall where the screws will go through the bracket.

Step 4

Drill into the wall.

> STEVIE: . . . Tessa!
>
> TESSA: Yes, hello.
>
> STEVIE: It says, 'Drill into the wall.'
>
> TESSA: I did think this chapter was very ambitious given the whole flatpack-bookcase-with-a-pan situation. OK, what kind of wall have you got?
>
> STEVIE: A white one?
>
> TESSA: Knock on it gently. Would you say that it feels as though if you were very strong it would be satisfying to punch through it, or that if you punched through it, it would break your hand?
>
> STEVIE: Break my hand.
>
> TESSA: Great, that's a brick wall. And you absolutely can drill through it, but it's going to take a little bit of time.
>
> STEVIE: What if I had one that felt more punchable?
>
> TESSA: That's a stud partition wall, so it's plaster and then hollow with spaced-out wooden posts (studs), and you want to drill into the studs.
>
> STEVIE: Great, I'll put my shelf on that wall instead. How do I know where the studs are?

TESSA: You need to knock.

STEVIE: Are you joking?

TESSA: No, you're supposed to knock all the way across until you hear the difference between knocking on wood and knocking on the bits that are hollow.

STEVIE: Good grief.

TESSA: You could also buy a stud finder. They're very cheap and you'll feel like Batman. It's a little handheld thing and it uses an electrical signal to tell you what's behind the wall. It can also tell you if there are live wires or pipes behind the wall (though if you're at all concerned about this part, do get a professional to come and check).

STEVIE: What about the actual drilling?

TESSA: You need a cordless hammer-action drill. Cordless drills have a battery, and hammer action means it's got the strength to drill into brick.

STEVIE: Look, I don't mind being the one to say it: this is quite hot.

TESSA: The cheapest ones are about £50 or you can always get one second-hand. Then you need to choose the right drill bit.

STEVIE: I chose this incredibly sharp and spiky one, like a spear for a mouse.

TESSA: Lovely choice, but that's actually a wood drill bit and it really won't like drilling into plaster or brick.

STEVIE: This one is gold, very fancy, like a staff for a mouse who is also a wizard. It's gold so it must be the best.

TESSA: Such reasonable logic, but that's actually a metal drill bit and is only for metal.

STEVIE: Oh GOD. This is exhausting. OK, this one with the big, flattened top, like a Hammerhead shark.

TESSA: That's the devil! He's a masonry drill bit for drilling into brick, concrete or plaster. Choose one that is the same width as your rawlplug and off you go!

STEVIE: Wait, wait, wait! What if I make a terrible mess?

TESSA: What's the first commandment of DIY?

STEVIE: 'Yes You Can.'

TESSA: And what's the second?

STEVIE: 'Oh gosh, well, not to worry, you can fix that.'

TESSA: If you make a mess and put a hole in the wall in the wrong place, fill it full of Polyfilla, scrape it flat with your least favourite knife, sand it down, paint over it and no one will ever know you were there. You got this!

Step 5

Drill your hole and then gently hammer in your rawlplug until it's flush with the wall. The rawlplug is like a hat for a screw, or a sheath for a sword. Or a condom.

Step 6

Put the brackets onto the wall and screw your screw through the bracket and into the rawlplug as tightly as you can. Redo the spirit level and reassess where the other bracket hole needs to be if necessary. Otherwise, stand back. Admire shelf.

How to Survive Your Stopgap Job

If you're working somewhere you hate in order to get enough money to one day do something you love, that is a stopgap job. It could be anything – from waitressing to welding. One person's dream job is another person's stopgap, and there's no judgement from either of us, no matter what you want to do or what you have to do to get there. Unless it involves murder.

While we can't tell you how to survive each individual job, we can certainly tell you about our own varying stopgap experiences and what we learnt from them, to give you a bit of a boost.

STEVIE

Box office at a small theatre
The job: Three-hour shifts ripping and selling tickets in a theatre an hour and a half away for £5 an hour. So that's £15 a shift, and by the time I'd got there, I'd already paid about £6 on public transport.

What it taught me: To work smart, not hard. Trudging all that way for essentially £9 was a bit of a blow. I should have found a job that paid me a higher hourly rate and wasn't so far away. I felt I could only get something small and cash-in-hand because the journalism MA I was doing at the time forbade students to have jobs to support themselves. The nine-month course cost £10k and I'm only just realising how hideous that was a decade later. Good God, that is some classist bullshit. No wonder everyone who works in women's magazines is called Polly Von Buffletown.

Copywriter for an escort agency
The job: Eight hundred words for various blogs on escort-agency websites. Yes, escort agencies – as in people pay people to have sex with them. I honestly believed escorts escorted people to parties and that it was nothing to do with sex until my unnerved parents informed me over the phone that this was not the case, casting doubt over the morals of my new 'writing job'. I was paid £10 for every eight hundred words, and had to write about things like the World Cup but get key words like 'busty blonde' and 'escorts' in as much as I could for the 'Google hittings' (as my employer put it).

What it taught me: LOOK AT THE WEBSITE YOU ARE WRITING FOR BEFORE YOU SAY YES. DO NOT JOBHUNT ON CRAIGSLIST. Also, if you have a unisex name and a picture of John Travolta as your Gmail image, people presume you're a man. Not saying that's a good or bad thing, but it certainly helped me freelance for men's magazines later on. When they found out I was a woman, a certain now-defunct men's mag asked me to do a 'getting ready photoshoot of you and your mates in your nighties', so I stopped freelancing for men's mags.

Waitress at numerous restaurants
The job: Regardless of which restaurant you're in, the job remains the same. Minimum wage, chefs screaming, no control over your shifts and rife sexism. At the end of each shift, the guys would sit and drink Peroni while the girls would clean the bar, despite the fact that girls weren't allowed to work behind the bar. So we ended up cleaning both the restaurant and the bar each night. Also, I ate customers' leftovers. Sorry, but I couldn't afford nice food on my measly wage, so, yeah, I scraped those plates of ratatouille into my mouth and I don't regret it.

What it taught me: The more you fight against your stopgap job, the worse it is. If you do the bare minimum and clock-watch, the day will pass in slow motion, but if you lean in and take pride in what you are doing – becoming the best at the coffeemaker, the quickest cutlery polisher and the most efficient waitress you can be – it will be more enjoyable. Waitressing also taught me that it's really hard to chase your dreams, babe, when you are working 17-hour shifts and unable to move or think on your days off. Try your best, spread out the dream-job hustle so you're not burnt out and slowly but surely you'll get there.

Social diarist for a broadsheet paper
The job: I would get a text saying, 'George Clooney is going to be at One Marylebone tonight – go NOW,' and would have to try to get a news story out of it. I was not paid unless something got published, and the fee was £30. You might think this sounds cool and not a stopgap at all because didn't I want to be a journalist?

But this was the worst job I have ever had – another attempt at funding my MA, kindly passed onto me by a fellow student who loved it. Shout-out to presenter Rick Edwards; I walked up to him at a party and – at this point having completely given up – said, 'Oh God, do you have any news?' and he replied, 'Are you doing that terrible gossip-column job? Oh, that is a HARD job!' and then gave me a quote before wishing me well. God bless that man.

What it taught me: Just because a job sounds close to something you want to do, this does not mean you will like it. And if you don't like it, it doesn't mean you're not cut out for the whole industry. You might be a terrible reporter, but a brilliant editor, or hate waiting tables, but love running a restaurant. You might want to work in films, but hate being on set. Your passion might be marine biology and you might be scared of the sea. I spent years thinking I wasn't cut out to be a writer because I couldn't do this one, badly paid, very morally bankrupt job, but I loved interning at magazines (when I could afford to do it – which was twice). Find your own path.

TESSA

Waitressing for a profoundly corrupt catering company
The job: I did this for many years, from the age of 14 'til long after I'd graduated. They operated out of a warehouse that is now an auction house for repossessed cars. The catering company was basically a front, we all got paid in cash and we weren't supposed to ask a lot of questions, but there was always work if you texted

and said I'm free this weekend. You made £7 an hour, double after midnight, and we went to some quite fun places and provided deeply adequate service. I was constantly getting sent home for backchat. Or, when they couldn't send me home because we'd all come in the same van, I was sent to the back of the kitchen to make the butter dishes.

What it taught me: I can say, 'This is a fucking nightmare,' in Polish, which is what the chefs used to say whenever we arrived anywhere and they were expected to cook for 200 people out of a small gazebo in a field with one gas canister.

Also, I can drive a van because sometimes everyone would get drunk and then throw me the keys even though I wasn't insured and I would drive so slowly everyone would be shouting, 'Please, Tessa! That old lady is overtaking you and she's on foot!' which I can also say in Polish.

Waitressing for a slightly less corrupt catering company
The job: I got asked to do this ten-day job in Paris (Paris!), working in the hospitality tent for British Airways at the Paris Air Show. They were going to put us up in a hotel, plus free food, and at the time I didn't have anywhere to live, and also, Paris! So I took the job. The hotel turned out to be in the most dangerous part of the city, way out of town, and we were instructed at the front desk not to leave at night under any circumstances. The only place we were allowed to go, in pairs, was across the intersection to visit the four-storey, 24-hour KFC.

Also, I thought the form said BA, as in British Airways, but when

I got there I discovered it said BAE. BAE turned out to be a multi-national aero-military defence company, and since no one would tell me what they did, or what BAE stood for, I decided it stood for Bombs and Everything. They sold weapons.

We ran a free and very classy bar and endless hospitality service and several Saudi princes came in and bought weapons.

What it taught me: On the third day a guy came in with a lot of equipment and I gave him a cup of tea and he said, 'Do you want to know how you check to see if a room is bugged?' and I said, 'Yes, please.' So I do know how to do that.

Cinderella in a children's toy shop

The job: I spent several weeks dressed as Cinderella, painting children's faces in a toy shop in London. I honestly wouldn't even call this a job because I liked it so much. I even bought myself some little silver ballet pumps and covered them with glitter because the children kept asking to see my glass slippers and they got quite aggressive about it. The shop had paid for a Gruffalo, so sometimes I would stand outside the shop and ask children if they would like to go in and see the Gruffalo, and then they came straight back out about seven seconds later, screaming, because he was so scary. The Gruffalo costume was about 12 foot tall and really hard to manoeuvre. The eyes didn't blink, the hungover teenager inside the costume couldn't see out and the head kept twisting backwards.

What it taught me: You don't have to hate the job. People will pay you to do a surprising number of things.

English as a foreign language teacher

The job: I was a substitute teacher wherever I was needed. Mostly I taught Italian teenagers on exchange trips who didn't give a single shit (*una sola merda!*) about learning English. I was left completely to my own devices, so we made a lot of posters about how we would save the world and wrote postcards home about Big Ben. Sometimes I had an interactive whiteboard that could bring up YouTube and then the class would descend into a karaoke session in which everyone took it in turns to sing me their favourite song while I sat on the desk and applauded. I could see them thinking, 'I can't believe we got away with this,' and I was thinking, '*You* got away with it?! I'm the one being paid!'

I worked a lot for a company in Greenwich who had named their school after the river in Oxford, so they'd called themselves ISIS, and we would take kids *on the Tube* in T-shirts that said 'I'm with ISIS'.

What it taught me: Do reconsider that name. But also that I loved teaching, and that you can love something and make money. Work doesn't have to be something you despise if you find something you're good at.

How to Be Single

Such an unbelievably popular topic that they made a film about it.

> TESSA: I want to tell you that the film is bad, which it is, but my truth is also that I once had seven gin and tonics on a plane and watched *How to Be Single* twice. Then I came home and painted a signature wall in my bedroom a deep yet vibrant shade of blue. I didn't ask permission from the landlord because I didn't want to explain that the film had had a profound effect on me and the main character paints her wall and now I wanted to. (The wall looked fantastic.)

Let us first address those who are Single and Thriving. For no matter how much you love being on your own, the world is built for two, and it can sometimes be really tough to be a One. You're constantly made to feel like you're On the Single's Table. You're priced out of living places because you can't afford the rent on your own and there's that awful Two Together railcard you can't get involved with.

STEVIE: My friend tried to do a Two Together railcard with
herself, using two pictures where she had slightly different hair.
It did not work.

The whole set-up from the moment you're born can feel like a
never-ending cycle of your PE teacher shouting, 'Get into pairs!'
and you thinking, 'I don't want to be in a pair! I want to climb the
rope on my own!' I want to have adventures and do my own thing,
and live my life, and move to Bogotá at the drop of a hat if the
mood takes me. I do not wish to get married and bicker about soft
furnishings and ask, 'What shall we do for dinner?' ad infinitum
until one of us dies.

If this is you, crack on and continue forging your own path.
Don't take it too hard if the friends you thought were just like you
develop a sudden and burning desire for comfort and stability.
Neither choice is right and neither is wrong. Everyone is entitled
to build whatever life they want.

If you are Single and Sometimes Thriving but also Perhaps Having
a Bit of a Wobble Occasionally, that's very normal. You're having a
great day and then out of nowhere you get blindsided by the realisation that you're nobody's favourite person (even though you
definitely are, you just don't fancy them back or even know they
fancy you. Also, you're forgetting all your friends and family here.
Look, you're doing VERY WELL). To return to the PE analogy, this
is the moment they shout, 'Get into pairs!' and when you look around
the room, everyone's eyes are already finding their person and no
one is looking at you.

That's tough, and it can often feel tougher when your best

friend/single partner-in-crime starts seeing somebody new. No one enjoys watching their friends get into another pair, and very few people manage to graciously transition into becoming the third wheel.

Be very brave and let them have their three months of passionate love-making before the chemicals start to wear off and they're available to hang out with you again. Admit your feelings to other friends and surround yourself with people you can be honest with. These wobbles are often much more about feeling left out than a marker of your own desperate desire for romantic love.

> TESSA: I once got very sad at a party because people kept coming up and asking me if I'd seen their partners. (They were right to choose me. I have a very good memory and I could say, 'Yes, they're at the buffet,' or, 'Yes, they're being sick out of the upstairs window.') I whispered to my friend Clare that I was sad that no one ever says, 'Hey, have you seen Tessa?' Which is very dumb and childish, but was also true in the moment, and she laughed a lot, and now whenever we go to a party she finds me to say, 'Hey, have you seen Tessa?' Which, as it turned out, was all I needed.

If you are Single and Definitely Hating It, that can be the most tough of all and you're not alone in your feelings.

Actively looking for love is really hard. It was hard a thousand years ago and it was hard a million years ago. It's hard if you're a human being or a krill or a giraffe. Sure, giraffes don't have to navigate Tinder, but in order to find out if a lady giraffe is into him, the male giraffe does have to drink her wee. So, you know, swings and roundabouts.

Don't beat yourself up, and admit that you're not enjoying being single. There's no point yelling, 'I'm actually FINE ON MY OWN!' because you think it makes you look weak to feel otherwise. You're fooling no one but yourself; the yelling unfortunately gave you away.

And, sure, you can be cynical and say that love is just a combination of chemicals evolved from the mammalian survival instinct to encourage hominid pair-bonding, and it is, but that doesn't stop it from feeling fantastic. It doesn't mean you're weak to want a piece of that pie. Own that pie. You'd like to be loved.

People can keep saying, 'The right person is just around the corner!' and you might be thinking, 'Could the corner hurry up? Is this the corner?!' while pointing to slight curvatures in a wall in an increasingly hysterical pitch, but – and this is unhelpful – you do need to chill out.

No one knows what's around life's corner, and waiting for it is a waste of time. Imagine if you met someone who said, 'I don't have any hobbies because I've been solely focused on attracting a mate.' You'd run for the hills. Now imagine they said, 'I gave up on looking for love and went travelling on my own and nearly fell out of a boat in the middle of the Atlantic – would you like to hear about it?' Yes, please, you would like to hear about it.

A whole sub-plot in *How to Be Single* (which really comes to life on the second viewing) is that Dakota Johnson's character wants to find someone to climb the Grand Canyon with at dawn on New Year's Day. She's been waiting years for someone to want to do it with her, and then what does she do at the end? She climbs it by herself.

This is your time to discover exactly who you are, what you love and what your passions are. If you don't learn to love life on your own, then you'll start a relationship with any old fool just to stop being single. If you're on Single Island, looking out to sea, desperately waiting to be rescued, you'll get into the first rickety leaking boat that comes along. If you turn around and see that the island is amazing and that you can make an incredible life here, then you won't get in a boat unless it's an absolutely knock-out, state-of-the-art cruise liner.

The ugly Catch-22 is that love arrives when you stop looking. Not pretend to stop looking, but truly stop looking. To return to *How to Be Single* just once more, Alison Brie's character has made herself a spreadsheet, built her own match-making software and is aggressively dating her way around the city. Then she gives up, has a meltdown in a library and decides to be single forever. And what happens? Jason Mantzoukas immediately falls in love with her.

TESSA: I was once ghosted by a ballet dancer and spent the weekend lying face down on the living-room carpet, only rising to do a 75-question online quiz called 'Why hasn't he texted you back?' (Mostly Bs: He's not that into you.) Then I got up, put on this massive diamond ring I found in Primark, went to a party and announced that I was done with love and I was 'married to comedy'. I was asked on a date *hours* later.

Worth pointing out that while you work yourself out and enjoy Single Island, those in intense long-term relationships might tell you how jealous they are that you get to sleep with whoever you want. This is crazy, because the pool of people you both can and want to sleep with is actually quite small, and not everyone in the pool wants to sleep with you.

Don't throw yourself into fervently sleeping around if you're not cut out for it, just because that's what you think you're supposed to do.

TESSA: Prior to the diamond-ring incident, in an attempt to be better at dating and less of a total prude, I invented something called the Dick Harvest, which lasted about six months and in which I managed to harvest exactly one dick. If it's not for you, it's not for you.

STEVIE: I was single for a while (the Great Drought of 2008–2012) and tried to harvest dick but my heart was never in it. It was like acting in a play, except the play involved actual sex, nobody saw it and I didn't get paid.

TESSA: I remember living with my two best friends – one straight lady, one gay man – who were, surprisingly for both of them, single at the same time. We were all laughing in the living room about how many people we'd slept with that week, and it felt like that bit in *The Lord of the Rings* when Legolas and Gimli are fighting orcs and happily shouting out how many they've killed. I felt like Strider, and no one's noticed but he's got his watch caught in that big dog or something, and he's about to go over the cliff.

STEVIE: Quite hard to follow if you're not a *Lord of the Rings* fan.

TESSA: To complete the metaphor, I forgot that what happens to Strider is that after he goes over the cliff, a magical white horse comes and rescues him. And it turns out *I* was the horse. I rescued myself.

There's no right way and wrong way to be single. We aren't going to give you hot tips like, 'Say yes to all parties!' and 'Download an app!' because you know all that. The point is that you need to feel your feelings, be honest and then get on with your life. Have single partners-in-crime where possible, but don't lose your mind when they find someone to pair up with. And always remember that you're not waiting to be rescued, you're going to rescue yourself. You are a magical white horse (please see anecdote above).

How to Budget

Good evening, my name is Stevie Martin, and it's an honour to be doing a TED Talk on How to Budget'.

(Water break.)

I am terrible at maths and have never worked in finance or, indeed, with budgets of any kind, so I'd be surprised to be doing TEDx, let alone a full-blown Theodore, but here I am. And despite being numerically underqualified for anything other than Counting On My Hands, I do know how to budget.

I could stand here before you all, in the O2 Arena – main stadium, not the indigo room or the bit where they have *Mamma Mia! The Party* – and tell you a complex formula. Apps to download to your phone. Apps to download to your eye (for anyone rewatching this talk in the future). I could ask my esteemed colleague for assistance –

(Tessa waves from the wings.)

– but if you ask her questions about maths she says things like, 'Isn't it interesting that we say eleven and not onety-one?'

(Tessa mouths, 'But why do we?')

I could tell you how huge corporations draw up their budgets, and how that software is necessary for you to work out how many times you went to Starbucks last month. But I won't. And not just because I genuinely can't, but because none of that matters when you're trying to draw up a simple budget.

There is only one way anyone can ever budget. The reason people don't do it, and read chapters like this hoping for some genius nugget that'll eliminate their financial woes, is the same reason we roll our eyes when an expert informs us that staying hydrated, getting plenty of sleep and regular exercise will make us feel good. It's boring. It works, but who cares? I'd prefer to take a pill every day that promises to banish my fatigue rather than do something stupid like assess my sleeping in order to make positive changes. If I do that, I'll come face to face with all my terrible habits and be forced to do things. I don't want to do things. I just want sleep to happen.

Budgeting is the same, because you already know how to do it, you just don't want to because it involves looking at what you're spending.

(Longer water break.)

For any sort of budget, whether you wish to save up a certain amount of money or you wish to simply pay all your bills and also stay alive, you need to take the amount of money you make monthly after tax is taken off, and then remove all the necessary outgoings, like rent, bills, bus fares and petrol, and see what you're left with.

Can you save what you need from that figure? If so, how much is left for you to spend on living? Have you got enough to pay the bills, put a little into savings and have a little leftover beer money? Fantastic.

If not, it's time to crack open the bank statements and categorise those outgoings. How much in total did you spend on supermarket shopping? And on lattes? Going out for drinks? Clothes? Make-up? Phone bill? Split them into categories that make sense to you – but a good starting point is 'necessary' and 'unnecessary'. 'Can't get out of it' and 'can get out of it'. Council tax is necessary. A bottle of wine at the pub is of course very necessary but unfortunately comes under 'unnecessary' because you could very easily get out of it. You must be brutal with the categorisation.

Once you've categorised, it's time to go through all of the outgoings and see where you can make cuts. Is it time to take the bus rather than the car for a bit? Do you need to start making your own coffee? It's depressing and gross and will make you embarrassed about what you spend. That's why lots of people are terrible at it – FEAR! Apologies for shouting.

It's also why there are loads of colourful budgeting apps with fun names like SQUIRRL, which seem fine until you realise that you still have to look at everything you've spent, it's just now there's a rodent burying a nut in the corner of your phone screen. Also, I made up SQUIRRL, but as you can see I removed a vowel, which is how you know it's modern, and if anyone is interested I would be prepared to sell a 20% share of the business for £10,000 and a 90% stake in the company for -5% APR (terms and conditions apply).

Keep the budget super simple, so you're able to adjust it as and when things change. May I suggest doing the thing in a spreadsheet, where you put all the numbers into a column, highlight the column and click 'sum' (the zig-zaggy Greek-looking backwards E thing). A self-updating spreadsheet is a real boon for people who are terrible at maths. It also recalculates as you progress through your week, so you can track your progress/lack of progress. Little tip: when I press 'sum' I like to say something impressively financial to give myself an edge, like 'hedgefundings' or 'the Dowager Jones is falling'.

(Water break where entire jug is consumed.)

Ultimately, this is between you and your bank account. And the calculator app on your phone. Once you've got into the habit of budgeting, you'll never again have that sinking feeling as the debit card makes the bad beeping sound. You'll always know when you need to pick up more shifts. You'll know when you can get a coffee and when you can't. But most importantly, you'll never be caught out having accidentally spaffed away your rent on a pair of leather dungarees. They look good, though, right?

To everyone here tonight who hasn't left the O2 Arena while booing, thank you for having me and for the free water. Goodnight.

How to Deal with Online Bullying

Online bullying is just as damaging as IRL abuse, but there's a curious response from people who aren't extremely online to 'just put your phone down' because 'it isn't real', which would have been great advice in 2007, but doesn't quite cut it when so much of our social and work interactions are online. Even in 2007, if you received something cruel as one of the eleven texts you could receive on your Nokia 3210, it would probably do a fair bit of damage.

Bullying can look, to others, like fun banter. People can even explicitly tell you it's fun banter, despite the fact that you're crying. The word banter has a lot to answer for, to be honest, but a good rule of thumb to test whether it's A Bit of a Laugh or Bullying is to ask yourself: 'Does this behaviour make me feel terrible, insecure, anxious, stupid, scared or like I'm going to start crying?'

If the answer is, 'No! I love it! Makes me chuckle!' then it's A Bit of a Laugh. If the answer is, 'Yes,' then it's bullying. Even if you add the caveat, 'But that's just me being oversensitive,' you still said yes. It's still bullying.

As you get older you realise life is literally the same as school, it's just that the bullies look older and have job titles like Marketing Director or bios telling you they're 'father to two beautiful daughters', making it harder to deal with. But remember that you're older, too, and you can get through this much better than you could at school, where there was literally no escape unless you pretended to be sick or hid in the toilets with your feet up so nobody could see you were in there.

> STEVIE: Or maybe you made an OUT OF ORDER sign and brought it in and stuck it on the toilet cubicle door so prefects and teachers wouldn't bother you.
>
> TESSA: Oh my God, Stevie.

We spoke to an extremely online person who would like to remain anonymous and who has experienced serious amounts of pile-ons, online harassment and trolling, to get some advice. Because an OUT OF ORDER sign doesn't really work on the internet.

1. Tell someone

'Trust me when I say that nothing else can come before this, and nothing that comes after it will help as much as it should, unless you've told someone you trust and have been honest about how it's making you feel. Not talking about it just suppresses it. Someone else being angry or upset for you makes you feel like your feelings are valid – which they are. My partner always knows the second I'm receiving abuse or have been dragged into something. Lean on the people around you. That's literally what they're there for.'

2. Identify what kind of bullying this is

'Is it about something you did or a job you had, or is it about you as a person? Is it about your identity or parts of it? Is it racist, misogynistic, homophobic, transphobic? To know this is to be able to identify when something crosses the line into a hate crime and it becomes a criminal offence.'

3. Screenshot. Everything.

'Even video the screen if you're sent pictures – which on some platforms disappear after one viewing. Get the evidence. Instagram and other platforms have a "delete this message/unsend" feature, which means if it goes down a serious route, the person bullying you can protect themselves. Don't let them! Keep the evidence of it, and preferably in an archived folder on your phone so you don't have to see it again.'

4. Remember that it doesn't matter what you've done

'There are very few things you could have done to justify the sheer volumes of abuse that can occur online. No human brain has evolved to be able to logically and healthily deal with bullying from multiple strangers, while at the same time sitting on the sofa or eating dinner with the fam. This is a completely new phenomenon, so it's going to feel awful, and if you aren't coping, that's not on you. It's your brain thinking, "What the HELL is this? How are 50 people screaming at me? It feels so dangerous even though I'm in a safe place!" so however you deal with it, you're doing fine.'

5. If you know you need to apologise, just do it

'Don't do anything because you're pressured into it, but if you've made a horrific gaffe, and you know it, then apologising sincerely and honestly is the way forward – without engaging with any of the abuse. If you've been dragged into something, done nothing wrong or people are just out to get you, then don't engage. There's no need to add to the fire while it's still burning.'

6. Set up all the tools social platforms offer to keep you safe

'Twitter hides keywords, phrases, numbers or emojis from you if you set it up, as does Instagram. This is the kind of thing Taylor Swift could have done during the infamous snake emoji period. Get rid of anything that could hurt you. Look up fixtheglitch.com and follow their brilliantly practical tips for online abuse.'

7. Delete the app from your home screen for a couple of days

'Nobody following you will notice anything unusual except a little less posting. Justify this by asking yourself: "If someone was saying this stuff to me on the street, what would I do?" You'd walk away. There's no way you'd stay standing there day and night, waiting for more to come your way or, worse, start seeking it out at 2 a.m. So leave. If you know you should delete the app but find yourself unable to (hello, social-media addiction), ask someone you trust to do it for you and change your password. You can even ask them to log into your account from their phone and field messages; they could screenshot them for you and delete them so that you don't have to see anything, but the evidence is logged. I can confirm this is *so* helpful.'

8. Later on, talk about your experience

'When you're through the worst of it – and only if you feel comfortable – talking about what happened either online (maybe on a different platform than the one you're receiving the most abuse on) or with friends outside of your immediate support system can help. Firstly, people should know about this problem, but also you'll find that people will share similar stories with you, or those who don't have them will see this as a moment to reach out and comfort you.

'A friend of mine once told me that her teacher said, "When teaching kids, you're supposed to give them three-parts positive praise to one-part constructive criticism, because the criticism is all they remember, but I actually think it's more like nine-parts positive to one-part criticism that actually works." Remember this. You are still that same kid inside, and you'll remember the mean messages way more than the good ones. So, don't be shy about letting people comfort you. We all need that, especially after being bullied online.'

Thank you to our extremely online person for her excellent advice. Remember: bullying isn't character building or a part of life. It's terrible, and you shouldn't put up with it. Report it, take yourself out of the situation if you can and definitely, definitely seek professional help if things are getting out of hand.

How to Quit Your Job

THE DREAM . . .

You get out of the car and cross the same grey car park, preparing yourself for another day of breathing recycled air while sitting at that stupid desk. And then, suddenly, as if from the very depth of your soul, a beat starts and there's music in the air. You step out of the lift and your ancient boss stands in the doorway of the stupid little separate room he has like he's in charge or something. He gets out a little pocket watch and looks at it with his monocle. 'Thirty seconds late again, I see,' he sneers, and the beat starts to build. You can hear it now – it's Aretha Franklin's 'R-E-S-P-E-C-T'.

'Just standing there? Are you stupid as well as late?' And you turn on your heels, look him dead in the eye. Everyone's watching now.

'You know what?' you say. 'I quit!' Your boss's mouth hangs open. 'I'm taking my stuff and I'm never coming back.'

You stride to your desk as Aretha brings the chorus home. All your possessions fit neatly into one small-to-medium cardboard box that you found under your desk so everything is over in under a minute. Someone starts to clap. The music builds until it almost dwarfs the sound of twelve people whooping and cheering as the lift doors close on you holding your box, cigarette in your mouth, sunglasses on.

As you cross the car park towards your new life, there are people hanging out of their car windows, clapping you. One woman gets out of her car and does a backflip. As she lands, it kicks everyone into a rendition of 'Freedom'. Employees from other offices appear at windows to harmonise and finger-click. You drive away with the top down – it wasn't a convertible when you drove in, but it sure is now. You've got a headscarf on like in *Thelma and Louise*, but instead of driving over a cliff, you drive into the sunset and the promise of a new life.

THE REALITY . . .

'Just standing there? Are you stupid as well as late?'

You take a deep breath, consider the difficult financial and legal position of walking out the door and sit at your desk.

You make a list of everything that would need to change for you to consider staying. A pay rise? A promotion? Changing desks so you're not next to the toilets? Moving sections so that old man with the monocle isn't directly in charge of you any more? If you think there might be some improvements, you set up a meeting to talk about it with your manager.

If there's nothing – not even a million pounds – that could keep you in this godforsaken hellhole, you calmly proceed with your day while quietly reading over your contract to double-check how much notice you need to give before leaving. If your computer screen faces the wall and no one can see, you start researching other jobs with a start date tallying up with your notice period. You send some messages and organise to have coffee with a few people. You schedule some 'doctor's appointments' that are actually job interviews. You get out your company calculator and work out how long you could last without another job.

> STEVIE: Be smart and don't walk out the door if you've got no money and no new job lined up. Don't screw yourself over like I did when I walked out on a restaurant shift because the manager was a sexist arsehole, realised I couldn't pay the rent and had to go back and beg for my job back while he smirked and said things like, 'Were you on your period?' to which I had to respond 'Yes,' because I needed the money.

Once you're confident you've got a new job lined up, or enough money saved to tide you over, and once you've really thought through your options and considered the situation from every angle, you send an email to your manager to organise a meeting.

Because you are calm and collected in the meeting, you don't get upset, you don't lie about why you're leaving and you avoid mentioning some of the gripes you have about the company. The goal is simply to leave, not to tell everyone that Mark is a bellend. Unless he really is a bellend, in which case go for it.

'I QUIT!' you scream. No, a small jest. You calmly say: 'After much consideration, I've decided I'd like to move on. It's been a really great experience working at the company, but I think it's time for some new challenges/I've decided to pivot into beekeeping/I've been offered a position at another company.'

'Oh,' your manager says, surprised. 'I was going to give you a promotion this year.'

'A-ha,' you think, 'a classic tactic deployed to confuse me into staying.' Happily, you've already asked yourself if you would like a promotion, and your answer was no. You have spent a long time putting everything in place. This is not a rash decision, so the prospect of more money doesn't blindside you into staying.

'No, thank you,' you reply. 'I do think it's important I have a change of scenery, but I really appreciate the offer. I will, of course, work my notice period.'

The same clear, decisive statement of departure is just as crucial, perhaps even more so, if you don't hate your boss; in fact, you love them, and you love your job. It's just that you've been offered something much better elsewhere, or you're ready to move on, or for whatever reason you're off. Don't be terrified about upsetting them or letting them down. This is a business, even if it's a small one. Even if everyone loves you and relies on you. You are still a person who deserves to lead the life you want, rather than staying at a job that's not right for you any more just because you don't want to be a bother. The same rules apply. Email ahead and, once you're in there, don't cry, don't get upset, don't start delivering a monologue, don't say, 'I wish I didn't have to go!' because they'll say, 'Well, don't then.' Just say it, nice and clear; get it over with. Don't freak out about them hating you; they'll probably be thrilled for you.

Once you've left the meeting, you continue to work until your notice period is up, all the time preparing for your new life in order to give yourself the smoothest transition period possible. If you find a job in that time, you tell the new company that you're leaving your old job a week later than you actually are so you get a Fun Week Between Employment. Obviously you're not paid for this, but if you're financially able to do it, then absolutely do it. If you don't find a new job, that's OK – you've got those savings and plenty of time, remember? Keep looking.

When your last working day arrives, you have forgotten to bring boxes, but you go out and buy some so you don't have to take the contents of your desk to and from the car in your arms like you're running a car-boot sale. You have been slowly downsizing and organising over your notice period and taking things home in stages so the process is calm and stress-free.

You have a surprising number of bulldog clips and notepads with 'MEETING' underlined twice on the first page followed by absolutely nothing because the meeting turned out to be pointless. You gift all of these to Mark.

Everybody in the office clubbed together and bought some chewy doughnuts and warm Prosecco, which you all awkwardly sip in thin plastic cups taken from the watercooler. Mark gives a speech about how great it's been having you in the office and his voice cracks. You walk out of the door at 5.31 p.m., a free agent. You have a little moment on your own in the lift where you put your sunglasses on and give the finger to nobody.

You pick up proper doughnuts on the way home and a bottle of champagne, which you drink that night from an actual glass. Well done you.

How to Restart a Dead Friendship

My quill trembles across the page as I write these words. Please forgive me, but what appears as carelessness is merely cold-blooded fear that shoots through my limbs and liquifies my stomach. 'Pon the divan, in the parlour of the East Wing, while taking my post-evening-meal constitutional turn around the grounds, I first laid eyes on the terrifying sight. A corpse! Lo! Prithee see those ink blots 'pon the page, and know they are caused by the sweat as it tumbles from m'brow, causing the words to run together like my racing thoughts. O! O! O! But to the sight – I must describe it, must set its countenance down in writing so as to OOOOOOOOOOOO! My apologies, I just thought upon't again.

    TESSA: What is this?
    STEVIE: How to restart a dead friendship. Don't interrupt.

It is, without a doubt, the countenance of my friend Katie from university. She hath the same dark hair, the same joyful smile playing 'pon her lips. O, we laughed together once! We shared secrets and spoke of high ambition and whimsy! We bonded o'er strawpedos and lovers of ill repute! But then she upped and left to Bristol,

298

became promised to a man of high standing (an accountant), whilst I tarried to the South to carve my way as an absinthe-soak'd poet, and whilst the letters from her began in earnest, soon, alas, they tail'd off. And I find myself confronted by the death of such a friendship, often yearning for the comfort of't in the dark nights as I wander the hallways of my surprisingly large house considering I just said I was a poet.

> TESSA: So it's all going to be written like a nineteenth-century gothic horror, is it?
>
> STEVIE: Very much so.
>
> TESSA. Right. If you're doing this, I'm going to write a rap about taxes.

But wait! My eye has been drawn to a book 'pon the table by the door. *How to Reanimate the Death of a Friendship.*

Marry, n'uncle! I open its pages to relay any chapters of relevance and/or n'uncles.

Chapter One: You must be the one to reach out

'But 'pon my ninny!' you may exclaim, if you are sat 'pon a ninny. She hath not reached out to me these five and twenty score years, so why should it fall to my hand to pen the missive and extend the withered hand of friendship? Why, you're the one reading this chapter, 'tis clearly bothersome to you! In the words of Chaucer, get over thyself and have a go. If they penned you a missive full of cheer and suggesting a luncheon, would you be filled with offence? 'Pon the contrary. 'O!' you would exclaim.

''Tis Katie! The last time I saw her she vomited in my graduation cap!'

Chapter Two: If therein lies old grudges you wish to settle, then, ye gods, settle them!

Did you drift apart from a boon companion because of long-forgotten resentments? Perhaps you found their lover dull or a braggart, and so allowed your friendship to slip away? Mayhaps they went through a darkened time and you did not care for them as you should have, and the guilt gnaws at your insides. Perchance you suffer'd from the glittering green eye of jealousy, 'til the very foundations of your union became a mist. Unless there has been a fearsome altercation, a cheery message of 'It's been so long and I'd love to catch up if you fancy a pint after work?' can undo much heartache.

Chapter Three: Ne'er expect them to be of their past likeness

Katie is not the same person she was three score and seven years ago. She was but a child. But no matter! A new friendship may be cast from the mould of the old. Perhaps you are destin'd to be no more than friendly acquaintances, perhaps you will speak once every few years. Perhaps you will drift apart again – it matters not. What matters true is that you tried to reanimate the bloated corpse of your relationship and must be saluted for't.

Chapter Four: If they live far away, never underestimate the power of an old-fashioned letter

Remember the beauty and delight one feels at receiving a letter?

Perhaps even a postcard depicting a humorous scene! Modern communications are the most effective for the initial declaration, but once you have reach'd out, use letters to liven up your missives to keep the friendship as new as a newborn babe.

Chapter Five: Ensure you create new experiences with your companion

Nostalgia is a comforting tavern-partner at first, but if you remain in the past your tongue will stall and you shall struggle to roam 'pon pastures new. Plough the fields, loom a hat, go to that terrible new ping-pong bar in the curious hipster part of the nearest town. Ensure you have more to talk about than old ghosts and you will ensure your friendship remains in the realm of the living. If the union goes well then why not bring your old friend to tarry with your newer acquaintances? Involve them in the merriment! That way you steer the ship into adventurous waters, bringing them into the life you live now rather than the child you were.

Chapter Six: If all else fails, write a chapter in your book in the hope that your old university friend Katie who isn't on WhatsApp or social media and with whom you share no mutual friends reads it and gets in touch

Behold, the door handle! It turns! O! The door swings open and there Katie stands, her pallor flushed with pink, her eyes glistening with life, her hand raised in half greeting, her mouth parted. O, speak to me, thou apparition from years gone by!

'So great to hear from you,' she says. Has she forgiven me for that most Ancient of Beefs? 'I'm free that evening, too – would be great to catch up! It's been ages!' O! O! OOOOOOO!

How to Be More Productive

To-do list:

• Be more productive.

The thing about modern life is that we're expected to be all of the characters on *Downton Abbey* simultaneously, while holding down a separate full-time job. We're supposed to cook and clean and run the estate and keep the house from falling down and raise the children while leaning out of the window looking beautiful and making quips.

There's genuinely not enough hours in the day to do all that successfully, especially the quips bit. Takes ages to work up a good witticism.

The main thing is never to let your productivity be a marker of your self-worth. Did you make it to the end of the day? Great. You smashed it.

Don't get addicted to the idea that, if you could just finish your to-do list, you will finally find peace. It's never going to happen, so take a breath and let that idea go. Now, let's try to get your day running more efficiently.

If you've got a normal number of things to do but just want a more efficient way to do them, skip right on over this next bit. This part is for anybody who's feeling completely overwhelmed, can't remember what they're supposed to be doing and keeps sporadically writing to-do lists on a napkin, immediately losing the napkin and finding it in a coat pocket months later and it just says 'Pigs?'

Get yourself a piece of A4 and draw as many columns as you have areas of your life.

> TESSA: Mine are Money, House, Work, Vibes (this is actually health, but I couldn't bear to write health), Ideas, Presents. Money is invoices I need to chase or send, and bills I need to pay, and currently says 'Pay IRS' in big letters. House is things I need to buy or fix. Presents is for when people make a passing comment about something they mildly like. Ideas is for ideas. It currently says 'Hotel for bees?'

Do your own categories, use felt-tip pens, make it look a bit nice. It can be anything, big or small. 'Do a marathon?' can sit right by 'Do the laundry?' Actually, not together, because one is in House and one is in Dreams. And now keep this A4 paper on your desk or in your bag at all times. As soon as you remember something, on it goes in the correct category. When something gets achieved, ceremoniously cross it out. This is bullet-journal adjacent, but it is not bullet journaling because we've all tried it and no one could do it.

It's important to have everything, no matter how much there is, all in one place so you can see it. Writing sporadic lists all over the shop is a recipe for disaster. Got your massive to-do list? OK, everybody else, welcome back.

The secret to being more productive is to break things down. Imagine you've got an assistant you've never met coming in to help you tomorrow, but you won't be there so you need to write them a list. Think of this not as your to-do list (which might be huge), but your to-day list.

If you just write 'Sort life out', your assistant is not going to know where to start or how to begin, and you'll probably have to fire them at the end of the day. Instead, you need to be specific.

9 a.m. – Laundry (dark wash) + hang it up

10 a.m. – Read papers (pages 12–24) ready for presentation on soil erosion

11 a.m. – Return ASOS package and pick up dinner (meatballs)

1 p.m. – Lunch (yesterday's lasagne in the fridge)

How calming does that look? When you write the list for somebody else, you think more rationally about what they can reasonably achieve and you can see where you need to clarify exactly what needs to be done. If you asked a stranger to pick up dinner, they would quite rightly say, 'Sure, but what?'

The key is clarity, being reasonable about how long a task takes and breaking things down into tiny, achievable chunks.

If you've lost morale and are feeling overwhelmed, the most helpful thing you can start doing is implementing the Two-minute Rule. If it can be done in two minutes, do it right now. If it takes longer than two minutes, just do two minutes of the task.

> STEVIE: This has changed my life and is my favourite piece of advice in the entire book.

The first part – 'If it takes less than two minutes, then do it now' – is from David Allen, in his bestselling book *Getting Things Done*. Just do it. Go. Right now. Fast as you can. Job done. The second part is from James Clear in *Atomic Habits*, who says it's all about getting into the habit of just showing up and starting. If doing the dishes is overwhelming, just wash one bowl. If folding the laundry is too much, fold one pair of socks. Plus, chances are you discover it actually wasn't as hard as you thought, and once you've started you might as well do a little bit more than two minutes, and then, oh whoops, it's finished. That's an occasional bonus, but not the goal. The goal is to truly look at things as tiny two-minute tasks and tackle them that way.

EAT THE DEAD FROG

Always do the worst thing on your list first. Here's your friend and mine, Mark Twain: *'If it's your job to eat a frog, it's best to do it first thing in the morning. And if it's your job to eat two frogs, it's best to eat the biggest one first.'*

DON'T FREAK OUT ABOUT PROCRASTINATING

Procrastinating is doing a different task to avoid the one you're meant to be doing. You're still getting a task done, but it's the wrong one. Procrastinating can be really healthy if it's occasional and you're aware that you're doing it, but if you're finding that it's stopping you from meeting deadlines and it's starting to annoy people then you need to address it.

Try the Pomodoro Technique, which was invented by Francesco Cirillo in the 1980s and involves breaking down the work into 25-minute stints, separated by short breaks of five minutes. Each burst of work is known as a 'pomodoro', from the Italian word for tomato, named after Cirillo's tomato-shaped kitchen timer!

You set a timer, the timer goes off, you get up and do something completely different for five minutes, you come back to it. After four pomodoro, you get a 30-minute break, then you start again.

STOP AVOIDING THINGS

Purposefully organising a house party when you need to get work done isn't procrastinating, it's avoiding. You'd be amazed at your ability to put off a task for six months that literally takes 20 minutes. 'Oh wow,' you'll think. 'I really let that hang over me for half a year. Maybe in the future I should run headlong at things and just get them done.'

When you receive an email, think of the Two-minute Rule and try to reply straight away. Just respond, instead of writing 'Respond to email' on your to-do list every day for the next six weeks.

If avoiding tasks is something you really struggle with, and the Two-minute Rule doesn't help, then this might be indicative of a bigger problem. Why are you avoiding this? Is it fear? Is it perfectionism?

> TESSA: OK, here are some truths. When it came to handing this book in, my instinct was to send a corrupted text file to buy us more time. I kept thinking of ways we could get round the deadline, and Stevie had to keep saying, 'Or we could just do

the work?' Just do the work, guys. It'll probably take you as long just to finish as it would to put the whole text into Wingdings and make it look believably corrupted. Guys. Just do your work.

ORGANISE YOURSELF

You're not going to be productive if you can't find anything. Sort out your workspace so everything is tidy and accessible, both on your desk and on your computer. Do you spend hours trying to find documents because you've put them all over the place and called them things like 'WORK??' and 'FINAL VERSION4___ DEFINITELY THIS ONE'? Sort yourself a neat and orderly filing system.

HAVE TIME OFF

If you are working all day and all night, you are going to burn out. If people know they can reach you 24/7 then they will. Choose some boundaries, maybe giving yourself evenings and weekends off, or not working on Wednesdays, and stick to it religiously. Give yourself bank holidays and actual holidays. Don't explain what you're doing. It doesn't have to be anything important. The working world is set up to punish rest and monetise hobbies, so there's a lot of internalised guilt about taking any time off, but it's yours to do with as you will. Oh, and take your lunch break. ALWAYS.

If things get too much, always tell someone. Don't suffer in silence, and if things are really out of control, consider getting professional help. Chronic unproductivity can be down to something deeper and more psychological. Your brain is trying to tell you something but doesn't quite have the words, so instead it's making you miss deadlines and feel completely overwhelmed at the thought of responding to an email. Listen to it. And if you can't work out what it's saying, escort it to a professional who can help you translate.

How to Break Up with Someone

If there's one thing you can guarantee, it's that nobody has ever been dumped and thought, 'Fair play to them, 10/10, that was a great break-up.'

Breaking up with someone, whatever the situation, is awful and will involve lots of hurt feelings, crying and swearing. Someone might throw something. Someone might throw up. Someone might say, 'By the way, I was lying when I said I like your moussaka. Your moussaka is shit.' You can't avoid this (no matter how hard you work on your moussaka recipe). What you can avoid is waking up five years from now at around 4 a.m. thinking, 'I screwed that up.' Or hurting someone more than you have to.

This is gleaned purely from our multiple break-up experiences. Which are as follows:

STEVIE

Broken up with tally: 3 (all by the same person, over the course of six months)

Broken up with someone tally: 4 (once over MSN Messenger in 2008, once at someone's parents' house, once at a bar but he didn't realise I was breaking up with him, once over the phone because I wanted to meet up and do it face to face but he could tell something was wrong and I blurted it out. Terrible business)

TESSA

Broken up with tally: 5 (three of those on October 3rd. Otherwise known as *Mean Girls* Day)

Broken up with someone tally: 0. Actually, that's not true at all. I had quite an intense long-distance fling with someone I met on holiday. Then, when we were both back in the country, we went on a few dates, and I fully intended to say, 'This has been very nice but I think we are wildly incompatible and every time one of us makes a joke they have to fully explain it to the other one,' but I chickened out, and then never messaged him again. I ghosted someone! I mean, this is awful. I was young and deeply emotionally unintelligent, but that's no excuse. If you're reading, G**** H****** – March to April 2012, I'm genuinely really sorry.

PART ONE: THE ACTUAL BREAK-UP

Below is a template for breaking up that you are welcome to use any time you need. First, we set the scene.

Location, location, location

> TESSA: I care quite passionately about this one because my first boyfriend broke up with me in a canoe.

People do all kinds of things when they're in shock, so make sure you have chosen somewhere calm and safe, with space for them to walk about if they need to. Their house is a good idea, so when it's all over you can leave and they're already safely home, as opposed to forcing them weeping out of your house and then closing the door on them as a physical manifestation of their removal from your life. Try not to do it somewhere they have no control, like right before you walk into a party together, or on the first night of a ten-day holiday. Or in a canoe.

Make sure you are face to face
This rule will be broken by people convinced they've got a really good excuse, and that they are the exception to the rule.

> STEVIE: Like me. The excuse I told myself was that I didn't mean it to be an over-the-phone break-up; he just managed to deduce it from my incredibly subtle 'We need to talk when I get back' message. Do not send a message like this. It is cowardly and you did it because you wanted them to work it out so you wouldn't have to sit down face to face and actually say it. I have learnt my lesson.

A phone call is not an acceptable way to break up with someone, but neither is a WhatsApp.

The one exception is, of course, if the person cheated on you mercilessly. In that instance, go one worse than WhatsApp and send them a text. Who texts? Companies requiring verification codes and you breaking up with an arsehole.

. . . Or virtual face to virtual face

If you're abroad or in a long-distance relationship, you can't wait eight weeks to break up. Don't waste somebody's time – arrange a Sadness Skype and break up with them face to virtual face instead.

Do not ghost them

What are you, a dickhead on Tinder who's never had a relationship that lasted longer than two months? Say what you like about the lad, but Jesus was bang on when he said, 'Do unto others as you would have them do unto you.'

TESSA: I'd like to discuss ghosting. I've been ghosted and, as discussed, I've also been the ghost. The older I get, the more I realise that breaking up with someone is unbelievably brave. It takes huge guts to go through that and give the other person the honour of a noble, swift end. Ghosting is for cowards (like me). It seems nice, because you don't have to say something hurtful, but it's actually much more cruel. Even if you've just had one date, don't leave them to tie themselves in knots wondering what's wrong with them. Like Sean Bean in *Game of Thrones*: 'He who passes the sentence shall swing the sword.' He who goes on the date shall send the text to say there will not be another date. She who gets too involved with a holiday romance shall be brave enough to say this has been really fun but I don't think we're right for each other in the Wetherspoons in Charing Cross, April 2012.

And now, the dialogue.

YOU: (enunciate clearly, do not mumble) I THINK WE SHOULD BREAK UP.
You have to go in hard, set out your stall from the off and don't leave any room for misinterpretation.

> STEVIE: I once tried to break up with someone in a bar and was so vague that he thought I was saying I didn't want to go for dinner that night, so he booked dinner for another night and I was so embarrassed that I went to dinner and then just continued going out with him.

RECENTLY I'VE BEEN FEELING LIKE [INSERT CLEARLY THOUGHT-OUT FEELINGS] . . .
Unless definite relationship crimes have been committed, keep to 'I feel' rather than 'You always . . .' It shows you're aware that this is just your perspective, but that your perspective does still count. Remember that when they try to counter by saying they see things completely differently.

Stick to broad reasons that you feel to be true, rather than specific pettiness, otherwise you risk hurting their feelings much more than you need to. It's all about being the bigger person. A giant. A giant breaking up with someone in a nice way.

HOW HAVE YOU BEEN FEELING? DOES ANY OF THIS CHIME WITH YOU?
This allows them to have their say and gives them a bit of agency

in a situation where they have very little. Showing that you're interested in how they feel is a lot better than just announcing your reasoning and walking out of the door.

Even if you're worried you can't cope with the answers, you owe it to the other person to at least try. If it gets too much and you have to leave, be sure to set a date ASAP to talk it through. ASAP as in the next day. Not doing this completely disrespects the other person's feelings and needs – they might have questions; they might need to get things off their chest. Let them. If clearly stating, 'I think we should break up,' is lancing the boil, this part is completely draining the boil. Get it all out, otherwise neither of you are going to heal.

This experience may take minutes and they might throw something and storm out. Or it might take all night, with both of you weeping and talking about your feelings 'til the sun comes up. False hope is an ugly thing, so make sure you make it clear that you are going through this break-up together, you will take care of them as best you can, but this is a final decision. If you start laughing, then they'll say, 'See! We're great together!' And then they'll start singing 'We Can Work It Out' by The Beatles. And also, they're soaking wet from the time they jumped out of the canoe and into the river.

PART TWO: THE AFTERMATH

Once you have said how you feel, there are a number of ways people will react to hearing the news, and please be aware that none of these ways will make you feel good. Consider the spectrum:

DENIAL	NOT BOTHERED	DEVASTATED
They will keep acting like you are together.	They secretly wanted to break up, too, which can feel oddly like rejection, even though you're rejecting them.	They will fall apart and need a lot of help dealing with this.

Regardless of where they fall, it's crucial to action the break-up immediately. We are using clinical office-speak like 'action' because that's what you both need. This doesn't mean cruel and cold, not responding to them or cutting them out, but you have to move out/ get your things/not stay the night. The wheels are moving. This break-up is being actioned otherwise you'll end up sticking around because you feel awful, making the end result so much worse. This is the ultimate in being cruel to be kind, so be kind, get your stuff and separate yourself as soon as possible.

The 'it's just not really working' break-up
One of the hardest break-ups. There may be nothing wrong with this person, so it could come out of the blue for them and is likely to fall on the 'DEVASTATED' side of the table. You might really love them, but you know that it is not going to work out. Don't blame yourself for wanting more from life than a relationship that's perfectly fine. So many people settle rather than being continually excited by someone, because they either aren't used to being loved, or because they're terrified of being single.

It's easy to find yourself wavering once you've broken up with someone if there isn't anything specifically terrible to focus on. In these shaky moments, ask yourself what is worse: this break-up, which hurts in the short term, or spending another 30 years with this person? This break-up, or never finding a relationship that makes you feel truly content and happy? You are respecting yourself and the other person enough to let them go and find someone who is crazy about them. And someone who is crazy about you.

> TESSA: Here's a truth. All my break-ups were absolutely awful, each in their own unique way, but every single one of them was the right decision and, in the end, I am genuinely grateful that the other person was brave enough to do it.

A 'yeah, I agree actually' break-up

Firmly situated in the 'NOT BOTHERED' camp, this break-up might leave you feeling oddly short-changed, because the person you are grandly breaking up with seems to want to have broken up with you all along. This shouldn't annoy you, but it will. You're only human. It's annoying because you can't work out the motive: is it mind games? A defensive tactic? Are they really not bothered about the relationship? Whatever the reason, get out quickly and be thankful you didn't have to prise their hands off your arm while they screamed, 'BUT I LOVE YOU!'

A 'prising their hands off your arm while they scream BUT I LOVE YOU' break-up

It's horrible, hurting someone, and it's doubly horrible hurting someone you used to love, or still love, just not enough to want to keep going out with them. This is where actioning that break-up comes into its own. You want to make it better, but if you make it better in the way they want you to, you'll ultimately have to leave again, making it so much worse. Get some space. A lot of advice says things like, 'Don't pick up their calls,' or, 'Instigate a no-contact rule immediately,' but it depends on the specifics. Talking it through as much as you can and answering their calls or texts is a nice thing to do, provided you are OK and you're ready to set the boundaries when the contact becomes too much. If they have questions about the break-up that you haven't clarified in the original chat, fine. If they want to call you every time they get drunk to beg you to get back with them, probably time to give them space, because even though they don't want it, they need it. It's tough, but they will never, ever get over you if you don't force space on them.

There's a big difference between being kind and stringing them along, otherwise known as I Don't Want To Go Out With Them But Nobody Else Can Either syndrome. Symptoms of this involve: seeing a picture of them looking happy without you and deep-liking twelve of their Instagram pictures, turning up uninvited to a reading of their new play 'to be supportive', or sending them a meme of a horse wearing a suit. Pictures of dogs (no matter how exquisite), an explicable 22-minute YouTube video about wooden puzzle boxes sent without context at 4 a.m. and the text message 'Hey, I had a dream about you last night' all fall under the banner of Official Bad Behaviour. This is not you wanting to make sure they're OK; this is you panicking that actually they're too OK without you.

When you break up with someone, mute them on social media and give yourself a chance to grieve the relationship, too, if you need it. But don't drag them back into it.

The 'can we still be friends?' break-up

This is a question for them to decide, not you, and if our experience is anything to go by, the answer should be, 'Absolutely not,' unless you were very young, or one party had a real rethink about their sexuality afterwards. Being really good friends after being in a relationship can sometimes happen in very rare cases, but not for years and not until both parties are completely over it. You have no idea when your ex will be over you, so don't go heavy on the friendliness until you're absolutely sure it is water under the bridge.

The denial break-up

You're going to have to stand your ground and Action That Break-up. See, it really is the key. Talking it over with someone who doesn't believe you can possibly feel what you said you feel is hardly the foundation for a stable and healthy conversation. It's desperate, unintentional gaslighting, and it's understandable because we've all done it.

> STEVIE: The first time my ex from university broke up with me I typed, 'I know you don't mean this,' on MSN Messenger; the second time I said, 'I know you don't mean this,' over the phone; the third time, I ran down a road full of broken glass with no shoes on, yelling, 'I KNOW YOU REALLY DON'T MEAN THIS!' while crying. There was not a fourth time.

PART 3: SOME TIPS THAT HELP WITH ALL BREAK-UPS

Go see a friend

Take yourself to a (preferably single) friend who you know will tell you exactly what they think. You need to remember why you instigated this break-up in the first place, otherwise you could end up freaking out and going back to them.

Don't sleep with them

We can't stop you, and God knows you're going to do it anyway, but all we can do is remind you that there is no situation whereby sleeping with an ex is positive. Unless you two are the sole survivors of an apocalypse and must procreate for the good of the human race. You also don't need to have sex 'one last time'. This will be a deeply traumatic disaster and one or both of you will cry. Good-bye sex isn't a thing. It's lose-lose, because it's either great and confusing or bad and confusing. Nobody wins.

Mute them on social media but don't block them

Blocking and unfriending seems cruel considering you've just cut them out of your life IRL, so make use of the handy mute button. It's an act of goodwill to give the person you've broken up with the chance to ceremoniously block you. Which they probably will do under a full moon and while burning some of your belongings.

If they still haven't blocked you and they start leaving horrible comments or writing tweets that are clearly about you, you're within your rights to pop them a quick message to say it's probably best if you unfollow each other to give you both some space. And then unfollow them. If it continues, then you can block them. Just give them a chance to block you first. Let that be your final parting gift.

LOOK AFTER YOURSELF

People doing the breaking up need time to heal as well. If that's throwing yourself into work or throwing yourself into the nearest bakery, go for it. Work out what you want from your new life, and congratulate yourself on having the strength to do something a lot of people dream of and never go through with and carry on leading miserable half-lives with someone they don't want to hurt, but also don't love any more. You've been very brave.

How to Pack

Whether you're off on a mini-break, constantly travelling for work or going to the Costa del Sol for a Big One, turning up to the airport with a bin bag full of clothes isn't going to cut it.

> TESSA: Also, some of the clothes in the bin bag were damp because in preparation I'd done a wash the night before – which I thought was very grown up – and had then forgotten to dry them. The lady at the checkout desk looked me in the eye and said, 'You have *got* to get it together.' So I did. Changed my life. Actually, now I say it, maybe she just meant I had to get the stuff together into one bin bag instead of two.

As with most things, the realities of mastering this ancient art are rooted in preparation. How are you going to pack properly when you start ten minutes before you are supposed to leave? Or the morning you are supposed to leave? Or any amount of time before you are supposed to leave that doesn't leave space for washing and drying pants because once again you have no clean pants? Give your future self a chance and pack at least 24 hours before you leave the house.

STEVIE: I will never forget my sister arriving in Edinburgh to see me at the Fringe Festival. She had gone out the night before, got home at 4 a.m., thinking she'd 'get up early and pack before the 9 a.m. train', slept in, realised she'd left everything, including her purse with the ticket in, at work, which was now locked for the weekend, cried so much at the station they just let her on the train, called me from various passengers' phones to tell me when she was arriving into Edinburgh and as she stepped off the train to greet me her boob fell out of the pyjamas she was wearing. It was, and still is, the most majestic entrance into a country I've ever witnessed.

Don't go hard the night before if you need to travel at 9 a.m. the next day – especially if you haven't packed. Unfortunately, this time gets later as you get older. Beyond 30, you'll struggle to make a 3 p.m. flight after a night out. And the night out was last week. Like the Brownie Guides, or the Scouts, or whoever it was, your motto for packing is 'Be Prepared'. So, you know, check your passport is in date before you get to the airport.

TESSA: Do you want to tell the story about your passport?
STEVIE: My passport needed to be renewed so I paid to get the passport renewal forms way in advance, which I thought was very grown up. While filling them out, I opened my passport and realised it still had four years left on it. I'd had *a dream* it was out of date. The passport office wouldn't refund me. And they certainly didn't laugh when I told them about my dream.

What's your suitcase situation? Has the zip broken? Has one of the wheels dropped off?

If you feel sick at the thought of dropping any more than £10 on a suitcase, think ahead to how you'll feel dragging it to a coach station at 2 a.m. when you're running late and one wheel is waggling instead of rolling. You lift it up to carry it in your arms like a heavy and emotionally draining child and all your possessions smash onto the floor, deodorant rolling into the road, lipsticks plopping down the drain. Once you've rescued as much as you can, you're sitting with it on a train, now so late you'll probably miss your flight. It's resting against your leg and you're thinking, 'Gosh, that's damp,' before realising your shampoo has split and is now seeping through the sides of the case and into your trousers. How much would you pay in that moment to have a suitcase that rolled along the floor smoothly while zipping up neatly?

Now we've got the best case our money can buy, let's get down to brass tacks. Here are some packing methods good travellers we know have taught us over the years that we largely ignored until very recently.

STEVIE'S DAD'S PACKING TIPS
Name: Roy Martin
Qualifications: Constantly away for work, rarely staying in one place for longer than a couple of days, very organised person.

How to Pack

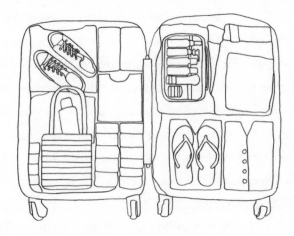

1. Pack the clothes you'll need first, last. For example, if you're arriving at the hotel at 3 a.m., don't pack your pyjamas first, otherwise they'll be at the bottom of the suitcase and you'll be swearing very loudly upon arrival.

2. Roy is a purveyor of the very flat, folded-over-once (if that) technique. This way, everything takes up about a millimetre of height and then doesn't need ironing on the other side. He has heard of rolling, but stands by the flat method.

3. He puts things in piles, so T-shirts in a (flattened) pile all on top of each other, sweatshirts next to them, etc., so you can easily find whatever you're looking for.

4. He leaves a gap in one side of the suitcase for his toilet bag, shoes and electrical stuff (razor, hairdryer, etc.) so he can see where everything is nice and quickly.

5. He stuffs underwear and socks around the outside of his clothing so they can be easily grabbed.

6. Because he travels from place to place so frequently, he 'can't be arsed' with sellotaping lids to liquids but makes sure they are

either in toilet bags or in shoes to conserve space. Also, if they explode, at least they explode in your wipe-clean shoes rather than all over your nice skirt. He concedes that sellotaping lids to liquids is a good idea if you are just travelling somewhere on holiday rather than hotel-hopping like he does.

7. He packs, at most, three shoes – one comfortable, one warm, one nice. Three pairs, sorry. He doesn't just pack three odd shoes.

8. In the WhatsApp voice note on which he relayed all this, he refers to tips as 'tiparoonies'. Wild.

9. Roy packs an empty tote bag for laundry so it doesn't mix with his nice clothes. As he puts it: 'If you don't have them separated, you might get your wine-soaked shirt also soaking into your smalls,' which is a fascinating insight into his on-the-road lifestyle. Stevie has also never heard him use the word 'smalls' before. Or 'tiparoonies'. This chapter is a real eye-opener.

TESSA'S DAD'S PACKING TIPS
Name: Tom Coates
Qualifications: Heard that Stevie's dad was doing tips.

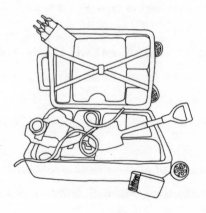

1. Rolling.

TESSA: That's it? Rolling?

TOM: Yeah, you know, roll your shit.

TESSA: OK, well, Stevie's dad did nine eloquent and well-thought-through tips.

TOM: All right, fold your shirts so it looks like you've just bought them, all neat and square with the collar on top, then roll carefully from the bottom. Shoes at the bottom, roll your shirts, separate bag for laundry. Always travel with your headtorch. And a length of rope.

TESSA: People don't need to know that.

TOM: Well, they'll be sorry when their plane crashes in the mountains.

TESSA: I'm just going to explain here that you're Canadian and were raised in the flatlands of Alberta where winter lasts for six months. And even though we live in England, the boot of the car has a blanket, candles, matches and a shovel for 'digging yourself out of a snowdrift'.

TOM: Probably put those in your suitcase, too.

ADVICE TESSA ONCE SAW PAINTED ON THE WALL OF A HOSTEL

Name: Hostel Wall

Qualifications: Very nice font, good colour scheme.

The hostel wall said: 'Put all your clothes and all your money on the bed before you pack, then take half as many clothes, and twice as much money.' Admittedly this was in the days when you carried cash, and in many ways the hostel wall did have a vested interest in you having more money than clothes, but the advice still stands. You don't need as many clothes as you think you do; think quality, not quantity. And for heaven's sake, take out those high heels 'in case you're invited on someone's yacht'.

TESSA'S MUM'S PACKING TIPS
Name: Debbie Coates
Qualifications: Loves to travel, always keen. If you're going somewhere, she'd like to come, too. Her memoir should be called *I'm In!*

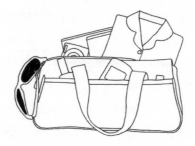

When going long haul, Debbie keeps all her pyjamas and a full change of clothes in her carry-on, so when – not if – the luggage gets lost, she at least has something to wear. This also means she doesn't have to unpack it all when she arrives, preferring to put her suitcase down, put her pyjamas on and leap straight into bed. Then, while everyone else is rooting through their suitcases looking for toothbrushes, she gleefully shouts, 'I'm in!' from the depths of the duvet.

TESSA'S GODSISTER'S PACKING TIPS

Name: Jessica Williams

Qualifications: She's a pilot. We were born exactly one week apart and one of us is a married pilot. No further questions.

Jess's number-one tip is that you want a wash bag that you never unpack. Rather than packing up all your cosmetics, creams, toothbrush, etc. and decanting them into the correct-sized bottles and then accidently leaving everything in the hotel, you want duplicates of all your things that are just for travel. Got a mascara that you love? Great, get one that's just for travel. Finally found your perfect moisturiser? Great, get a miniature one that lives in the wash bag. Sun cream, mosquito spray – everything you might need. This way, you never forget any crucial things, and you don't race around panicking trying to think of what you're missing when you should be walking out of the door. You just pick up your wash bag and you're off! *Bon voyage!*

How to Go to Therapy

Who should go to therapy?

Everyone.

If we had our way, the whole population would have been seeing a therapist once a week, for free, since they were old enough to talk. We would call it 'mind gym', so going was as cool and celebrated as going to the normal gym. It would be well funded and supported by the Government, and there wouldn't be a hint of stigma around things going awry inside the only organ complex enough to truly understand its own mortality. Of course things go wrong up there! And the only thing you have to fix it with is the thing that's gone wrong. Of course you need an extra pair of hands. Or, rather, an extra brain that can look at your brain and say, 'You need to sort out your relationship with your parents.'

If you're thinking, 'Do I need therapy?' the answer is 100% yes.

I don't need it, though.

If you've never done therapy before, it will knock your socks off with what it actually involves. It's not just lying on a couch talking about your absent father, nor is it being wrestled into a straitjacket. It's a space that you have nowhere else in your life, for a person to

330

listen to you without any judgement whatsoever, and help you make sense of what's going on. Maybe you have fantastic friends, and you're really good at talking to each other, or you're really clued up on the jigsaw that makes up your personality and you know why you are the way you are. But it's not the same as a professional with ten years of experience pointing at pieces of the jigsaw and asking if you've tried putting them in the other way around. You'll discover things about yourself that you had no idea were there, and it will make you infinitely better at being a person. That's why it's called mind gym. A personal trainer can show you the best way to lift weights; a therapist can show you an easier way to live.

I'd like to go but I'm 'not mad enough'.

It can feel like therapy is only for people in desperate crises, but it's absolutely not; it's for everybody. You don't need to be ashamed that other people might have it worse than you. Sure, they do, but you're still going through it, and you're still deserving of someone to go through it with you.

I'd like to go but I'm scared I'm 'too mad'.

You're not alone if your worry is that when you finally reveal to another person what's going on up there, they'll be so horrified they'll press a secret panic button and the men in white coats will come for you. Therapists have seen things you can't even imagine – nothing you can come up with is going to shock them. Go in there, lay your own personal horror show on the table and they won't even bat an eyelid.

I tried it and I hated it.

Very common. But if you find the right person, it'll all click into place. Keep shopping around and know that it's pointless working with the wrong therapist. You might as well chat to the tree outside your house – pleasant in the moment, but ultimately useless. It could also be that the type of therapy they offered doesn't work for you, or that you simply don't gel with the person your friend swears by. That's OK! You need to feel like this is a good fit, so keep looking until you find a therapist who really works with you. It'll be different for everyone, but you'll know what works for you when you find it.

STEVIE: I went to see a therapist my friend recommended in a grand surgery in Marylebone with a chandelier and decided therapy wasn't for me because I felt so stupid and intimidated in my scruffy jeans. Everything was so pristine and she said words I didn't understand. Then a different friend recommended another therapist who looked like he'd died and been stuffed moments before I walked in and said nothing other than, 'I see,' which made me REALLY believe therapy wasn't for me. A third friend finally convinced me to go to her therapist, and the room was filled with lots of books and comfy chairs and she let me cry for half an hour before providing an absolutely bang-on summary of my issues in a voice that sounded like an extractor fan. I still see her four years later and honestly she has saved my life, my friendships and my relationships. I have also now developed a fondness for extractor fans.

I know I should go but don't want to open that box.
Sometimes we can shove everything into the basement, double-bolt the door and safely get on with the day. We're going to have to go into the basement eventually, but right now it feels too overwhelming. That's OK, you don't have to go in right this second. But be careful of putting things off for too long, because those padlocks aren't going to hold forever. There's weird black steam pouring out from under the door and one day everything is going to come exploding out. It's going to be tough whenever you do it, so one day might as well be today.

I can't afford it.
This is a genuine barrier and the Government needs to do so much more to make mental-health services accessible, BUT there is some hope. Firstly, the NHS offers counselling and CBT, which stands for Cognitive Behavioural Therapy. At the time of writing, the service is called IAPT (Improving Access to Psychological Therapies) and each area throughout the UK has its own IAPT contact number. You don't need a referral from your GP; you can just call them, talk to someone about what you've been going through and they'll figure out the best sort of therapy for you to have. There may be a waiting list, but hang in there, it'll be worth it.

If the waiting list is too long or, as in Stevie's case, you finally get an appointment with a therapist but he decides two weeks in to quit his job, so you are put back to the start of the waiting list, private therapy isn't as eye-wateringly pricey as you might think. If you want to pay full whack, it can be anywhere from £65 an hour to £300, but private practices have trainee therapists charging as little as £20 a go, so it's worth calling and asking about their trainee schemes just in case. They'll be properly trained and supervised, but just needing experience one on one with clients – like going to the hairdresser and having a trainee give you a trim.

Alternatively, there are online therapies where you can chat, MSN Messenger style, to a qualified professional. We would always advocate for being in the room – you'd be surprised how much you can hide behind a screen – but online can be a marvellous starting point or a great work-around if distance and time are making meeting impossible.

OK, I'm going. What happens when I get there?

First off, a therapist is different to a counsellor. Counselling is often shorter term than therapy and focused on just giving you a space to talk freely about difficult experiences you've been through, such as depression or bereavement, and is less focused on tools and coping strategies.

Therapy tends to be longer term, and can continue long after the initial problem you came with has been resolved. It's a talking-based solution, helping you to make links and notice patterns, although practical tools and coping mechanisms can often be incorporated into the sessions. A therapist won't offer you medication, although if this is something you're interested in trying, have a chat with your GP.

The sessions will mostly be talking, and you getting to grips with the ground rules of therapy. Like how it ends after 50 minutes and that's that, no matter how much you're crying. And no one seems interested in asking you what you can see in an ink blot.

TESSA: We did picture cards once, not ink blots, actual pictures, and then my therapist took them away because I was 'way too into it'.

It's also called 'work' for a reason, because therapy really is work.

STEVIE: My therapist gives me homework. I refuse to do it because it's 'stupid' and then, after months of cajoling, I try it and find it very illuminating. Such is the cycle.

Write down what you hope to get from therapy, no matter how simple or complex it sounds, and relay this to your therapist. It's a good starting point for them. They can explain to you the process and what they can offer. Remember that the first session is as much for you as it is for them. This isn't a test; you're just figuring each other out. It can feel weird talking about yourself for an hour, and it can also feel slightly unreal.

STEVIE: I felt like Tony Soprano for the first few months.

Accept that the thing you don't want to talk about will probably be the thing you most need to talk about. Don't know what to say? Tell them you don't know what to say. Don't want to answer that question because it feels too hard? Be open with them. You'll get used to talking about yourself for an hour. Where else are you allowed that freedom? Or allowed to say something you've never admitted before and not have to follow it up with, 'But don't worry, I'm fine! How are you?'

Turn up to every session, even though sometimes you won't want to. Explain that you didn't want to turn up. Everything's useful, even if you feel like it isn't. If you can't leave the house because things have got really bad, call them and request a phone appointment. Remember who you're doing this for (you).

Trust the process, and trust that it might take a while. You don't get ripped after one session in the gym. Some people choose to continue with therapy on and off for their whole lives. You might decide you're ready to finish, only to need it again a few months later. You might find one course of therapy is enough. Whatever happens, you know you've done the right thing for you. Just keep going: one session at a time, one foot in front of the other.

How to Have a Live-in Lover

Congratulations on deciding to take a live-in lover (otherwise known as 'moving in with your partner')! Here is your celebratory houseplant that will die within three weeks. If you're apprehensive about what to expect, underneath the plant is an ancient scroll, upon which is inscribed the following commandments for making life as harmonious as possible. What a treat.

THE TEN COMMANDMENTS OF LIVING WITH THY LOVER

Thou Shalt Not Kill
Pretty self-explanatory – don't murder your partner.

Thou Shalt Discuss Thy Flaws Openly
If you are messy, and you've always hidden this from them by throwing every possession you own into a wardrobe and then saying, 'Don't go in the wardrobe!' this won't fly when you're cohabiting. You'll probably be sharing a wardrobe, but even if you're not, firstly, well done on your impressive storage solutions, and secondly, you still need to talk to them about how messy you are. Get them to

talk about their flaws, too, and make sure you approach it clearly looking for ways to improve. Saying, 'I leave socks on the floor and will not be putting them away ever,' is quite unhelpful. Having a live-in lover is all about compromise.

> STEVIE: I wrote a list of things I was worried my boyfriend would find out about me (very messy, bad sleeper so liable to walk around like a phantom for most of the night, hate eating while watching TV, eat weird food combinations, own too many coats), and it turned out to be quite fun. He did one, too, and we laughed about it. Sure, the fact that I still sometimes leave a room looking like I spontaneously combusted and nobody can move for puffer jackets can be a problem, but none of it is a surprise, which is the main thing.

Thou Shalt Share Thine Housework

Whether you want to divide it by room, or whether you prefer having a weekly blitz together, do not get into the habit of having one person do the majority of the work. If you're the messier one, pick some specific household chores and make sure you keep on top of them. Nobody likes bitching about housework, especially not when you're supposed to be live-in lovering, so create some sort of system that you both understand, both feel is fair and can both stick to.

Thou Shalt Communicateth

It's one of those pieces of advice you hear over and over again, but it's so vague that you never actually know how to implement it.

Basically, it means never having an elephant in the room, but always calmly and openly being able to say, 'Hey, shall we discuss this elephant?'

> TESSA: Sometimes the elephant in the room will be the large antique ceramic elephant that you keep carting everywhere and they absolutely hate.

It's being able to say, 'It really upset me when you said . . .' or, 'I know you're messy, but recently it's gone turbo,' without fear of a screaming match. Difficult topics should be approached with care and 'I feel like . . .' statements, rather than 'YOU ALWAYS DO THIS . . .' statements, with plenty of room for the other person to respond.

Really try to see it from their point of view, and aim to get to a stage where you both compromise because your relationship is more important than winning. Nine times out of ten this conversation is only successful after the disagreement, or at least when one of you has gone for a little walk to cool off while the other stood in the kitchen and stress-ate an out-of-date bagel.

Learning how to communicate with your partner never stops; it's an ongoing process that you get better at as time passes. They might be the sort of person who needs to get accustomed to change, so you'll learn to give them a couple of days rather than demand a resolution to a problem immediately. They might feel particularly defensive about some topics and not others, so you'll have to approach them with the appropriate sensitivity. They might need reassurance after an argument, whereas you prefer space. Don't panic after the first massive row and decide it's never going to work out. The only time it's never going to work out is when one of you no longer wants to try to learn how to communicate with the other one. You'll be amazed how much you continue to learn about a person even after years together. Many of these communicating conversations involve something like, 'Sorry I do that, it's because I once saw a dog when I was seven and when you laughed at my bow tie it reminded me of that,' or something equally incoherent, which you could never have guessed in a million years because you're not a mind reader.

Thou Shalt Organise Dateth Nightseth

You'll think this definitely doesn't apply to you because your relationship is *alive* and *passionate,* until one day you wake up and realise you have transitioned seamlessly into a stereotype and only hang out together watching Netflix while scrolling through your phones. Which is nice, sure, lovely to hang out, but you used to go places and dress up and do things.

Having new experiences with a partner and making new memories is one of the quickest and easiest ways to deepen your bond (lame) or get the spark back (flame). Go outside the house, somewhere you've never been before. Doesn't have to be fancy or expensive; does have to involve putting on proper trousers and brushing your hair. The aim is creating memories rather than just doing the same thing day in, day out. It's all about the mems.

Thou Shalt Maketh Thine Interior Decorating Decisions Togethereth

Because opposites attract, it's possible that one of you is a minimalist and one of you is a maximalist. One of you wants to live inside the Gryffindor common room and one of you wants to live inside an Excel spreadsheet. Don't just plough ahead with your own ideas, because you are building this space *together*.

If you love a bit of interior design and your partner seems laidback about the whole thing, it's easy to just buy all the rugs/cushions/giant bronze dogs you fancy because they'll probably be fine with it. This attitude risks a gentle building of resentment until one day they'll say, 'I'd actually like to hang one of my prints, but you've bought so many there's no wall space left and we've only been living together for a month,' and you'll say, 'BUT YOU DIDN'T SHOW AN INTEREST!' and they'll say, 'OK, but you didn't ask me,' and boom – you've got yourself into an Interior Decorating Argument.

Whether it's some new forks or painting an entire wall, it's always good to talk it through with the other person before you launch ahead. And be prepared to find a compromise if they say, 'Aquamarine feels a bit much for the living room.' It's important to feel like a team. If you are the more minimalist of the two, make sure you're using language like, 'Aquamarine feels a bit much, but how about a different shade of blue?' rather than just putting your foot down, otherwise you risk the more creative soul exploding and bellowing, 'Why won't you LET ME LIVE?'

Thou Shalt Setteth Boundaries and Respecteth Others Boundarieseth

Go into this being aware that they're going to say insane things like, 'I can't sleep without the window open, even when it's -2 degrees,' or, 'If you don't take the foil bit off the yoghurt and throw it away, I feel sick,' or, 'My greatest fear is you leaving a glass in the sink, because what if one of us accidentally punches it and our hand comes off?'

STEVIE: That last one is, surprisingly, real.

Over time you will slowly morph your weirdness into one nebulous blob of strange; you'll realise you also quite like having the window open, and they'll begin to get over their fear of yoghurt foil with the exposure therapy you provide by never, ever removing it even when there's only a tiny bit of yoghurt left. They will have an incredibly precise way of loading the dishwasher, which eventually you'll learn. In turn, they will eat dinner later even though they used to prefer it on the dot of six, because you're not hungry at six and it doesn't kill them to wait another hour and a half because you're not 80 years old. These things are superficial, but they feel like a big deal when you first move in, so don't worry, they will fade and become normal soon.

Some things, however, require proper boundary setting to establish how, together, you're going to make something work. Are they constantly taking their work home with them to the extent that you don't feel you're ever getting downtime together? Do you socialise much more than them, leaving them feeling a bit lonely? Does one of you work from home, and so is expected to do all the housework all the time? That doesn't seem fair, so talk about it. The challenge is to find the middle ground where neither of you loses out, and sometimes that might result in you saying, 'OK, if you need space to sleep, I understand that me wrapping my limbs around you in a death grip until 4 a.m. may impact your health and wellbeing. I understand that this small alteration in sleep positioning doesn't mean you don't love me any more.' For example.

Thou Shalt Be Reasonable About Thy Sleepingeth

If we ran a dating app that's sole purpose was to find people for a harmonious marriage, we would probably match people by how much they like hugging, how they like to sleep and what time they want to get to the airport before a flight. It is rare that the person you fancy and love most in the world also has the same sleeping pattern as you. This will result in you lying awake at night, staring at the ceiling and thinking, 'What, so I fall in love and now this fucker is just going to be in my bedroom forever, are they?' and other such irrational thoughts. Spend money on the nicest, biggest mattress you can afford. You'll think, 'Not worth it,' followed by, 'Oh golly, that was worth it.' And if you possibly can, work out either having a spare room (unlikely) or a pull-out sofa bed, or just somewhere so that if one person is sick or working late, or in any way just needs some space to do their own weird sleeping thing for a bit, they can do it in perfect peace, before returning to the marital bed refreshed and once more full of love.

STEVIE: My parents remain happily married and very much in love, but when I go home I often find my dad sleeping bolt upright in an armchair in the living room.

TESSA: What are you doing in the living room in the middle of the night?

STEVIE: Trying to find an armchair I can sleep bolt upright in because I am my father's daughter.

If nothing else, adopt the Scandinavian sleeping method of having two duvets. Then one person can sleep under the eight weighted blankets they like to cover themselves with, and the other can sleep under the flimsy prison rag they inexplicably seem to love. Everyone's happy!

Thou Shalt Focuseth on the Little Things

Never underestimate the power of making someone breakfast for no reason. Or picking up a Snickers on the way home because it's their favourite. Big, romantic gestures are all very well and good if you've got the money and the time and in-date passports, but it's all meaningless if you don't plug their phone in for them when they've fallen asleep or charge up their toothbrush, or leave them stupid notes to make them laugh after you've left for work.

Thou Shalt Not Try to Change the Other Personeth

Compromise is one thing. Wanting your partner to like everything you like and live exactly the way you like to live is . . . not going to happen. If this is what you need in a relationship, then consider moving in with a cardboard cut-out of yourself? You are two separate people working out how to coexist peacefully, not clones of each other. They might love watching sport all Saturday afternoon, whereas you prefer to go hiking. This does not mean they have to come with you, or you have to stay in. Enjoy your differences – it gives you something to talk about! Think of your lives as a giant Venn diagram – there should be a sprinkling of crossover, with a healthy dose of differences on each side. By all means take an interest in things they like. Go along to that *Star Wars* convention or a ramble in the woods even though you're not the rambling type; you'll find so many new interests once you start living with your lover, but there's no need to panic if they don't want to go to a reading of your best mate's play. *You* don't even want to go to a reading of your best mate's new play.

Thou Shalt Not Covet Thy Neighbour's Ass

Not worth it. Keep your eyes up here. No looking at the neighbour's butt. Or donkey. Or donkey's butt.

How to Go Travelling Alone

Whether it's a weekend trip to a new city or six months trekking in the wilderness, the magical thing about not being a kid any more is that, if you've got the money and you've got the time off work, you don't need to ask anyone's permission to go anywhere – you can just go! You don't need to coerce others into going with you or compromise the adventure you want to have – you can pack up your treasures in a little red handkerchief and hit the road.

TESSA: I've done this extensively and with much contentment. I like my own company. I like going places. If you're having a wedding anywhere in the world, I will travel and I will attend.

STEVIE: I've never been travelling and I've certainly never been travelling on my own. Mainly because I was too scared and now I feel like the travelling boat has sailed without me.

TESSA: Stevie, you're not too old and it's not too late! You can go travelling at any time!

STEVIE: I know, I know, but I think I'm too nervous about not making any friends or getting killed.

TESSA: Both valid concerns. You can't ever truly protect yourself

346

from anything, even in your own country, but you can take plenty of steps to stay as safe as possible, and you will 100% make friends.

1. Stick to the beaten track

If you're nervous and this is your first time travelling alone, now is not the time to start trying to find an undiscovered city. Accept that you're a beginner and surround yourself with other travellers. Rather than attempting an experience no one has ever had before, go to the cool famous restaurants, visit the classic attractions, stay in the most popular hostels. Don't set fire to your *Lonely Planet* and march into the jungle.

2. Tell people where you are

For you, but also for them. Even if you want to be free and wild and unshackled, people worry. If your mate just disappeared for six months, you might start to feel quite stressed. Update people regularly, whether that's via Instagram, emails, texts or relentlessly WhatsApping pictures of you up a mountain. People want to know you're OK. Download the Find My Friends app so people can see where you are.

3. Keep multiple forms of ID in different places

Your passport should be in a secret place and on you at all times, but you also want several colour photocopies of your passport in different places, and your driver's licence somewhere else. Nothing worse than losing your passport and having no way of proving who you are to get a new one. Absolute nightmare.

4. Get an embarrassing bumbag

Keep your most important valuables on you at all times but separate from each other. Some things in the bumbag; your phone around your neck on a string; cash in a little zipped-up pocket. Sew a secret extra credit card into the lining of your backpack so if it all goes wrong, you've got a back-up plan. Spread out your money so if the worst happens and someone's stolen your bag, they haven't got everything all at once. You've still got some cash tucked into your butt crack. Or the pocket of your other bag. Or somewhere else sensible (maybe not your butt crack).

5. Plan everything before you go

Know where the embassies are and what the emergency number is if you find yourself needing medical help. What's the region's number for the police? What's your contingency plan if you need someone to wire you money or send you a new debit card? All of these things are helpful to sort out before you go; who wants to land in a new country and start thinking about contingency plans? Boring. Do all the boring stuff before you get there so you can focus on having fun/finding yourself, man.

6. Arrive/depart places during the day

Train and coach stations can feel scarier than they actually are at night. Plus, if you get stuck or lost in the daytime, there'll be more people around to ask for help.

7. If you're worried about people looking at you sideways because you're alone, no one does that

If anything, they're thinking, 'Wow, what an incredibly powerful traveller steering their own path through life.' Take a book and don't worry about eating alone at a restaurant. Keep a Moleskine journal and document everything; then it doesn't feel like alone time, but crucial journal time. Those beautiful train tickets aren't going to Pritt-stick themselves.

> TESSA: I backpacked by myself for six months and I don't think I ever ate dinner alone. I made great friends, travelled with them for a bit, then we went our separate ways. If you're sticking to the beaten trail, you're surrounded by other travellers. You always get chatting on the bus, or people say, 'Would you like to join us?' if they see you eating alone. People want to chat. You're all doing the same thing and everyone wants to hear about other people's experiences and where to go and what to do.

8. You will make friends!

Hang out in the hostel bar and by law the hostel must provide you with a jovial Australian man to hang out with. He'll use expressions you cannot quite understand, but you'll admire his general enthusiasm and zest for life. Hostels are designed around people hanging out with other people, and the most popular ones will have themed nights and organised activities and all manner of opportunity to find like-minded souls to hang out with. Most people you meet will look like the best of friends but actually only met each other a few days ago and teamed up to make things cheaper. Go for the largest multi-person dorm room – it's the cheapest option and it'll give you the highest chance of finding people to be friends with.

'Where are you guys from?' 'Where are you headed?' 'How long have you been travelling?' – these will become your daily bread and conversational butter. Practise saying, 'Hey, do you mind if I join you?' as many times as it takes for it not to feel like sand in your mouth, and then you can always join new people.

9. Have a purpose

This is why weddings abroad are so useful, because then it's an excuse to travel either side of the wedding date. Even just booking a flight into one end of a country and a flight out from the other is a purpose. You've got to keep going every day and get to the other side! A purpose keeps at bay those feelings of, 'What on earth am I doing here?' 'Going travelling' seems overwhelming. 'Going to see the Terracotta Army' is a clear purpose. Or 'going to see the Northern Lights'. Or 'buying a horse off a Mongol tribe and riding into the forest to find Genghis Khan's grave'.

10. Don't put off travelling just because you're scared

You'll never do it if you don't take the plunge! If you've got a dream place you've never visited, commit to the decision that this is your year. Take a sabbatical, use up all your holiday, arrange to start a new job three months after you leave your old one – find some time and just go.

STEVIE: Otherwise you'll end up like me.

TESSA: Stevie, go! GO.

STEVIE: I'M GOING.

How to Survive the Post-education Wasteland

Dear Traveller,

If you have found this note, it means you have landed in the Post-education Wasteland. By our estimate you've arrived here about a month after you left school, or finished your training, or graduated university, and now you're out in the real world. You spent that month going 'Wayoh!' and partying and burning your revision notes and now, here we are.

Stevie has drawn you a map.

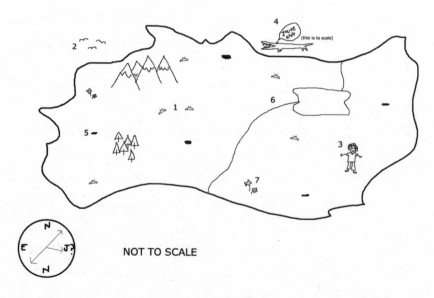

We lived here longer than we'd care to admit, and so we've left you this letter in the hope that you navigate the barren terrain and desolate mountains better than we did.

What are you even supposed to do here? What are the rules? In education the rules weren't great, but at least they made sense: you revised, you did the exam, you passed or failed, you tried again. How are you supposed to get an A* at life? How does everyone else seem to know what to do?

At first it will seem that you are the only one here. Everyone else seems to have gone straight into a proper job or a graduate scheme or somehow become 'a consultant' even though only weeks ago they were gaffer-taping bottles of Strongbow to their palms and calling themselves 'Edward Ciderhands'.

You are not alone. It took us a long time to work this out, but if you give the special call, you can find other people sheltering in the wasteland. The call is three short hoots, like an owl, then one long, continuous scream. If that doesn't work, try, 'I'm actually finding this very hard,' or, 'I don't know what I'm doing.' The call that will come back is: 'Me too! Me too!'

The only way out of the wasteland is through, but unfortunately there are infinite paths you could take. That's part of the problem (note the directionless compass on the map). You could be anything, do anything, and that choice is both exciting and suffocating.

The choice you make now doesn't have to be the one you stick with forever. Pick an industry, pick a career, pick a vague sense of what you want to do and start walking.

Beware! Sorry, we should have said that before you started walking. There are so many dangers in the wasteland.

1. Money Crabs

They're everywhere. It was a barren but ultimately peaceful waste-land until these things were introduced to the ecosystem. It's hard enough as it is, wandering about, trying to work it all out, and now you're being attacked as well. Their name suggests they feed on money, but really they feed on joy. You just want a moment to regroup? Sorry, you owe rent. You want a little treat after a bad job interview? Sorry, you can't afford it. New pair of shoes for the job interview? Uh-oh, that's taken you into your overdraft.

Build yourself a crab-proof suit by regularly checking your bank balance, drawing up a budget and seeing what you can cut out. Can you split the rent by sharing a bed with a friend, sleeping on someone's sofa, moving back in with your parents? Get yourself any temporary job you can find and do it very intensely for a month. That buys you a month of charging headlong into the wasteland wearing your crab-proof suit. When the suit falls apart, start the process again.

Don't waste your time counting how many people seem to be wearing state-of-the-art crab-proof suits called Daddy's Money. Life is unfair; it serves you nothing to complain.

2. False-Promise Birds

Oh man, these are even worse than the Money Crabs. They circle overhead all day every day, calling out, 'Oh yeah, I'm sure I can help you out – drop me an email, I'll see what I can do!' and, 'Paul's brother works in that industry, I'm sure he can get you a job!' You must always follow up on the bird's suggestion, because legend has it that one in every flock will actually get you a job, but take everything they say with a pinch of salt. Send a polite and professional email, follow up a week later, know that their intentions were good, but don't let them get your hopes up.

3. Your Aunt

What's she doing in the wasteland? Nobody knows, but she drops by occasionally and keeps asking if you've got a job yet and saying how easy it was in her day and she doesn't understand what the problem is. To get everybody off your back at family gatherings, you can just make up a job that sounds vague but important, like Accounts Manager, or say you work for the Government and you're not at liberty to reveal any more information.

4. The Giant Crocodile of Self-Doubt

Crocodiles aren't that fast, clocking up around 12–14 mph in short bursts, but this one is persistent and it won't stop moving. It follows you all day and then it catches you up at night when you're trying to sleep and starts chatting shit in your ear. It whispers things about how you're too old, and not talented, and what do you think you're playing at trying to forge a career? It wants you to just forget it and give up. Don't listen! You've got one shot at life. You might as well keep striving for something you love.

5. Due-to-the-volume-of-applicants-we-cannot-provide-feedback sinkholes

Absolutely everywhere, and you will fall in one eventually. You will put your heart and soul into applying and you will keep getting rejected. Keep brushing off the faceless rejection emails and keep

355

going. Stay strong, otherwise you'll be straight in that sinkhole, wailing, 'What's the poooooooint?' at the moon, and it can take weeks to climb out.

6. The River of Unfairness

The river looks like a one-way ticket out, but it's actually a very large, circular lake. You'll think you're finally out of here, only for the current to carry you round to exactly where you started from. Plus it's saltwater, so you can't even have a nice sup while you're going round in circles. There will be placements and internships that come to nothing, everyone in the office will love you, you'll finally think, 'This is it!' and the job will go to someone else. The lake will send you mad with bitterness at the sheer unfairness of it all, but don't let that happen. Accept the circular lake for the literal learning curve that it is, take what you can from the experience and keep moving.

7. Your-Career-is-Not-your-Life Forget-Me-Nots

These aren't a danger; in fact, they're the only nice thing in the wasteland, and the more you plant, the more will grow. These flowers are very small but very beautiful, and they're there to remind you that your career is not the be all and end all. Set yourself goals that nobody can take away from you and nobody can reject. Learn to do a handstand, learn to cook, learn to do a press-up, learn to knit, learn to code, plant a garden, whittle a spoon. When your life becomes all about trying to impress other people enough for them to take a chance on you, it's always good to have projects on the go that belong to you and no one else. It's perfectly possible that during this time you will get so heavily into your side project that you become obsessed with stop-motion animation, or close-up magic, or quilt-making. Point anyone who's worried about you to this key piece of information: it's just a phase, and it will pass.

That's everything we know, young traveller. You've got your map, you know it's going to be tough and all you can do now is start walking. You'll stay here longer than you'd like, but we swear on our lives you won't stay here forever.

From two wasteland survivors to another, we promise you'll make it out. Good luck x

How to Be Creative

If you're a relentless torrent of ideas and imagination, please be on your way – there's nothing for you here. Stay if you feel like you used to be creative and now that muscle has seized up, or you're going through a dry spell, or you feel like you've never been a creative person (not true) or that you don't have time to be creative (also not true).

But I'm not a creative person!

Creativity isn't just painting or performing slam poetry. It's anything you imagined and then brought out of your mind into the world: cooking is creative, engineering is creative, designing a sudoku is creative, building a bike is creative. Redecorating your flat, planting a garden, coding a website, building a fence – it's all creative. If you're still thinking, 'Yeah, but not me,' we bet an adult casually said that about you as a child. 'Oh so-and-so isn't creative, he's good at maths,' or something. And you lodged that straight in your brain as a defining feature of your personality.

But you *were* creative as a child, and you certainly didn't judge the quality of your output. You served mud pies in your thriving garden restaurant, and you barely stopped for breath as you ran to present your crayon creation and insist it was not only put on the fridge, but faxed to Grandma. So what happens as we get older? Fear of judgement? Thinking that messing around is a waste of time? You have a very nice career in sales and business accounting – who do you think you are, posting poems on Instagram? Edgar Allan Poe?

> STEVIE: Edgar Allan Hoe! Amiright?! Hahahahahaha.
> TESSA: Creativity is hard.

Pick something you'd like to make, and go right ahead and make it. Not *for* anything. Just because it's nice to do.

But what if it's crap?
Yeah. It probably will be. Don't judge how it turned out against the vision of how it looked in your head. Free yourself from trying to make something good, and just make something. It's about the creating, not the creation. You don't have to show anyone and you certainly don't have to put it on Instagram. Make something bad – who cares?

What's that? Popular-music icon Cher has something to say about all this? Take it away, Cher!

> CHER: Until you're ready to look foolish, you'll never have the possibility of being great.

Thank you, Cher. You've got to start, you've got to make bad things, you've got to be foolish.

Yes, yes, very nice, but I simply don't have the time.

Schedule the time. Into the next gap in the calendar add some space to 'dick about' or 'mess around' or any other turn of phrase that reminds you that this is fun. If any moment away from work feels like a waste, remember that taking the time to check out and be creative will make you better at your job. Google famously give their employees a budget that they have to spend on learning a skill outside of work. Maybe take a holiday day and feel the thrill of being paid to do nonsense. If the possibility of a whole day off work is laughable, find stolen moments. Let your mind wander on the train, staring out of the window. In the shower is prime creative retail because it's the only time you can't touch your phone.

If you know you won't do it without some help, sign up to a course. Maybe you need the rigid structure and companionship of the basket-weaving class. Maybe you're more of a YouTube-tutorial-at-home-go-at-your-own-pace sort of person.

Oh hello? Tchaikovsky has something he would like to share?

TCHAIKOVSKY: A self-respecting artist must not fold his hands
on the pretext that he is not in the mood.

Very wise, Mr T. You might not be feeling it, but keep showing up to your scheduled creative time, to your classes, to the ten minutes you've found at lunchtime. Keep going. Fill the time that you have carved for yourself.

I'm in a creative rut and I can't get out.

Creative block is a horrible feeling. And you're not alone if you used to be an oasis of ideas and now you're standing in a barren, dry desert. Oh God, here comes Kafka. How's it going, Franz?

> KAFKA: How time flies; another ten days and I have achieved nothing. It doesn't come off. A page now and then is successful, but I can't keep it up, the next day I am powerless.

Thanks for sharing, man. Sounds very tough. But here's the thing, it will come back.

Your muse is not, as Enlightenment artists would have you believe, a sexy woman sat on your shoulder who you simply ask to help you, she complies, you write a delightful phrase for your lute and then have sex with her. Your muse is your brain. And sometimes your brain is really tired and doesn't want to be creative. While you're waiting, give your brain a boost by completing something totally different, like ironing your smalls.

You might find that by the time you come back the creative dam has burst, and if it hasn't, at the very least you'll have very smooth smalls.

Oh hello Hilary Mantel, you want to share something quite specific to writing but you hope it will still resonate? Take it away.

> HILARY MANTEL: If you get stuck, get away from your desk. Take a walk, take a bath, go to sleep, make a pie, draw, listen to music, meditate, exercise; whatever you do, don't just stick there scowling at the problem. But don't make telephone calls or go to a party; if you do, other people's words will pour in

where your lost words should be. Open a gap for them, create a space. Be patient.[15]

Thank you, H-Dog. Don't panic and think you need to be living a more interesting lifestyle to be creative. The concept of the tortured artist is a myth. Yes, Edgar Allan Poe was drunk most of the time, but imagine how productive he could have been if he wasn't? He also married his 14-year-old cousin. Point is, you don't need to be deliriously painting through the night. If you love a routine, you'll convince yourself you're not doing your best work because you're not riddled with opium, and if you're a hard-partying insomniac, you'll convince yourself this lifestyle is the inevitable result of your *profound* creativity. Everybody chill out.

EDGAR ALLAN POE: I have absolutely no pleasure in the stimulants in which I sometimes so madly indulge.

All right, mate.

EDGAR ALLAN POE: It has not been in the pursuit of pleasure that I have periled life and reputation and reason. It has been in the desperate attempt to escape from torturing memories, from a sense of insupportable loneliness and a dread of some strange impending doom.

---

15 https://www.theguardian.com/books/2010/feb/22/hilary-mantel-rules-for-writers

Keep it LIGHT, Edgar! We're trying to help people be creative here!

  EDGAR ALLAN POE: I wish I could write as mysterious as a
    cat.

Sure. Why not?

How to Go to a Wedding

Weddings are a social, emotional and financial minefield for everyone involved, and after a lifetime of not attending any, there will suddenly come a time when everyone you've ever met starts getting married.

To help you crest majestically through the day, here are our Dos and Don'ts for the modern wedding guest, with additional advice from the fifteenth-century bestselling handbook *Etiquette for the Medieval Wedding Guest*.

Don't freak out about what to wear.

As long as you're not wearing a long, white wedding dress, you'll be fine. Don't spend too much time worrying about it, and for heaven's sake, don't think you have to wear a different outfit to every wedding. If you've got a cracker, wear it everywhere.

TESSA: A very good business idea I had is a website called what-shalliweartothiswedding.com and it asks you questions like, when is it? Where is it? What's your relationship to the couple? Is your ex going to be there? How do you feel about sleeves? And then it would present you with a whole outfit. Unfortunately, it's pointless, because the answer would always be 'Is it not a long, white wedding dress? Do you feel nice? Wear it!' so the business was doomed to fail from the start. You can have this idea if you want. My ideas are nothing but a burden.

Check in with the bridesmaids beforehand in case you're accidentally dressed the same, and consider having a back-up outfit just in case – for you, or it could come to the rescue of a friend who arrives at the church only to disappear into her body and whisper, 'Oh my God, I'm dressed as the mother of the bride.' (True story.)

If you've had a good year selling tallow candles, dye your wool tunic for the occasion.
The bride will probably be wearing blue, the colour of purity, and the origin of 'something blue', so avoid that like the plague. The groom will probably be in green, the colour of young love, so avoid that one, too. Black is unlucky, pure white is physically impossible, red means you've slept with the groom. Royal blue suggests you have ideas above your station and purple takes 10,000 shellfish to make one gram of dye. Look, just stick to whatever wool colour you've already got (dirty brown or grey) and shut up.

Do get in a team.
Being single at a wedding isn't difficult. Being the *only* single person at a wedding is a nightmare. Nothing will send you into an existential white-wine meltdown quite like being excitedly told that you won't believe this, but you and that six-year-old pageboy are the only single people at this wedding! Before you know it you're

on a one-way ticket to counting your eggs and crying round the back of the marquee.

Ideally, there's another single friend there and the two of you can pair up. Then you've got someone to sit with, someone to dance with and someone to go off and partake in an extremely elaborate photoshoot with until the official photographer has to ask you to get out of the background of his shots. If you're the only solo participant in a big group, quietly say to the person you like best that you might need someone to keep an eye on you. Like a buddy system. If someone's rented an Airbnb and everyone else is a couple, be ready for them all to get double beds, and for you to have to go in the attic in a cot, because 'you're just a one, and everyone else is a two'.

Do be ready to get married if the groom doesn't like the look of the bride.
If you're a bridesmaid, be ready to present yourself to the groom if the original bride runs away. Keep your veil on unless you're called up and don't make a fuss about what you're wearing – you're dressed the same to confuse the evil spirits.

Do bring your A-game.
If you're on your own and don't know anybody except the bride and groom, the only way through is for this whole experience to be a Tits and Teeth affair from start to finish. That means your very best listening skills and your very best bravery in going up and starting conversations. 'Your dress is amazing, where is it from?' 'How do you know the bride and groom?' 'I'm on my own,

do you mind if I sit with you guys?' 'If forced to fight a thousand geese in hand-to-hand combat, how long do you think you could last?' Just your essential wedding-day patter. It seems like everyone is best friends and you're the odd one out, but even the bride and groom don't know everybody here. Plus, everyone's drunk so won't remember what you say in about an hour anyway. Sort of perfect for introverts, really.

Alone or otherwise, it's crucial that you GET INVOLVED. Yes, weddings are expensive and time-consuming, but if you've decided to attend, your motto needs to be 'Well, we're here now!' You've been invited to celebrate something very important to somebody you love, which is quite magical when you think about it. It's not your day, it's not how you would have done anything, but if your friend wants to get married in a rat-infested barn with no heating and, crucially, no seating, then that's her prerogative. Do not complain. Get drunk and get involved.

STEVIE: I'll never forget my amazing friend Gabby who saw that the wedding dance floor was getting fatigued and immediately kicked into a high-octane dance workshop. Within minutes there were a hundred people on the dance floor following her moves. It was like a religious experience.

Do write your complaint on the door of the church before sundown. If you know of a reason the marriage can't go ahead, you need to get it in quick. If the clergy have stuck the marriage warrant to the door and you've not marked your name with an X (you can't write) by sundown, then the wedding is going ahead.

Do keep your opinions to yourself.

> TESSA: OK, listen. So I know from experience that you keep your
> mouth shut at weddings and simply Do Not Have Opinions.
> Keep them 'til you're driving safely home the next day, and
> definitely don't use them as a friend-hunting tool. Once, I was
> watching a man who looked *exactly* like Nigel Farage earnestly
> playing guitar on a hay bale and I said to the boy next to me,
> 'What a dickhead!' at the exact same time the boy said, 'That's
> my dad!'
>
> STEVIE: This also applies to pre-wedding WhatsApp groups.
> Sure, the bride and groom might not be in the group, but your
> pal who is getting married next year is, and if everyone starts
> bitching she'll be having a meltdown that everyone is secretly
> doing this behind her back as well. It's just a wedding – let's
> all keep our pants on (or not, if it's a nudist ceremony).

Do remember to bring confetti.
As the bride walks out of the church, all the unmarried women of
the town will want to try to rip a bit off her wedding dress for
good luck; distract them by throwing large handfuls of rice at them
so they can't get a purchase.

Don't give a speech.
Unless you have been specifically asked to give a speech, or the floor
has definitely been opened for impromptu speeches, do not allow
the mood just to take you, no matter how confident you are that
this one is really going to blow the roof off. It won't. An actor we

know once got up during the speeches, unannounced and unre-
quested, and performed the monologue from *Hamlet*. CAN YOU
IMAGINE?

> STEVIE: At my friend's wedding, the wedding singer they'd hired
> stopped the band halfway through and proposed to his girlfriend
> (the bassist). It went down terribly. The groom's mum screamed,
> 'NO!' and drowned out the girlfriend's answer (which might
> have also been 'NO!').

Do be ready to defend the groom.
If you've been chosen as the best man, it doesn't mean you're the
best friend, but the best man with a sword in the local area. If
this is a 'marriage-by-capture', you're there to defend the groom
if the bride's family come for her. That's why she stands on his
left in the church, so he has his sword arm free. You've probably
never even met the couple before today, so be nice, and if you're
handy with a weapon, you can make a fine living as a best man
for hire.

Do get drunk, don't go feral.
Weddings are designed around a steady flow of drinking, so by all
means lean in, but do pace yourself and remember that several
grandmas are here and this is ultimately a family affair. You don't
want to be in a situation where the best man has to plug their iPod
in because someone bottled the DJ and he's rightly gone home and
the bride is in tears. (True story.)

Don't boo the minstrel performing the love poem.
Sure, you don't like the cut of his jib and his poetry is derivative, but keep your opinions to yourself. It's very disrespectful to boo.

Don't worry about a cash contribution.
Your presence is much more valuable than your presents. If you can't afford it, you can't afford it. If you're worried, hand-make something, or frame a photo of them, or make a lovely card. Don't turn yourself in knots if you don't have the money.

Do wear a hat if you want to wear a hat.
If you want to wear a hat, for God's sake wear a hat.

Do wear a bonnet.
If you are a widow or a middle-aged unmarried woman, for God's sake let everyone know by wearing your bonnet.

Do eat whatever's on your plate.
Obviously if there's a vegetarian option going round and you've been served a steak, politely ask if you can swap, but if you've been given something more niche that you don't eat or can't eat, just gently slide it to one side and say, 'Absolutely delicious, thank you.' Someone has gone to unimaginable lengths and costs to sort out this meal, so don't start making a scene because you don't like figs. You're not going to starve – there'll be pavlova in a minute.

Do bring a bottle in a gift bag.
If it's a cash bar, sneak your alcohol in by putting it in a jazzy gift bag and pretending it's a present.

Don't take the bouquet-catching too seriously.
If you are the Single Lady at the Wedding, all eyes will be on you for the bouquet toss. Your only option is to play along in a way that is both serious and 'a bit of a laugh'. Say you don't want to play and everyone will boo you for being a spoilsport; take your shoes off and ask someone to rugby-lift you into the air without cracking a smile and everyone will feel very tense.

> TESSA: I'm well practised at this light-but-deadly-serious fine line of bouquet-catching – I wasn't goal defence in netball for nothing – though you'd be surprised how dangerous it can get in the scrum. Once, as I went to jump, I was punched in the throat by the (married) mother-of-the-bride, who then proceeded to snatch the bouquet out of the air and take it on a victory lap of the dance floor.

Don't take the stacking of the buns too seriously.
The stacking of the sweet buns will be the highlight of the day, but don't get too competitive. The buns must be stacked between the couple as tall as possible by the wedding guests, but if the couple can still kiss over the buns, the marriage will be fruitful. Squash your bun down a bit if you can – give the marriage a chance. And may their union be long and filled with love!

How to Be Brilliant at Public Speaking

Because we go onstage and tell jokes for people, like court jesters, you'd be forgiven for thinking we are naturally good at public speaking. We are not.

Our very first time performing together, in our sketch group Massive Dad, we were introduced by an old man who ran the gig in the back of a pub, who said, 'And now some women! They all work for the BBC.' (This was not true then, and remains not true to this day.) 'Should women even be allowed to do comedy? It's illegal in many parts of the Middle East. And rightly so. Well, here they are!' (This is a true story.)

We got onstage and Tessa whispered, 'Here's our first sketch if you would like.' Then we performed our entire sketch at breakneck speed and looking directly at the floor.

Very few people are born public speakers. In fact, nobody is; it's just that some people are better at controlling their nerves than others, or better at remembering the techniques and phrases and gestures that make it all look effortless, thereby giving them the confidence to sail through something that might provoke someone else to wet themselves.

While comedy is an extreme form of public speaking, because

372

it lives or dies by whether or not people laugh, it's no different to doing a presentation, a speech, or anything else that requires you to talk to a group of people for a period of time. No matter how carefree others may look on the outside, they're feeling that same sweaty panic on the inside. To help you through, here is what the lead-up to a show looks like for both of us, and how we cope. Maybe you can take some of these techniques away with you, and hopefully they'll help.

STEVIE

The nerves start about a week before, which means I go to the toilet four times as much – and I mean the kind that makes you google 'how to stop shitting please help'. On the day, I can't sit still and walk around the flat saying 'Right' and 'OK'. I eat lots of disjointed snacks (spoons of peanut butter, pieces of dry bread, fists of dry cereal) while standing in the kitchen saying 'Right' and 'OK' with my mouth full. I spend an hour putting on too much make-up, like war paint. I'm so terrified of being late that I arrive far too early and spend ages wandering around the venue losing confidence and cutting material before realising that if I don't say those things I just cut, the gig will be 30 seconds long. As I'm waiting to go on, my body goes into fight-or-flight mode, like I'm about to go on a rollercoaster (I hate rollercoasters).

Do the preparation

Never bury your head in the sand and avoid prepping, because not only does it delay the inevitable, but you'll end up having to prep on the day when the serious nerves have kicked in with a face full of sand. A lot of people I know (including Tessa) work best under pressure, but I just panic and go blank. So if you're like me, give yourself plenty of time. If you're like Tessa, probably ignore everything I'm saying and skip straight to her bit.

It's not fear, it's just adrenaline

I came across an interview with Dutch footballer Virgil van Dijk, who, when asked how he manages to remain so cool under pressure all the time, said: 'You need to turn nerves into more excitement.' I didn't realise I could simply change my perspective on being frightened – how novel! That seventeenth toilet trip isn't nervousness about messing up, it's excitement at going out there and having a go. The shaky hands or dry mouth is just adrenaline, so have a sip of water and, hey, nobody's looking at your hands. What's the point in being alive if you're not going to put yourself in new and exciting positions that challenge you? Adrenaline doesn't dictate whether you'll do a good job or not, unless you let it. The saying is that 'Fear is like fire; it can heat your home or it can burn it down'. I used to let it burn the house down, but now it's just crackling away in my fireplace.

Have cue cards

For some reason, I got it into my head that having a script or a notebook in my hand onstage was lazy and unprofessional. I have no idea why, and the moment someone reminded me, 'You know, you can just take your script with you,' it calmed me down SO MUCH. Ignore the fact that some people can rattle off presentations without a single cue card or riff all night long. Who cares? People are all different, so bring cue cards if you need to. Jot some clear notes down in a notebook. Take a moment to look at them during the speech or presentation. Don't pretend you aren't using them; everyone can see you're using them. Whatever you're doing, own it. It's like getting worried that people will think you look silly while going for a run, when in fact everyone's just thinking, 'God, I really need to go running.'

Do not fear the pause
When I'm doing new material, I record myself on my phone and then force myself to listen back to see what worked and what didn't. I tend to race through when I'm not sure about the joke, and sometimes there'll be a moment onstage when I've totally forgotten where I am and will falter for what feels like 10–12 years. It feels terrible. But when listening back, it usually turns out it was only a second or two and sounds perfectly natural. People take pauses all the time; it just sounds like you're taking the time to think about what you're going to say. Sloooooooooow down. Take sips of water throughout. Have a breathe. A person talking at breakneck speed is actually quite stressful to watch. Have a lovely professional pause. It puts people at ease.

TESSA
I get very, very nervous beforehand and have to go to the toilet about a hundred times. Also, my palms get extremely hot and my hands cramp up and I get completely dressed about seven hours ahead of schedule. When I was seven, I was in a swimming gala with some local schools at the Didcot Wave – in retrospect,

probably an extremely relaxed and casual affair, but in my seven-year-old mind it might as well have been the Olympics. My race was not until about two in the afternoon, but I became totally convinced that they would call my race early and I would have to run to the start line, where they would blow the whistle even though I wasn't ready and I would be forced to dive in with my towel wrapped around my legs. So convinced was I that this might happen that while all the other children laughed and played and didn't bother to get changed until it was a bit closer to their race, I sat on my seat, as close to the start of the race as I could possibly get, in my swimming costume, hat *and goggles,* staring stoically ahead for the entire day.

This completely reasonable attitude pervades to this day and I don't feel calm until I'm totally dressed and ready. Ideally with my goggles on. When we were doing Massive Dad I would whisper, 'My towel is wrapped around my legs,' and Liz and Stevie would know I needed to go and get dressed now and put the props out and there was no point talking to me until I had.

Thank somebody if you can
When I do a mixed-bill gig, I like to thank the MC as soon as I get onstage. It's nice to do and nobody says thank you enough these days, but saying, 'Give it up for your host . . .' also gives me a chance to breathe while people are clapping for somebody else. Don't start every board meeting by saying, 'Give it up for our CEO! Am I right!?' but thanking the person who introduced you, or in some way pushing the focus away from you, gives you a chance to ground yourself, rather than just starting straight out of the gate.

It's all absolutely meaningless

The most freeing thing in the world is to remember that, ultimately, nobody cares. Even if it feels like the most important thing to you, it's not really a life-or-death situation. The planets will not realign because your speech didn't go as well as it could.

Of course, take it seriously, but remember that in the grand scheme of things, this is not actually that big a deal. Take a breath, take some of the pressure off.

Don't reference the fact that you hate public speaking

We don't need to know that. In fact, we need to know exactly zero of the thoughts that are going through your head. When I started doing stand-up I kept saying things like, 'Gosh, this microphone stand is so much heavier than you think!' which, while true, is not necessarily comedy per se.

The overhead projector might not work and your thought might be, 'I wish for the sweet release of death,' but instead of saying that out loud, try, 'OK, we'll give that a few seconds and see if we can get that working.' No one really cares. It's all absolutely meaningless, and no one knows how this speech was supposed to go so we won't know things are going badly unless you explicitly tell us. Everyone is looking to you for cues. If you are going, 'I WANT TO DIE,' they will feel second-hand embarrassment. If you appear absolutely fine, they will too.

As a teenager I saw the production of *Joseph and the Amazing Technicolor Dreamcoat* with Lee Mead (star, and indeed winner, of TV talent show *Any Dream Will Do*) on its opening night. In the first half the rotating camel came halfway out and promptly stopped working. The Narrator finished her song in the middle of listing Joseph's brothers, beamed and walked off the stage. The curtain came down, the lights came up. I looked about in horror because I, a super-fan, knew that things had gone severely wrong. I made eyes at the sound-desk staff to clearly convey that if they needed me, I was available to help. I thought the audience would be rolling in aisles wailing, 'But the camel!' But everyone just applauded the interval, got out of their seats and said, 'Shall we get a drink?' Nobody even knew!

My point here is that if you don't tell us, we'll never know! Don't keep up a running commentary of your real-time inner monologue. As far as you're concerned, this speech is going fantastically, no matter what's happening inside.

Be Sasha Fierce

If Beyoncé needs an alter ego to go onstage, then, by Jove, you can have one too. Leave yourself at the door, and adopt the spirit of any famous person, real or fictional, who's a confident public speaker. Stand tall, eye contact, warm smile, open body language.

As philosopher Eddie Izzard famously said in her *Dress to Kill* stand-up show, it's 70% how you look, 20% how you sound and 10% what you actually say.

If you look like you're in control, speak calmly and with confidence, and you look like you're happy to be there, then you really have to work very hard to get people to remember the 10%. I can't remember a single word of the best best man speech I ever heard, all I remember is that he looked like he was having a brilliant time and I was really enjoying the piña colada I was drinking.

If you look calm, we're calm. If you're smiling, we're smiling. If you breathlessly apologise for being shit before you've even said anything, we will be very, very tense.

Even at its very worst, you will be fine

I tell you this story not to scare you, but to convey that even if things go spectacularly wrong (which they won't), you will survive this. When I first started doing stand-up, for my *second ever solo gig* I got asked to come up to Swansea for a gig I believed would be above a pub, to perhaps ten people. I was booked to do seven minutes and I thought I could probably manage it and I gamely hopped on the train to Swansea. I had – and I can't stress this enough – no material. For my first gig I had told a story about my grandma who lived on Vancouver Island and kept a dead owl in the freezer, and I thought I'd probably talk about that again. I arrived to discover that it was in fact in the Swansea Grand, to a sold-out crowd of 300 people. There were huge, big famous names on the bill.

I've generally got through life on the sort of whimsical self-confidence of turn-of-the-century aristocrats. 'Oh yeah,' I think when presented with something I clearly cannot do, 'I can do that.' But this was one of the rare times when I thought, 'Oh, I truly am out of my depth here.' I went onstage and made a few . . . well, jokes is a strong word, but certainly passingly amusing comments about Swansea. I told the story about Grandma and the owl, which had absolutely no punchline and, crucially, no jokes. These were greeted with ripples of polite and muted laughter and after that I was out of material. I thought, 'What shall I say now?' and my mind was empty and limitless. I stood onstage blinded by the stage lights and looked out into the pitch-black, silent void. It felt like that episode of *Buffy the Vampire Slayer* where all the nightmares come to life. I was living an actual anxiety dream. But then – and this is important – then I took a big breath, looked at my watch (I wasn't wearing a watch) and said, 'That's my time, you've been amazing, thank you so much, goodnight!' The people of Swansea, God bless them, gave me a warm and genuine round of applause (I imagine largely fuelled by relief). I beamed, I waved and I got off the stage. And here's the thing, nothing happened. Maybe some of them thought to themselves, 'What a weird girl,' but then they forgot about me. I've been down to the very bottom of the nightmare, and then I just came back up. I'm not saying I ever want to go down there again, but I am saying there's nothing down there. You will survive it. You just take a big breath and you come right back up. I tell you this in case I've described your nightmare, to say that I've been there, I've actually done it, and then it was over. There's nothing down there.

How to Work Out What You Want to Do with Your Life

Ah, yes. Maybe the hardest chapter of all.

The reason we love the idea of the Sorting Hat, or Grandmother Willow, or *Buffy the Vampire Slayer*, or really any young-adult fiction, is because someone walks into the protagonist's life and says, 'You're a wizard,' or, 'You're the Slayer,' or, 'You should bring destruction to your people by pissing about with John Smith, even though Kocoum seems kind and sensible and extremely handsome.'

This is the person you are, this is the house you are in, this is the life you are destined to lead. And then one of the hardest kicks of adult life is realising that there is no path, there is no destiny, and you appear to be showing no signs of magical powers whatsoever.

It's tough, and it's easy to hurtle from person to person, desperately asking, 'What am I supposed to be doing?' 'Who am I supposed to be?' But the freeing, if scary, thing is that they don't know the answer and you get to make it up.

There is no Magic 8-Ball, and it can be a long and winding process to work out what you want to do. Maybe you never work it out! Take comfort from the immortal words of Baz Luhrmann in 'Everybody's Free (to Wear Sunscreen)':

Don't feel guilty if you don't know what you want to do with your life.

The most interesting people I know

Didn't know at 22 what they wanted to do with their lives.

Some of the most interesting 40-years-olds I know still don't.

If you are very young, this was a song when we were in primary school in 1997. We only had this, Aqua's 'Barbie Girl' and 'Tub-thumping' by Chumbawamba.

Anyway, don't worry if you don't know. The coolest people don't know.

In life, everybody gets to pull their skills out of a hat at random, and you get what you get. Sometimes your skills don't line up with your greatest dreams.

TESSA: My greatest dreams are 1) Olympic gymnast and 2) country and western singer, but I can't sing, I can't play an instrument, I've got no rhythm and I'm terrified of going upside down. I didn't pull out spatial awareness, time-keeping or basic maths. But I did get imagination and reckless overconfidence. You get what you get.

Don't berate yourself for what skills you didn't get, or congratulate yourself too much either. Just keep searching until your skill set starts to match up with something you're passionate about.

Ask yourself what you would do if you had limitless money. After you'd partied and bought houses and boats and paid off all of your family's debts, what then? What would you fill your time with?

Ask yourself what you would do if you knew you couldn't fail.

Ask yourself what you did when you were very small. Wrote stories? Put all your animals in a row and pretended to be a teacher? Put all your animals in bandages and pretended to be a doctor? Built Meccano? Designed rockets? Made mud pies? What did you do when you could still do anything?

We were sitting in the garden writing books and look at us now! Though let me tell you, we were a lot faster then. You could have a book written, illustrated and bound, and a soft launch organised with extracts read out to your dad by lunchtime. This thing has taken *months*.

Look at your past jobs and work out what you hated and what you loved about them. Do you need to be in a team? Do you hate the general public? Are you visually minded? Do you love to be in charge? Every job is just teaching you something new about yourself until you realise who you are and what you're best at and, crucially, what you actually like doing.

After that, it's just about trying on all the hats in the shop until one of them fits. Until a spark lights back up again and you think, 'Ah yes, OK, *this* is my thing. My thing is working in a hat shop.'

It might be easier to let it happen in reverse, to be closing doors and saying, 'OK, not that.' Crossing things off a list is just as helpful as adding to it.

TESSA: I once left an internship, and they very kindly gave me a good-luck card. It was probably the only good-luck card in the shop, probably no thought had gone into it at all, but I've kept it with me ever since. It says, 'Go for it!' with a little cartoon man looking up at a crossroads, and one way says 'It!' and one way says 'Not it!' It's just a cute way of saying go for it, but it profoundly stuck with me. It's hard to find 'it', but at least knowing 'not it' gets you a bit closer.

Sometimes that can be enough. Just keep trying things out and say, 'Not it!' if it's not right.

And if you find 'it', if you find your dream, for heaven's sake, follow it.

You have one wild and precious life; if you have a secret passion, show it. If you find something you love, who cares if it's 'not a real job'? Who cares if you've been an accountant all your life and now you want to be a deep sea diver. Who cares if you've always been a circus clown and now you want to be a lawyer. You get to choose what you do, but you also get to change. Nothing is permanent. You can change careers even if you've been somewhere so long you don't know how to do anything else.

When we first started the podcast, we had one listener and it was Stevie's mum. Stevie's mum left us positive reviews under different names about how we were very nice girls having a very interesting chat and retweeted every episode. She's always doodled and been too frightened to show anybody, and then this year she finally decided to put herself out there. She tentatively put her drawings on Instagram (@wigglydoodles) and now . . . well, remember that drawing of us in the intro to this very book? That's her! Illustrator extraordinaire, Margie Martin!

It's never too late and no dream is ever too big, too small or too silly; we want you to finish this book and immediately go forth and doodle. Or go back to school, or quit your job, or go see the world, or whatever it is you've been meaning to do and haven't got round to doing yet.

And you never find the perfect answer, by the way. You never get the A* at life. You never sit back and say, 'Wow, I've absolutely smashed this.' It's not about one enormous, insurmountable goal. It's about total commitment to tiny improvements.

You never get to the top of the mountain. Every time you think you're nearly at the summit, it turns out to be just another ridge, but you just have to keep climbing. And waving, because we're all up there. Up, down, sideways, often backwards. On we all go. Keep climbing, keep searching for your thing, for your people. Keep doing things that scare you.

We can do it.

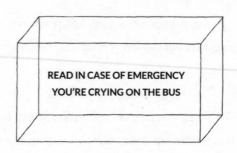

READ IN CASE OF EMERGENCY
YOU'RE CRYING ON THE BUS

Doesn't have to be the bus. We've just done a lot of crying on the bus.

We are extremely pro-meltdown. You're feeling your feelings – let them out! Consider moving to the front seat, top deck, so fewer people can see you and also you've got more of a panoramic vista of the rain (we're assuming it's raining), and then really let it out. Don't fight it. Who cares? Sometimes it's all just too much.

> STEVIE: My therapist once said, 'Emotions are never negative, but the way we react to them can be' – and that has helped me so much. Crying is fine, but beating yourself up about crying is not fair. You're sad! Be sad.

Sad, happy, overtired, hormonal, hungry, broke, too much to do, too little to do, the bank was shut, your feet are wet, you forgot leeks and you only went out to get leeks. There are so many reasons for a cry.

> TESSA: I once cried because, and I quote, there were 'too many countries'.

STEVIE: I used to put my hair over my face while crying in public, which made me feel like nobody could see me, but in retrospect it made me look like the girl from *The Ring*.

Cry this cry out, or if you feel like it's becoming too intense for the bus, maybe walk to a pier, a bridge or even just behind some bins, and really commit. Then call someone who never tells you to stop crying or says, 'Oh, don't be sad!' but who just lets you have a meltdown. Then have one of the following: a portion of chips from the fish and chip shop; toast with butter; soup; an outrageous hot chocolate or elaborate coffee called Winter Pumpkin Baby Hehe that you would never normally buy; a McDonald's Quarter Pounder with cheese and/or a cheeseburger (look, we're sorry, we don't make the rules).

STEVIE: My personal favourite is a 12-inch from Subway. And a large sandwich. Just a gentle penis joke there to help you stop crying.

If there is an online purchase you've been considering for a while, you may now buy it. And if you see anything at all fun between now and home, you may buy that too.

What if the cry is happening at work?
If you're reading this in the toilets at work, know that we've reviewed your case and you are completely in the right and Janet is a bitch. All the above still applies: cry it out, but then you're going to have to visit the pier/bridge/bins in your mind. Even if you're on a crip-

pling deadline, take five minutes, go once around the block or into the stairwell and take a deep breath. Channel the tears into anger and ride that fury for the rest of the day.

If the cry is happening mid-meeting, you've probably lost valuable time reading this far to check what to do, but here it is:

STEVIE: I witnessed a woman tell our boss he was incredibly rude in a meeting, but her eyes filled up so she said calmly, 'My eyes are watering because I'm having an emotional reaction, but they do not undermine the words I'm saying to you,' and continued to make her point. It was the most powerful thing I've ever seen.

The cry belongs to you. You must never apologise for having a physical reaction you can't control. If you're too upset to speak, announce that you're going to take five, get some air and come back to discuss this, because you want to give this topic the care and attention it deserves.

If you're crying at work for non-work reasons, acknowledge this. If someone hands you a pen and you start weeping, best to confront it head on and say, 'Sorry, I've got some things going on at home and became overwhelmed by this Bic.' If you aren't able to get the words out, send a quick email and thank them for understanding. Even if they weren't particularly understanding. In general, people don't know how to act when someone cries, so it's best not to lash out at them for it – just focus on damage control and ultimate professionalism.

What if the cry is happening at someone else's party?
OK, champ, it's time to go home. If it's your do then go to town.

There's a whole song dedicated to your right to cry at your own party. Lock yourself in a room and summon select people in to provide counsel as though you are a queen.

If, however, it's someone else's big day then you need to be very brave and take yourself out of the picture. As ever, there is no shame in this emotion, and no shade from us, but pop yourself out of the spotlight and let it all out without pulling focus.

> STEVIE: I once left a party after having a panic attack because my dress was too tight and messaged my friend, who was still there, 'I'M SO SORRY, I couldn't breathe out! I feel absolutely terrible for leaving so early. God, so embarrassing,' and she said, 'Stevie, when someone leaves a party the most that happens is someone goes, "Oh, I think Stevie went home," and the party continues.' This was helpful. I now do not main-character myself at parties unless they're mine, and I'm too uptight to have parties, so . . .

If it's a wedding and you can't actually leave, go round the back of the marquee for a regroup.

> TESSA: I once calmly escorted myself out of a wedding to have a cry round the back of the marquee and there were THREE OTHER WOMEN doing the same thing. Once I left the marquee and let myself into the family home during a wedding and had a bath. Then I returned to the dance floor, completely refreshed (and very clean) and ready for a second wave.

If it's a big party –

> TESSA: Sorry, it's all coming back to me now – just remembered that when I had that mid-wedding bath I found some very strong European-looking shampoo under the sink and thought 'God, this is strong' and only sometime later did I realise I'd washed myself with carpet shampoo.

If it's a big party you can simply ghost everyone by sliding out the door. Don't message unless people ask where you've gone, and certainly don't message the host saying that their party upset you so much you had to leave.

> STEVIE: I was at a wedding last year and my friend went to bed early because she got some bad personal news, but she did it so swiftly, coolly and decisively that we all just presumed she was tired and let her go off. I found her up at six the next morning, meditating while holding a large crystal ball, and found out that the news was that 'her chakras felt wrong', but that's beside the point.

If it's a smaller gathering, announce that you're going to the shops to buy limes (people always need limes at parties) and have a lovely cry in the street and/or explain the situation to the man in the corner shop who doesn't give one shit about it.

> TESSA: I once showed up to a birthday party having just been dumped outside the Tube station. I was in no position to talk

about it, but I did want to stay at the party, and my very under-standing friends, who've been ignoring me crying since we were twelve, said, 'Do you want to stay and we'll just ignore the fact that you're crying?' and I said, 'Yes, please.' I was then led around the party like a regal weeping monk, while they said, 'This is Tessa, she's just been dumped outside the Tube, but she's not ready to talk about it.' It was actually a very good party.

What if I'm crying, but I really need to get my shit together?
Please refer to the Katy Perry documentary, *Part of Me*.

Halfway through this documentary, Katy is going through her divorce from Russell Brand and is backstage having an absolute meltdown. The crowds are already filling up the stadium and she's still in her pyjamas (we think they've played fast and loose with the timings here, but we respect the creative decision). The crowd is chanting her name and she isn't even dressed and she's *sobbing*. Her manager comes in while she's throwing something away and the make-up lady whispers, 'It's a necklace Russell got her from the fair.' Her manager asks: 'Are you OK?' which is unintentionally very funny because she is absolutely hysterical. And then he says: 'You've got two options: you can cancel the show, or you can do your best,' and she takes a long pause and a deep breath and then says something in such a funny voice that we had to rewind it maybe 20 times to try to understand what she was saying before eventually putting the subtitles on. It turned out to be 'Start time'.

She's led to the stage in all her gear – wig on, party dress – and she's wracked with sobs.

She's holding the sound man's hand because she can't stand up straight. He puts her in a tube, ready to be raised up to the stage. Someone hands her a glittering red microphone, her candy-cane nipple tassels start rotating, she takes a huge breath, stands up tall, puts on her biggest smile, the tube starts going up, and by the time she hits the stage she's Katy Perry.

The point of this is that you can cancel the show or you can do your best.

Sometimes you've just got to take a big breath, get your candy-cane nipple tassels rotating and launch into your 2014 hit, 'Dark Horse' feat. Juicy J. You can do it, champ. You will get through this.

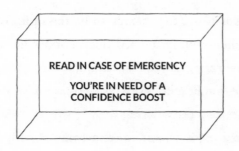

READ IN CASE OF EMERGENCY

YOU'RE IN NEED OF A
CONFIDENCE BOOST

Firstly, your hair looks really nice today.

Secondly, you've got very nice taste and people don't compliment you on that enough.

Thirdly, let's get out there and FAKE IT FAKE IT FAKE IT. You're going to do an impression of a confident person until you feel like a confident person.

Everybody is born confident. Babies come out blindsiding bystanders with the magnitude of their charisma when they can't even speak. Toddlers parade around presenting you with bits of ham they just found on the floor. We come out believing ourselves to be bulletproof and we remain that way until someone or something drains it out of us.

Maybe this happened when you were a kid. Maybe you made it all the way to 47. Either way, after it's gone, you'll always be trying to get back to being that bulletproof baby.

'Confident' people have just figured out, subconsciously or otherwise, how to pretend to be confident, which ultimately increases their confidence. They plant their feet and look the other person in the eye, giving them their full attention. They sweat, they get shaky hands, they feel like a little nervous prawn, but they don't let that feeling take over. They just recognise the signs of adrenaline – not fear, adrenaline – take a sip of water and keep going.

They don't subscribe to the maxim 'Never apologise, never explain', because sometimes you must apologise, and you really must explain, but they don't wring their hands and say, 'This is a piece of shit, I'm a piece of shit,' anytime they do anything. They admit when they are wrong or could have done better, but they never over-apologise. They ask for help, delegate jobs and show weakness. Remember that, all the while, they still feel like a prawn.

So what's coming up? Date? Exam? Job interview? Speech? Competition? Party where you don't know anyone? Presenting your work for the first time? Going back to school? You might want to back out right now and not go through with it but:

IF YOU DON'T DO THE THING, THE FEELING OF REGRET AT HAVING NOT DONE IT WILL BE SO MUCH WORSE THAN DOING IT. EVEN IF IT GOES BADLY.

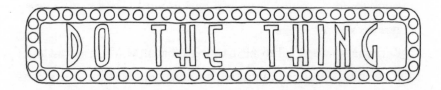

That's twice we've said this in the book, and if we had our way we would start every chapter with it. Train your brain to recognise that while this might be an anxious situation, it's not a life-or-death situation. So it goes badly? Who cares? Give it a go!

Think of this one thing as just a practice for the next thing. It's not about saying, 'You're going to be great out there!' It's about saying, 'Who cares what happens? Have a nice time!'

Here's a line from a poem by Erin Hanson that is forever popping up on Instagram:

'What if I fall?'
Oh but my darling,
What if you fly?

May we suggest an alternative version?

'What if I fall?
Oh but my darling,
SO WHAT?!

So you fell! Who cares? You did it! You learnt something! You'll be even better next time! And crucially, next time you won't be so afraid, because you've already done it. The fear will still be there, but it'll be like a radio on in the background – audible, but easy to ignore.

But what if there is no next time? What if you're the best man at a wedding, you're reading this book under the table and there's only one shot at this! Grab a friend, go round the back of the marquee, do it out loud to them right now. What if this is the interview for your dream job? This is to see if they are the right fit for you, not the other way around. They've already made their decision, just have a nice time. What if this is the Olympics and you're about to go on! You made it to the Olympics! Holy shit who cares what happens next! You made it this far! Everything else is bonus!

Feel the fear and recognise it as feeling alive. Everyone wants you to do well, and if you mess up, just smile and try again! If it is a disaster (it won't be), nobody will think about your failure. At most, if it's very public, someone will notice and then immediately start thinking about whether they have enough chopped tomatoes at home to make a pasta sauce tonight. Everyone is obsessed with themselves and only themselves.

> STEVIE: When I'm really frightened, I plan something excellent
> to do afterwards (even if that's just drinking a glass of wine
> that's not the cheapest on the menu) and remind myself that
> when I look back on my life I want to be proud that I did things
> I was frightened of. I don't want to feel bad because I let the
> fear take over.

Get out there, stand tall, make eye contact, take deep breaths, fake it 'til you make it, enjoy the feeling and KICK SOME ASS!

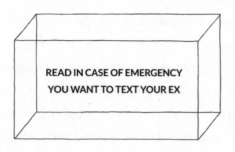

READ IN CASE OF EMERGENCY
YOU WANT TO TEXT YOUR EX

Did you break up with them? Great. The answer's no. You may not text them. Not about your dream, not about missing them, not about a sock you found that reminds you of them, not about a dog you just saw. Leave them alone and let them heal.

Did they break up with you? OK. Let's talk it through.

Firstly, there is no rush to send this message. You could send it right now, or you could send it tomorrow morning. Have a sleep, have a think, and if you still want to send the message, do some light market research by asking three close friends, who are aware of the context, if they think you should message them.

If all of your friends say no . . .

DO NOT SEND THE MESSAGE.

They're not going to realise what they've been missing and come back to you. This message is not going to win them back. You're not breezily ready to be friends with them yet (you just did market research: the definition of non-breezy) and this stage is all about moving forwards rather than backwards.

The moment you send that message, you will have relinquished all your power. The ball will be in their court. You'll just be standing there in the receiving position, anxiously bouncing from foot to foot, but they will not hit the ball back the way you want, because they literally told you they didn't want to play tennis with you.

They'll just leave your ball sitting there while you wither away on the other side of the net, hating yourself for having hit it across to them. You will watch them on social media (because of course you haven't blocked them) hitting balls into other people's courts, while yours sits alone and rotting. A bird will do a shit on your ball. They may at some point lazily throw it back and it'll feel like their heart isn't in it. Because it isn't. And your heart will break.

What shall we do instead?

How about you don't send the message, and you continue to heal with all of your power intact? Oh, they want you to go crying to them, do they? Well, you're not going to give them the satisfaction. We bet they're amazed at how well you're coping. We bet they sometimes think, 'Whoa, OK, I underestimated this person.' And you're going to keep them thinking that until the moment when you inevitably bump into them at a soirée looking fabulous and, for a moment, pretend not to recognise them before saying an airy, 'Oh, hey,' and swanning off to fetch another drink. You can also achieve the same effect while wearing food-stained pyjamas in Tesco. It's not the setting or the aesthetic, it's the devastating way in which you say, 'Oh, hey,' before selecting that frozen pizza. But you cannot pull this off if you won't stop texting them at 3 a.m.

If most of your friends say no and one says, 'Errrrr yeah?' unconvincingly . . .

DO NOT SEND THE MESSAGE.

If all your friends say, 'Oh God, yes, they're dying to get back with you but don't know how to tell you so they've been desperately hoping you'll message them . . .'

Send the message, but know that you are having a fever dream, and when you wake up you need to NOT SEND THE MESSAGE.

> STEVIE: This chapter is very close to my heart because I always send the message. Always. And I've never once been glad that I have. I regret it every single time, whether that's immediately after, the next morning or years later.

DO NOT SEND THE MESSAGE.

ACTUALLY USEFUL RESOURCES

National Domestic Abuse Helpline: 0808 2000 247 (available 24/7)

Samaritans: 116 123

Shout: (for mental health crises – either yours or for advice to help someone you know) text SHOUT to 85258

National Bullying Helpline: 0300 323 0169 (Mon–Fri, 9–5 p.m.)

Counselling (online): Betterhelp.com

Mind (for help with mental-health issues, treatment options, where to find more help): 0300 123 3393 (Mon–Fri, 9–6 p.m.)

Citizens Advice Bureau (for renting woes, council tax woes, benefits, debt advice – basically most important things): England: 0800 144 8848, Wales: 0800 702 2020, Scotland: 0800 028 1456, NI: 028 9026 2532, Ireland: 0761 07 4000 (opening times vary)

Acknowledgements

First and foremost, thank you to Myfanwy Moore and Bea Fitzgerald at Hodder for taking a chance on us, for gently walking us back from our more avant-garde ideas and for their considerate and endlessly thoughtful notes. Thank you to Emma Cowlam, our wonderful illustrator, and Joanne Myler for creating the front cover.

Thank you to our wonderful contributors, Phoebe O'Donnell, Rachel Wilson, and Melissa Creese among many others, all our friends who's hard-earned wisdom we've used, and all the experts of all the excellent books we've referenced.

Thank you to Kat Buckle at Curtis Brown, and Katie McKay and Julien Matthews at Avalon, who read the first draft of this book in a weekend. You'd think, 'Fair enough,' but it was four times longer and every other line was a niche reference to *Pocahontas*.

STEVIE: I would also like to thank my parents and the residents of my flat for dealing with the various bennies I have thrown.

TESSA: I'd like to thank my Mum and Dad, and Pig, and all the gewls, for their support, and Amy, my biggest air conditioning unit.

This book wouldn't exist without the podcast, and the podcast wouldn't exist without so many people. Thank you to Ben Williams and Naomi Parnell at Plosive for rescuing us once we'd gone independent, for being such incredible professionals and for being so much fun to work with. Without you the podcast wouldn't exist.

Thank you Producer Tom, our very first producer back when we were *The Debrief*. We got to record at a fancy studio and Producer Tom would stay late after work to record it with us. We found out after about a year that he wasn't getting paid any extra to do this. Thank you, Producer Tom, for being brilliant.

Liz, sorry you had to have front-row seats to everything in this book.

Everybody who has ever messaged or emailed. We read every single one and they make us so happy.

Everybody who listens to the podcast. Thank you so, so much.